FIFTEEN THOUSAND USEFUL PHRASES

A PRACTICAL HANDBOOK
OF PERTINENT EXPRESSIONS, STRIKING SIMILES,
LITERARY, COMMERCIAL, CONVERSATIONAL, AND
ORATORICAL TERMS, FOR THE EMBELLISHMENT OF
SPEECH AND LITERATURE, AND THE IMPROVEMENT
OF THE VOCABULARY OF THOSE PERSONS WHO
READ, WRITE AND SPEAK ENGLISH

By

GRENVILLE KLEISER

AUTHOR OF
How to Speak in Public

First published in 1910

This edition published by Read Books Ltd.
Copyright © 2019 Read Books Ltd.
This book is copyright and may not be
reproduced or copied in any way without
the express permission of the publisher in writing

British Library Cataloguing-in-Publication Data
A catalogue record for this book is available
from the British Library

One cannot always live in the palaces and state apartments of language, but we can refuse to spend our days in searching for its vilest slums. —William Watson

Words without thought are dead sounds;
Thoughts without words are nothing.
To think is to speak low;
To speak is to think aloud.
—Max Muller

The first merit which attracts in the pages of a good writer, or the talk of a brilliant conversationalist, is the apt choice and contrast of the words employed. It is indeed a strange art to take these blocks rudely conceived for the purpose of the market or the bar, and by tact of application touch them to the finest meanings and distinctions.
—Robert Louis Stevenson

It is with words as with sunbeams,
The more they are condensed,
The deeper they burn.
—Southey

No noble or right style was ever yet founded but out of a sincere heart. —Ruskin

Words are things; and a small drop of ink, falling like dew upon a thought, produces that which makes thousands, perhaps millions, think. —Byron

A good phrase may outweigh a poor library.
—Thomas W. Higginson

CONTENTS

INTRODUCTION

HOW TO USE THIS BOOK 14

SECTION I. USEFUL PHRASES 19

SECTION II. SIGNIFICANT PHRASES............... 139

SECTION III. FELICITOUS PHRASES 206

SECTION IV. IMPRESSIVE PHRASES 234

SECTION V. PREPOSITIONAL PHRASES............ 255

SECTION VI. BUSINESS PHRASES.................. 312

SECTION VII. LITERARY EXPRESSIONS............ 329

SECTION VIII. STRIKING SIMILES................. 386

SECTION IX. CONVERSATIONAL PHRASES........ 447

SECTION X. PUBLIC SPEAKING PHRASES......... 484

SECTION XI. MISCELLANEOUS PHRASES.......... 604

AIMS AND PURPOSES OF SPEAKING

It is obvious that the style of your public speaking will depend upon the specific purpose you have in view. If you have important truths which you wish to make known, or a great and definite cause to serve, you are likely to speak about it with earnestness and probably with eloquence.

If, however, your purpose in speaking is a selfish one—if your object is self-exploitation, or to serve some special interest of your own—if you regard your speaking as an irksome task, or are unduly anxious as to what your hearers will think of you and your effort—then you are almost sure to fail.

On the other hand, if you have the interests of your hearers sincerely at heart—if you really wish to render a worthy public service—if you lose all thought of self in your heartfelt desire to serve others—then you will have the most essential requirements of true and enduring oratory.

-GRENVILLE KLEISER
Model Speeches for Practise, 1920

INTRODUCTION

The most powerful and the most perfect expression of thought and feeling through the medium of oral language must be traced to the mastery of words. Nothing is better suited to lead speakers and readers of English into an easy control of this language than the command of the phrase that perfectly expresses the thought. Every speaker's aim is to be heard and understood. A clear, crisp articulation holds an audience as by the spell of some irresistible power. The choice word, the correct phrase, are instruments that may reach the heart, and awake the soul if they fall upon the ear in melodious cadence; but if the utterance be harsh and discordant they fail to interest, fall upon deaf ears, and are as barren as seed sown on fallow ground. In language, nothing conduces so emphatically to the harmony of sounds as perfect phrasing—that is, the emphasizing of the relation of clause to clause, and of sentence to sentence by the systematic grouping of words. The phrase consists usually of a few words which denote a single idea that forms a separate part of a sentence. In this respect it differs from the clause, which is a short sentence that forms a distinct part of a composition, paragraph, or discourse. Correct phrasing is regulated by rests, such rests as do not break the continuity of a thought or the progress of the sense.

Grenville Kleiser, who has devoted years of his diligent life to imparting the art of correct expression in speech and writing, has provided many aids for those who would know not merely what to say, but how to say it. He has taught also what the great HOLMES taught, that language is a temple in which the human soul is enshrined, and that it grows out of life—out of its joys and its sorrows, its burdens and its necessities. To him, as well as to the writer, the deep strong voice of man and the low sweet voice of woman are never heard at finer advantage than in the earnest but mellow tones of familiar speech. In the present volume Mr. Kleiser furnishes an additional and an exceptional aid for those who would have a mint of phrases at their command from which to draw when in need of the golden mean for expressing thought. Few indeed are the books fitted to-day for the purpose of imparting this knowledge, yet two centuries ago phrase-books were esteemed as supplements to the dictionaries, and have not by any manner of means lost their value. The guide to familiar quotations, the index to similes, the grammars, the readers, the machine-made letter-writer of mechanically perfect letters of congratulation or condolence—none are sententious enough to supply the need. By the compilation of this praxis, Mr. Kleiser has not only supplied it, but has furnished a means for the increase of one's vocabulary by practical methods. There are thousands of persons who may profit by the systematic study of such a book as this if they will familiarize themselves with the author's purpose by a careful reading of the preliminary pages of his book. To speak in public pleasingly and readily and to read well are accomplishments acquired only after many days, weeks even, of practise.

Foreigners sometimes reproach us for the asperity and discordance of our speech, and in general, this reproach is just, for there are many persons who do scanty justice to the vowel-elements of our language. Although these elements constitute its music they are continually mistreated. We flirt with and pirouette around them constantly. If it were not so, English would be found full of beauty and harmony of sound. Familiar with the maxim, "Take care of the vowels and the consonants will take care of themselves,"—a maxim that when put into practise has frequently led to the breaking-down of vowel values—the writer feels that the common custom of allowing "the consonants to take care of themselves" is pernicious. It leads to suppression or to imperfect utterance, and thus produces indistinct articulation.

The English language is so complex in character that it can

scarcely be learned by rule, and can best be mastered by the study of such idioms and phrases as are provided in this book; but just as care must be taken to place every accent or stress on the proper syllable in the pronouncing of every word it contains, so must the stress or emphasis be placed on the proper word in every sentence spoken. To read or speak pleasingly one should resort to constant practise by doing so aloud in private, or preferably, in the presence of such persons as know good reading when they hear it and are masters of the melody of sounds. It was Dean Swift's belief that the common fluency of speech in many men and most women was due to scarcity of matter and scarcity of words. He claimed that a master of language possessed a mind full of ideas, and that before speaking, such a mind paused to select the choice word—the phrase best suited to the occasion. "Common speakers," he said, "have only one set of ideas, and one set of words to clothe them in," and these are always ready on the lips. Because he holds the Dean's view sound to-day, the writer will venture to warn the readers of this book against a habit that, growing far too common among us, should be checked, and this is the iteration and reiteration in conversation of "the battered, stale, and trite" phrases, the like of which were credited by the worthy Dean to the women of his time.

Human thought elaborates itself with the progress of intelligence. Speech is the harvest of thought, and the relation which exists between words and the mouths that speak them must be carefully observed. Just as nothing is more beautiful than a word fitly spoken, so nothing is rarer than the use of a word in its exact meaning. There is a tendency to overwork both words and phrases that is not restricted to any particular class. The learned sin in this respect even as do the ignorant, and the practise spreads until it becomes an epidemic. The epidemic word with us yesterday was unquestionably "conscription"; several months ago it was "preparedness." Before then "efficiency" was heard on every side and succeeded in superseding "vocational teaching," only to be displaced in turn by "life extension" activities. "Safety-first" had a long run which was brought almost to abrupt end by "strict accountability," but these are mere reflections of our cosmopolitan life and activities. There are others that stand out as indicators of brain-weariness. These are most frequently met in the work of our novelists.

English authors and journalists are abusing and overworking the word intrigue to-day. Sir Arthur Quillercouch on page 81 of his book "On the Art of Writing" uses it: "We are intrigued by the process of manufacture instead of being wearied by a description of the ready-made article." Mrs. Sidgwick in "Salt and Savour," page 232, wrote: "But what intrigued her was Little Mamma's remark at breakfast," From the Parliamentary news, one learns that "Mr. Harcourt intrigued the House of Commons by his sustained silence for two years" and that "London is interested in, and not a little intrigued, by the statement." This use of intrigue in the sense of "perplex, puzzle, trick, or deceive" dates from 1600. Then it fell into a state of somnolence, and after an existence of innocuous desuetude lasting till 1794 it was revived, only to hibernate again until 1894. It owes its new lease of life to a writer on The Westminster Gazette, a London journal famous for its competitions in aid of the restoring of the dead meanings of words.

One is almost exasperated by the repeated use and abuse of the word "intimate" in a recently published work of fiction, by an author who aspires to the first rank in his profession. He writes of "the intimate dimness of the room;" "a fierce intimate whispering;" "a look that was intimate;" "the noise of the city was intimate," etc. Who has not heard, "The idea!" "What's the idea?" "Is that the idea?" "Yes, that's the idea," with increased inflection at each repetition. And who is without a friend who at some time or another has not sprung "meticulous" upon him? Another example is afforded by the endemic use of "of sorts" which struck London while the writer was in that city a few years ago. Whence it came no one knew, but it was heard on every side. "She was a woman of sorts;" "he is a Tory of sorts;" "he had a religion of sorts;" "he was a critic of sorts." While it originally meant "of different or various kinds," as hats of sorts; offices of sorts; cheeses of sorts, etc., it is now used disparagingly, and implies something of a kind that is not satisfactory, or of a character that is rather poor. This, as Shakespeare might have said, is "Sodden business! There's a stewed phrase indeed!"*

The abuse of phrases and the misuse of words rife among us can be checked by diligent exercises in good English, such as this book provides. These exercises, in conjunction with others to be found in different volumes by the same author, will serve to correct careless diction and slovenly speech, and lead to the art of speaking and writing correctly; for, after all, accuracy in the use of words is more a matter of habit than of theory, and once it is acquired it becomes just as easy to speak or to write good English as bad English. It was Chesterfield's resolution not to speak a word in conversation which was not the fittest he could recall. All persons should avoid using words whose meanings they do not know, and with the correct application of which they are unfamiliar. The best spoken and the best written English is that which conforms to the language as used by men and women of culture—a high standard, it is true, but one not so high that it is unattainable by any earnest student of the English tongue.

Frank H. Vizetelly.

Footnote:

* Troilus and Cressida, act iii, sc. 1.

HOW TO USE THIS BOOK

The study of words, phrases, and literary expressions is a highly interesting pursuit. There is a reciprocal influence between thought and language. What we think molds the words we use, and the words we use react upon our thoughts. Hence a study of words is a study of ideas, and a stimulant to deep and original thinking.

We should not, however, study "sparkling words and sonorous phrases" with the object of introducing them consciously into our speech. To do so would inevitably lead to stiltedness and superficiality. Words and phrases should be studied as symbols of ideas, and as we become thoroughly familiar with them they will play an unconscious but effective part in our daily expression.

We acquire our vocabulary largely from our reading and our personal associates. The words we use are an unmistakable indication of our thought habits, tastes, ideals, and interests in life. In like manner, the habitual language of a people is a barometer of their intellectual, civil, moral, and spiritual ideals. A great and noble people express themselves in great and noble words.

Ruskin earnestly counsels us to form the habit of looking intensely at words. We should scrutinize them closely and endeavor to grasp their innermost meaning. There is an indefinable satisfaction in knowing how to choose and use words with accuracy and precision. As Fox once said, "I am never at a loss for a word, but Pitt always has the word."

All the great writers and orators have been diligent students of words. Demosthenes and Cicero were indefatigable in their study of language. Shakespeare, "infinite in faculty," took infinite pains to embody his thought in words of crystal clearness. Coleridge once said of him that one might as well try to dislodge a brick from a building with one's forefinger as to omit a single word from one of his finest passages.

Milton, master of majestic prose, under whose touch words became as living things; Flaubert, who believed there was one and one only best word with which to express a given thought; De Quincey, who exercised a weird-like power over words; Ruskin, whose rhythmic prose enchanted the ear; Keats, who brooded over phrases like a lover; Newman, of pure and melodious style; Stevenson, forever in quest of the scrupulously precise word; Tennyson, graceful and exquisite as the limpid stream; Emerson, of trenchant and epigrammatic style; Webster, whose virile words sometimes weighed a pound; and Lincoln, of simple, Saxon speech,—all these illustrious men were assiduous in their study of words.

Many persons of good education unconsciously circumscribe themselves within a small vocabulary. They have a knowledge of hundreds of desirable words which they do not put into practical use in their speech or writing. Many, too, are conscious of a poverty of language, which engenders in them a sense of timidity and self-depreciation. The method used for building a large vocabulary has usually been confined to the study of single words. This has produced good results, but it is believed that eminently better results can be obtained from a careful study of words and expressions, as furnished in this book, where words can be examined in their context.

It is intended and suggested that this study should be pursued in connection with, and as a supplement to, a good standard dictionary. Fifteen minutes a day devoted to this subject, in the manner outlined, will do more to improve and enlarge the vocabulary than an hour spent in desultory reading.

There is no better way in which to develop the mental qualities of clearness, accuracy, and precision, and to improve and enlarge the intellectual powers generally, than by regular and painstaking study of judiciously selected phrases and literary expressions.

PLAN OF STUDY

First examine the book in a general way to grasp its character, scope, and purpose. Carefully note the following plan of classification of the various kinds of phrases, and choose for initial study a section which you think will be of the most immediate value to you.

I. USEFUL PHRASES
II. SIGNIFICANT PHRASES
III. FELICITOUS PHRASES
IV. IMPRESSIVE PHRASES
V. PREPOSITIONAL PHRASES
VI. BUSINESS PHRASES
VII. LITERARY EXPRESSIONS
VIII. STRIKING SIMILES
IX. CONVERSATIONAL PHRASES
X. PUBLIC SPEAKING PHRASES
XI. MISCELLANEOUS PHRASES

There are many advantages in keeping before you a definite purpose in your study of this book. A well-defined plan will act as an incentive to regular and systematic effort, and incidentally develop your power of concentration.

It is desirable that you set apart a certain convenient time each day for this study. Regularity tends to produce maximum results. As you progress with this work your interest will be quickened and you will realize the desirability of giving more and more time to this important subject.

When you have chosen a section of the book which particularly appeals to you, begin your actual study by reading the phrases aloud. Read them slowly and understandingly. This tends to impress them more deeply upon your mind, and is in itself one of the best and most practical ways of acquiring a large and varied vocabulary. Moreover, the practise of fitting words to the mouth rapidly develops fluency and facility of speech.

Few persons realize the great value of reading aloud. Many of the foremost English stylists devoted a certain period regularly to this practise. Cardinal Newman read aloud each day a chapter from Cicero as a means of developing his ear for sentence-rhythm. Rufus Choate, in order to increase his command of language, and to avoid sinking into mere empty fluency, read aloud daily, during a large part of his life, a page or more from some great English author. As a writer has said, "The practise of storing the mind with choice passages from the best prose writers and poets, and thus flavoring it with the essence of good literatures, is one which is commended both by the best teachers and by the example of some of the most celebrated orators, who have adopted it with signal success."

This study should be pursued with pencil in hand, so that you may readily underscore phrases which make a special appeal to you. The free use of a pencil in marking significant parts of a book is good evidence of thoroughness. This, too, will facilitate your work of subsequent review.

The habit of regularly copying, in your own handwriting, one or more pages of phrases will be of immense practical value. This exercise is a great aid in developing a facile English style. The daily use of the pen has been recommended in all times as a valuable means of developing oral and literary expression.

A helpful exercise is to pronounce a phrase aloud and then fit it into a complete sentence of your own making. This practice gives added facility and resourcefulness in the use of words.

As an enthusiastic student of good English, you should carefully note striking and significant phrases or literary expressions which you find in your general reading. These should be set down in a note-book reserved for this exclusive purpose. In this way you can prepare many lists of your own, and thus greatly augment the value of this study.

The taste for beauty, truth, and harmony in language can be

developed by careful study of well-selected phrases and literary expressions as furnished in this book. A good literary style is formed principally by daily study of great English writers, by careful examination of words in their context, and by a discriminating use of language at all times.

GRENVILLE KLEISER.
New York City, July, 1917

SECTION I

USEFUL PHRASES

A

abandoned hope

abated pride

abbreviated visit

abhorred thraldom
  [thraldom = enslaved or in bondage]

abiding romance

abject submission

abjured ambition

able strategist

abnormal talents

abominably perverse

abounding happiness

abridged statement

abrogated law

abrupt transition

absolutely irrevocable

absorbed reverie

abstemious diet
  [abstemious = eating and drinking in moderation]

abstract character
abstruse reasoning
absurdly dangerous
abundant opportunity
abusive epithet
abysmally apologetic
academic rigor
accelerated progress
accentuated playfulness
accepted littleness
accessible pleasures
accessory circumstances
accidental lapse
accommodating temper
accomplished ease
accredited agent
accumulated burden
accurate appraisement
accursed enemy
accusing glance
accustomed lucidity
aching desire
acknowledged authority
acoustical effects
acquired timidity
acrid controversy
acrimonious warfare
actively zealous

actualized ideals

acutely conscious

adamantine rigidity
  [adamantine = unyielding; inflexible]

adaptive wit

adduced facts
  [adduce = cite as an example]

adequate execution

adhesive quality

administered rebuke

admirable reserve

admissible evidence

admittedly inferior

admonitory gesture

adolescent youth

adorable vanity

adroit flatterer

adulated stranger

adventitious way
  [adventitious = not inherent; added extrinsically]

adventurous mind

adverse experience

affably accommodating

affected indifference

affectionate approval

affianced lady

affirmative attitude

affluent language

affrighted slave
aggravated faults
aggregate body
aggressive selfishness
agile mind
agitated imagination
agonizing appeal
agreeable frankness
aimless confusion
airy splendor
alarming rapidity
alert acceptance
algebraic brevity
alien splendor
alleged reluctance
allegorical vein
allied subjects
alliterative suggestion
all-pervading influence
alluring idleness
alternating opinion
altogether dissimilar
altruistic ideal
amatory effusions
   [amatory = expressive of sexual love]
amazing artifice
ambidextrous assistant
ambiguous grimace

ambitious project

ambling pedestrian

ambrosial essence
  [ambrosial = fragrant or delicious; worthy of the gods; divine.]

amiable solicitude

amicable arrangement

amorous youth

ample culture

amusing artlessness

analogous example

analytical survey

ancestral creed

ancient garb

angelic softness

angry protestations

anguished entreaty

angular features

animated eloquence

annoying complications

anomalous appearance

anonymous benefactor

answering response

antagonistic views

antecedent facts

anticipated attention

antiquated prudery

anxious misgiving

apathetic greeting

aphoristic wit
  [aphoristic = Tersely phrased statement]

apish agility

apocalyptic vision

apocryphal lodger
  [apocryphal = questionable authenticity]

apologetic explanation

apostrophic dignity

appalling difficulties

apparent significance

appealing picture

appointed function

apposite illustration

appreciable relief

appreciative fervor

apprehensive dread

apprentice touch

appropriate designation

approving smile

approximately correct

aptly suggested

arbitrarily imposed

arch conspirator

arched embrasure
  [embrasure = flared opening for a gun in a wall or parapet]

archeological pursuits

architectural grandeur

ardent protest
arduous quest
arid formula
aristocratic lineage
aromatic fragrance
arrant trifling
arrested development
arrogant imposition
artful adaptation
artificial suavity
artistic elegance
artless candor
ascending supremacy
ascetic devotion
ascribed productiveness
aspiring genius
assembled arguments
asserted activity
assiduously cultivated
assimilative power
assumed humiliation
assuredly enshrined
astonishing facility
astounding mistakes
astute observer
athletic prowess
atmospheric vagueness
atoning sacrifice

atrocious expression

atrophied view

attending circumstances

attentive deference

attenuated sound

attested loyalty

attractive exordium
   [exordium = introduction of a speech or treatise]

audacious mendicant
   [mendicant = depending on alms; beggar]

audible intimations

augmented force

august tribunal

auspicious moment

austere charm

authentic indications

authoritative critic

autobiographical pages

autocratic power

automatic termination

autumnal skies

auxiliary aids

available data

avaricious eyes

avenging fate

average excellence

averted calamity

avowed intention

awakened curiosity
awed devotion
awful dejection
awkward dilemma
axiomatic truth
azure sky

B

babbling gossip
bacchanalian desires
bachelor freedom
bad omen
baffled sagacity
  [sagacity = farsighted; wise]
balanced capacity
baldly described
baleful glances
balmy fragrance
bandying talk
baneful impression
banished silence
barbarous statecraft
barefaced appeal
barest commonplaces
barren opportunities
base intrigues
baseless assumptions

bashful modesty
basic principles
battered witticism
beaming countenance
bearish rudeness
beatific vision
beautiful modesty
beckoning horizon
becoming diffidence
bedraggled wretch
befitting honor
beggarly flimsiness
beguiling voice
belated acknowledgment
belittling fears
bellicose humanity
beneficent career
benevolent regard
benighted sense
benignant pity
   [benignant = favorable; beneficial; kind]
beseeching gesture
besetting heresy
besotted fanaticism
bestial ferocity
bewildering maze
bewitching airs

beyond peradventure
  [peradventure = perhaps]
bibulous diversions
  [bibulous = consumes alcoholic drink]
bigoted contempt
binding obligation
bitter recrimination
bizarre apparel
blackening west
blameless indolence
blanched desolation
bland confidence
blank misgivings
blasphemous hypocrisy
blatant discourse
blazing audacity
blazoned shield
bleak loneliness
blended impression
blessed condolence
blighted happiness
blind partizan
blissful consciousness
blistering satire
blithe disregard
bloated equivalent
bloodless creature
bloodthirsty malice

blundering discourtesy

blunt rusticity
  [rusticity = rustic; awkward or tactless]

blurred vision

blustering assertion

boastful positiveness

bodily activity

boisterous edification

bold generalization

bombastic prating
  [prating = idle talk]

bookish precision

boon companion

boorish abuse

bored demeanor

borrowed grace

bottomless abyss

boundless admiration

bountiful supply

boyish appreciation

braggart pretense

bravely vanquished

braying trumpet

brazen importunity
  [importunity = insistent request]

breathless eagerness

brief tenure

briefless barrister

bright interlude

brilliant embodiment

brisk energy

bristling temper

brittle sarcasm

broadening fame

broken murmurs

brooding peace

brutal composure

bubbling frivolities

bucolic cudgeling
   [bucolic = about shepherds or flocks; pastoral]
   [cudgeling = beat with a short heavy stick]

budding joy

bulky figure

buoyant pluck

burdensome business

burly strength

burning zeal

bursting laugh

busily engrossed

business acumen

bygone period

C

cabalistic phrase
   [cabalistic = secret or hidden meaning]

cadaverous appearance

calamitous course

calculating admiration

callous indifference

calm resignation

calumnious suspicions
   [calumnious = harmful and often untrue; discredit]

cantankerous enemy

canting hypocrite
   [canting = monotonous platitudes; hypocritically pious]

capacious mind

capricious allurements

captivating speech

cardinal merit

careless parrying

caressing grasp

carping critic

castellated towers
   [castellated = with turrets and battlements like a castle]

casual violation

cataclysmic elements

causelessly frightened

caustic remark

cautious skepticism

cavernous gloom

ceaseless vigilance

celebrated instance

celestial joy

censorious critic

centralized wealth

ceremonious courtesy

cerulean blue
  [cerulean = azure; sky-blue]

challenge admiration

chance reflections

changing exigencies
  [exigencies = pressing or urgent situation]

chaotic plans

characteristic audacity

charitable allowance

charming radiance

chary instincts
  [chary = cautious; wary]

chastened hope

chatty familiarity

cheap resentment

cheery response

chequered career

cherished objects

childlike ingenuousness
  [ingenuous = frank; candid.]

chilled cynicism

chirpy familiarities

chivalrous spirit

choicest refinements

choleric temperament
  [choleric = easily angered; bad-tempered]

choral chant

chronic frailties

churlish temper
   [churlish = boorish; vulgar; rude]

circling eddyings

circuitous information

circumscribed purpose

civic consciousness

civilizing influence

clammy death

clamorous vibration

clangorous industry

clarion tone

class demarcations

classical objurgation
   [objurgation = harsh rebuke]

clattering accents

clear insight

climactic revelation

clinching proof

cloaked nature

cloistered virtue

close condensation

cloudy magnificence

clownishly insensible

cloying sweetness
   [cloying = too filling, rich, or sweet]

clumsy talk

clustering trees
coarse necessity
coaxing eloquence
coercive enactment
cogent statement
coherent thinking
coined metaphor
cold formalities
collateral duties
collective wisdom
colloquial display
colonial character
colossal failure
comatose state
combative tone
comforting reassurance
comic infelicity
commanding attitude
commendable purpose
commercial opulence
commingled emotion
commodiously arranged
common substratum
commonplace allusions
compact fitness
comparative scantiness
compassionate love
compelling force

compendious abstract

compensatory character

competent authority

competitive enterprise

complacent platitudes

complaining sea

complaisant observation

complete aloofness

complex notions

complicated maze

complimentary glance

component aspects

composed zeal

composite growth

compound idea

comprehensive design

compressed view

compromising rashness

compulsory repetition

compunctious visitings
   [compunctious = feeling guilt]

concatenated pedantries
   [pedantries = attention to detail or rules]

concealed advantage

conceivable comparison

concentrated vigor

concerted action

conciliating air

concomitant events

concrete realities

concurrent testimony

condemnable rashness

condescending badinage
  [badinage = frivolous banter]

conditional approval

confessed ardor

confidently anticipated

confirmed misanthrope
  [misanthrope = one who dislikes people in general]

conflicting influences

confused mingling

conjectural estimate

conjugal felicity

connected series

connotative damage

connubial love

conquering intelligence

conscientious objection

conscious repugnance

consecrated endeavor

consequent retribution

conservative distrust

considerate hint

consistent friendliness

consoling consciousness

conspicuous ascendency

constant reiteration

constitutional reserve

constrained politeness

constructive idealists

consuming zeal

consummate mastery

contagious wit

contaminating influence

contemplative nature

contemporary fame

contemptuous disrespect

contented indolence

contingent reasons

continuous endeavor

contorted expression

contracted view

contradictory theories

contrary tendencies

contrasted types

controversial disputant

contumelious epithet
  [contumelious = Rudeness or contempt arising from arrogance]

convenient footing

conventional verbiage

conversational decorum

convincing forcefulness

convivial habits

convulsive agony
cool confidence
copious materials
coquettish advances
cordial approval
corporate selfishness
corporeal constituent
correct forecast
corresponding variation
corroborated truth
corrosive effect
corrupting tendency
cosmical changes
cosmopolitan position
costly advantages
counterbalancing power
countless barriers
courageous eagerness
courteous solicitude
courtly bearing
covert curiosity
coveted honors
cowardly concession
cowering agitation
coy reluctance
crackling laughter
crafty deception
craggy eminence

cramped energies
crass stolidity
craven determination
creative faculty
credibly informed
creditable performance
credulous superstition
creeping progress
criminal negligence
cringing smile
crisp dialogue
critical judgment
crouching culprit
crowning indiscretion
crucial instance
crucifying irony
crude affectation
cruel handicap
crumbling precipice
crunching jangle
crushing sorrow
cryptic saying
crystalline sky
crystallized conclusions
culinary myrmidons
   [myrmidon = one who carries out orders without question]
culminating fascination
culpable behavior

cultivated ferocity
cultured idleness
cumbrous fragments
  [cumbrous = cumbersome; difficult to handle or use]
cumulative tendency
cunningly contrived
curbed profligacy
curious coincidence
current gossip
curry favor
cursed inactivity
cursory acquaintance
curt formality
curtained embrasure
cutting directness
cycloramic sweep
cynical disregard

D

damaging admission
damask cheek
  [damask = rich patterned fabric; wavy pattern on
  Damascus steel]
dampened ardor
dancing sunshine
dangerous temerity
dappled shadows

daring candor

dark superstition

dashing gallantry

dastardly injustice

dauntless courage

dawning instinct

dazed brain

dazzling triumph

deadly virulence

deaf tribunal

deathless structure

debasing tendency

debatable point

debilitating features

decadent poets

deceiving mists

decided superiority

decisive manner

declamatory treatment
    [declamatory = pretentiously rhetorical; bombastic]

declared brotherhood

decorously adorned

deepening dusk

deep-seated curiosity

deep-toned lamentations

defective construction

defenseless innocence

defensive alliance

deferential regard

defiant coldness

deficient vitality

definite conception

deformed visage

deft evasion

degrading tendencies

delectable speculations

delegated power

deliberate abnegation
  [abnegation = self-denial]

delicate discrimination

delicious vagueness

delightful variation

delirious ecstasies

delusive charm

demagogic style

democratic institutions

demoniacal force

demonstrable conclusion

demoralizing luxury

demure composure

denunciatory terms

departed glories

deplorable decay

deprecatory shrug

depressing concomitants

depthless forest

derisive voice

derogatory denial

descriptive power

desecrated ideals

deserted desert

deserved approbation
  [approbation = warm approval; praise]

desirable distinction

desolating dread

despairing austerity

desperate defiance

despicable vices

despondent exaggeration

despotic rulers

destructive radicalism

desultory vacillation
  [desultory = disconnected; haphazard; random]

detailed portraiture

detected hypocrisies

determinate swing

detestable purpose

dethroned princes

detrimental result

devastating effect

devilish sophistries

deviously subtle

devitalized personality

devoted attachment

devouring ambition

devout thanksgiving

dewy coolness

dexterous impudence

diabolical passion

dialectic power

diametrically opposite

dictatorial manner

dictionary significance

didactic exposition
   [didactic = intended to be morally instructive]

different distortion

difficult portraiture

diffident civility
   [diffident = lacking self-confidence; shy; timid]

diffuse verbosity

dignified austerity

digressional adventure

dilettante mind
   [dilettante = dabbler in a field of knowledge]

diligently propagated

dim comprehension

diminished efficacy

diminutive stature

diplomatic skill

dire consummation

direct obligation

disappointing attitude

disarmed criticism
disastrous termination
discarded reminiscences
discerning critic
disciplined mind
disclosed insincerity
discomfited opponent
disconcerted conjecture
disconnected fancies
disconsolate opinions
discordant sounds
discredited statement
discretional opinion
discriminating homage
discursive staggerings
disdainful comment
diseased hallucinations
disembodied personality
disengaged air
disfiguring disguise
disgraceful plight
disgruntled pessimist
disguised contempt
disgusted protest
disheartening facts
dishonorable submission
disillusioned youth
disintegrating tendency

disinterested motive
disjoined reminiscences
dismal seclusion
dismantled appearance
disordered imagination
disparaging criticism
dispassionate judgment
dispelling fear
displeasing softness
disproportionate ideas
disputative philosopher
disquieting thrill
disreputable aspect
dissenting opinion
dissimilar laws
dissipated illusion
dissolute audacity
dissolving years
dissonant jargon
distant adherent
distasteful notion
distempered feeling
distinct desideratum
distorted vanity
distracting babble
distraught air
distressing laxity
disturbed equanimity

diurnal rotation

divergent calculations

diversified attributes

diverting interests

divine potentialities

dizzy precipice

documentary evidence

dogged determination

doggerel expressions
    [doggerel = crude, humorous verse]

dogmatic assurance

doleful forebodings

domestic endearment

dominating influence

domineering insolence

dormant capacities

doubly odious

doubtful authenticity

downright nonsense

downtrodden drudge

drab apology

dramatic liveliness

drastic action

dread presence

dreaming adventurer

dreamless rest

dreary disrelish

droll incongruity

droning world
drowsy tranquillity
dubious success
ductile language
dulcet tone
dull aversion
dumb surprise
dumbfounded amazement
durable impression
dusky obscurity
dutiful compliance
dynamic energy
dynastic insolence

E

eager animosity
early servitude
earnestly espoused
earthly splendor
easy garrulity
   [garrulity = excessive talkativeness]
eccentric casuists
   [casuistry = excessively subtle reasoning intended to mislead]
ecclesiastical rule
echoless silence
economic absurdity
ecstatically happy

edifying exhortation

educational enterprise

effective embellishment

effectual stimulus

effeminate grace

effervescent multitude

effete aristocracy

efficacious power

efficient education

efflorescent style
  [efflorescent = bursting into flower]

effulgent daybeams
  [effulgent = radiating light]

egoistic sentiment

egregious mistake
  [egregious = outrageously reprehensible]

ejaculatory prayer

elaborate composition

elastic ductility

electric effluvium
  [effluvium = invisible emanation; an aura]

elegant mediocrity

elemental emotions

elephantine footsteps

elevated enjoyment

elfish grace

eloquent refutation

elusive charm

emancipating labors

embarrassing variety

embellished truths

embittered gaze

emblazoned pinnacles

embryo enterprise

emerald scintillations

eminent nonentity

emotional warmth

emotive power

emphatic earnestness

empirical corroboration

empty phraseology

emulative zeal

enamored troubadour

enchanted garden

encircling embrace

endearing appellation
   [appellation = name, title; act of naming]

endless dissertation

enduring charm

energetic enthusiasm

enervating humility
   [enervating = weaken or destroy the strength]

enfeebled activity

enforced silence

engaging affability

engendered feelings

engrossing purpose

engulfing waters
enhanced reputation
enigmatical silence
enlightened solicitude
enlivened monotony
ennobling personality
enormously outbalanced
enraptured attention
enriched experience
entangled subject
enthralling charm
enthusiastic adherents
enticing odors
entire domain
entrancing sadness
enveloping presence
envenomed attacks
enviable superiority
environing conditions
ephemeral duration
   [ephemeral = markedly short-lived]
epicurean taste
epigrammatic sallies
   [epigrammatic = terse and witty]
equable composure
equally efficacious
equitably governed
equivocal compliment

erotic poem

errant thoughts

erratic flight

erroneous assumption

erudite labors
  [erudite = having or showing profound knowledge]

eruptive violence

esoteric doctrine

especial pleasure

essential prerequisite

estimable qualities

eternal hostility

ethereal azure

ethical wisdom

euphuistic affectations
  [euphuistic = affected elegance of language]

evanescent glances
  [evanescent = vanishing like vapor]

evangelic doctrine

evasive answer

eventful circumstance

eventual failure

everlasting mysteries

everyday reality

evident authority

evil necromancy
  [necromancy = communicating with the dead to predict the future; black magic; sorcery]

eviscerating shrieks

exact antithesis

exacting taskmaster

exaggerated estimate

exalted imagination

exasperating coolness

exceedingly acceptable

excellent discernment

exceptional magnitude

excessive zeal

excitable temperament

exclusive pursuit

excretory secretion

excruciating accents

excursive fancy

execrable villainy
  [execrable = hateful; extremely inferior; very bad]

executive efficiency

exemplary conduct

exhaustless energy

exhilarating charm

exoteric scorn
  [exoteric = easily comprehensible; popular; outside]

exotic appearance

expansive benevolence

expectant throng

expeditionary force

expeditiously secreted

experimental suggestion

expiatory sacrifices

explicit injunction

explosive violence

expressionless visage

expressive lineaments
    [lineaments = distinctive shape, especially of the face]

exquisite tact

extemporaneous effusion

extended magnitude

extenuating circumstance

external cheerfulness

extraneous ideas

extraordinary vivacity

extravagant caprice

extremely picturesque

exuberant mirth

exultant condition

F

facetious mood

facile criticism

factitious propensity

faded magnificence

faintly sinister

faithfully perpetuated

fallacious hopes

false illusions

faltering tongue
familiar sacredness
famished voracity
fanatical admiration
fanciful alliance
fantastic display
farcical expedient
far-reaching influence
fascinating illusiveness
fashioned symmetrically
fastidious taste
fatal disclosure
fatalistic belief
fathomless powers
fatiguing assertion
fattening servitude
fatuous pedantry
   [pedantry = attention to detail or rules]
faultless taste
favorable augury
fawning flatteries
fearful imprecations
fearless integrity
feasible mode
feeble dribble
feigned reluctance
felicitous expression
feminine capriciousness

ferocious foe

fertile fancy

fervent invocation

fervid enthusiasm

festive illuminations

fetid dampness

fettered tyranny

feverish bewilderment

fickle fancy

fictitious pretext

fidgety impatience

fierce resentment

fiery indignation

figurative eloquence

filial tenderness

final enthronement

fine sensibilities

finished artistry

fireside delights

fitful desire

fitting opportunity

fizzing flame

flaccid faith

flagging popularity

flagitious attack
  [flagitious = extremely brutal or cruel crimes; vicious; infamous]

flagrant boasting

flamboyant brilliancy
flaming zeal
flashing wit
flat denial
flattering aspect
flaunting insolence
flawless constitution
fleecy clouds
fleeting intimation
flickering conscience
flighty obstinacy
flimsy organization
flippant ease
floating blackness
florid oratory
  [florid = ornate; flowery]
flowery circumlocution
flowing imagery
fluctuating light
fluent sophist
fluffy indignation
fluid ideas
flushed embarrassment
fluttering laugh
focused attention
foggy notion
fond enthusiast
foolish frenzy

forbearing silence

forbidding air

forceful audacity

foregone conclusion

foremost opponent

forensic orator

forest stillness

forgotten graveyard

forlorn desolation

formal acquiescence

formidable barrier

formless jottings

formulated conclusions

fortified selfishness

fortuitous circumstance

foul calumny
   [calumny = maliciously lying to injure a reputation]

fragile form

fragmentary facts

fragrant reminiscence

frail craft

frank admiration

frantic ardor

fraternal pity

freakish humor

freeborn soul

freezing disdain

frenzied haste

frequent digression

fresh impetus

freshening breeze

fretful discontent

friendly familiarity

frightened sense

frightful apparition

frigid disdain

frisky lightness

frivolous expedient

frolicsome extravagance

frozen wonder

fructifying thought
   [fructifying = make fruitful or productive]

fruitful indignation

fruitless repining

fugitive thoughts

full plenitude

fulsome praise

fumbling endeavor

functional disparity

fundamental principles

funereal gloom

furious invective
   [invective = abusive language]

furrowed cheeks

furtive glance

fussy enthusiasms

futile babble

G

gabbling reminiscences
  [gabbling = speak rapidly or incoherently; jabber]

galling thought

galvanic jumpings

gaping chasm

garbled information

garish decorations

garnered experience

gathering gloom

gaudy embellishments

gaunt specter

gay defiance

general acclamation

generative influence

generic characteristics

generous abundance

genial tolerance

genteel parlance

gentle blandishments
  [blandishments = coax by flattery]

gentlemanly personage

genuine cynicism

geological enigma

geometrical progression

germinal idea

ghastly loneliness

ghostly apparitions

giant height

giddy pleasure

gifted intelligence

gigantic sagacity
   [sagacity = discerning, sound in judgment; wisdom.]

girlish sprightliness

gladdening influence

gladiatorial exercise

gladsome glow

glaring impropriety

glassy smoothness

gleaming escutcheon
   [escutcheon = shield-shaped emblem bearing a coat of arms]

gleeful spirit

glibly condoned

gliding measures

glimmering idea

glistening dewdrop

glittering epigram

gloomy musing

glorious freedom

glossed faults

glowering countenance

glowing anticipations

gnawing thoughts

godlike independence
golden opportunity
good-humored gibes
gorgeous splendor
gossiping opinion
governing impulse
graceful demeanor
gracious immunity
graduated sequence
grandiose nomenclature
graphic portrayal
grasping credulity
gratuitous rudeness
grave reticence
greedy grasp
gregarious humanity
grievously mistaken
grim swiftness
grinding despotism
grinning ghosts
griping fascination
grizzled warrior
gross exaggeration
grotesque perversion
groundless fear
groveling servility
growing tension
grudging thanks

grumbling monotone
guileless zeal
gullible humanity
gurgling brooks
gushing enthusiasm
gusty clamor
guttural incoherence
gymnastic agility

H

habitual deference
hackneyed statement
hairbreadth difference
halcyon innocence
  [halcyon = tranquil; prosperous; golden]
hallowed stillness
halting praise
hampered power
handsomely recompensed
haphazard ostentation
happy intuition
harassing anxiety
hardened indifference
harmless mirth
harmonious grace
harrowing details
harsh jarrings

hasty generalization

hateful malignity

haughty composure

haunting despair

hazardous enterprise

hazy recollection

headlong vehemence

healthful vitality

heartfelt amity

heartless perfidy
  [perfidy = breach of faith; treachery]

heartrending outcry

hearty contempt

heated discussion

heathen hordes

heavenly ecstasies

heavy handicap

hectic tittering

hectoring rant

heedless love

heightened charm

heinous enormity

helpless innocence

herculean monster

hereditary arrogance

heretical opinions

hermetically sealed

heroic fortitude

hesitating courage
heterogeneous mass
hidden pitfalls
hideous phantom
high-flying theories
highly meritorious
hilarious outburst
hillside mist
hissing murmur
historic edifice
hoarded vengeance
hoary antiquity
hollow joys
homebred virtues
homeless wind
homely pathos
homespun play
homicidal mania
homogeneous whole
honest admiration
honeyed eloquence
hooligan wind
hopelessly befogged
horrible swiftness
horrid significance
hortatory moonshine
hospitable courtesy
hostile partizan

hot frenzy

hovering presence

howling chaos

huddled faculties

huge aspiration

human derelict

humanitarian impulse

humbly propitiating
  [propitiating = appeasing]

humdrum inconsistencies

humid luster

humiliating discomfiture

humorless variety

humorous urbanity

hungry satisfaction

hurrying years

hurtful indulgence

hushed laughter

husky shrillness

hybrid emotions

hypnotic fascination

hypochondriacal terrors

hypocritical pretense

hysterical agitation

I

iconoclastic attitude

icy smile

idealistic type

identical mode

idiomatic propriety

idiotic obstinacy

idle jesting

idolatrous fervor

idyllic nonsense

ignoble domination

ignominious retreat

ill-concealed impatience

illiberal superstition

illimitable progression

illiterate denizens

illogical interruption

illuminating insight

illusive touch

illustrative anecdote

illustrious era

imaginative warmth

imbittered controversy

immaterial connection

immature dissent

immeasurable scorn

immediate abjuration
  [abjuration = renounce under oath]

immemorial bulwark

immense complacency

imminent perplexities

immitigable contempt

immoderate grief

immortal creation

immovably silent

immutable law

impaired prestige

impalpable nothingness

impartial justice

impassable serenity

impassioned impulse

impatient yearning

impeccable felicity

impecunious exile

impelling movement

impending fate

impenetrable calmness

imperative necessity

imperceptible deviation

imperfect equipment

imperial authority

imperious mind
   [imperious = arrogantly domineering or overbearing]

imperishable renown

impersonal compliment

impertinent drollery

imperturbable gravity

impetuous zeal

impious defiance

impish humor

implacable resentment

implicit faith

implied concealment

implored pardon

imponderable air

important epoch

importunate questions
  [importunate = insistent request]

imposing mien
  [mien = manner revealing a state of mind; appearance or aspect]

impossible contingency

impotent desperation

impoverished age

impracticable obstinacy

impregnable fortress

impressionistic stroke

imprisoning limitations

improbable conjecture

impromptu utterance

improvising powers

imprudent indebtedness

impudent knowingness

impulsive gratitude

inaccessible dignity

inadequate appreciation

inadmissible expression

inadvertent remark

inalienable right

inanimate existence

inapposite blandness
  [inapposite = inappropriate or misapplied nature]

inaptly designated

inarticulate lispings

inaugural discourse

inborn refinement

inbred taste

incalculable mischief

incarnate hate

incendiary opinions

incessant volume

incidental duty

incipient fancy

incisive critic

incoherent loquacity
  [loquacity = very talkative]

incommunicable gift

incomparable excellence

incompletely apprehended

inconceivable absurdity

incongruous contrast

inconsiderable trifle

inconsistent conduct

inconsolable cares

incontestable inference

incontrovertible proof

incorrigible merriment

incorruptible constancy

increasing clamor

incredible swiftness

indecent saturnalia
  [saturnalia = unrestrained revelry; an orgy]

indecorously amused

indefatigable diligence
  [indefatigable = tireless]

indefeasible title
  [indefeasible = cannot be annulled]

indefinable reluctance

indefinite yearning

indelible obligation

indelicate impetuosity

indented outline

independent research

indescribably lugubriou
  [lugubriou = exaggerated gloom]

indestructible atoms

indeterminable value

indifferent promise

indigenous growth

indignant denunciation

indirect interrogation

indiscriminate censure

indispensable requisites

indisputable chronicler

indissoluble compact

indistinct association

individual valor

indivisible aspects

indolent neglect

indomitable pride

indubitable signs

indulgent construction

indwelling delight

ineffable disdain

ineffaceable incongruity
  [ineffaceable = indelible]

ineffectual blandishment

ineradicable coquetry

inestimable honor

inevitable corollary

inexcusable laughter

inexhaustible abundance

inexorable authority
  [inexorable = incapable of being persuaded]

inexplicable reluctance

inexpressible benignity

inextricable confusion

infallible judgment

infamous pretense

infantile simplicity

infectious hilarity

infelicitous arrangement
inferential method
infernal machinations
infinite deference
infinitesimal gradations
infirm purpose
inflamed curiosity
inflated optimism
inflexible integrity
influential voice
informing feature
infuriated demagogues
ingenious trick
inglorious victory
ingrained love
ingratiating exterior
inharmonious prelude
inherent dignity
inherited anxieties
inimitable felicity
iniquitous fortune
initiatory period
injudicious yielding
injured conceit
inky blackness
inmost recesses
innate forbearance
inner restlessness

innocent amenities

innocuous desuetude
  [desuetude = state of disuse or inactivity]

innovating spirit

inoffensive copiousness

inopportune condition

inordinate ambition

inquisitional rack

inquisitive observer

insatiable vanity

inscrutable austerity

insecure truce

insensate barbarism

insensibly flattered

inseparably associated

insidious tendency

insignificant blot

insincere profession

insinuatingly pursued

insipid tameness

insistent babel

insolent placidity

insoluble riddles

inspiring achievement

inspiriting spectacle

instant readiness

instantaneous cessations

instinctive disapproval

insufferably dull
insufficient appeal
insular strength
insulting invectives
   [invective = abusive language]
insuperable difficulty
insurmountable obstacles
intangible something
integral element
intellectual integrity
intelligent adaptation
intemperate scorn
intense perplexity
intensive cultivation
intentional garbling
interior spirit
interlocking directorate
intermediate link
interminable question
intermingled gloom
intermittent threats
internal dissension
interpolated speech
interpretative criticism
interwoven thread
intimately allied
intolerably tedious
intoxicating hum

intractable temper

intrenched privilege

intrepid dexterity

intricate interlacings

intriguing braggart

intrinsic fecundity
  [fecundity = productive or creative power]

intrusive brightness

intuitive perception

invaluable composition

invariable kindness

inveighing incessantly
  [inveighing = angry disapproval]

inventive jealousy

inveterate antipathy

invidious mention
  [invidious = rousing ill will or resentment]

invigorating discipline

invincible optimism

inviolable confidence

involuntary yearnings

involuted sentences
  [involuted = intricate; complex]

involved pomposity

invulnerable solemnity

inward disinclination

irascible doggedness

irate remonstrance

iridescent sheen

irksome task

iron resolution

ironic iciness

irradiating spirit

irrational awe

irreclaimable dead

irreconcilable parting

irrecoverably lost

irrefragable laws
  [irrefragable = indisputable]

irrefutable argument

irregular constellations

irrelevant suggestion

irremediable sorrow

irreparable injury

irrepressible excitement

irreproachable exterior

irresistible will

irresponsible gossip

irretrievable blunder

irreverent audacity

irreversible facts

irrevocable verdict

irritable impatience

isolated splendor

J

jaded sensibility
jagged outline
jarring discord
jaundiced opinion
jaunty confidence
jealous animosity
jesting allusion
jingling alliteration
jocular mirth
jocund host
   [jocund = sprightly; lighthearted]
jostling confusion
jovial fancy
joyful alacrity
joyous stagnation
jubilant antagonist
judicial impartiality
judicious candor
just rebuke
juvenile attempt

K

kaleidoscopic pictures
keen insight

kindled enthusiasm
kindly innocence
kindred sympathies
kingly generosity
knavish conduct
knightly achievement
known disingenuousness
   [ingenuous = frank; candid.]

L

labored levity
labyrinthian windings
lacerated feelings
lachrymose monotony
lackadaisical manner
laconic force
lagging footsteps
lamentable helplessness
languid impertinence
large receptivity
lashing scorn
latent conviction
laudable zeal
laughable absurdity
lavish liberality
lawless freedom
lazy acquiescence

leaden steps

leaping ambition

learned gravity

leering smile

legal perspicacity
   [perspicacity = perceptive, discerning]

legendary associations

legislative enactment

legitimate inference

leisurely composure

lengthening shadows

leonine powers

lethargic temperament

lettered coxcomb
   [coxcomb = conceited dandy; jester's cap]

liberal contemplations

lifeless imbecility

lifelong adherence

lightless eyes

lightly disregard

lightning glare

limpid twilight

lingering tenderness

linguistic attainments

liquid eloquence

lisping utterance

listening reverence

listless apathy

literal exactness
literary research
lithe contortions
little idiosyncrasies
lively susceptibility
livid lightning
living manifestation
loathsome oppression
local busybody
loftiest aspirations
logical precision
lone magnificence
longing fancy
looming probabilities
loquacious assurances
   [loquacious = very talkative]
lordly abhorrence
loud vociferation
   [vociferation = cry out loudly, especially in protest]
lounging gait
loutish rudeness
lovingly quizzical
lowering aspects
lowest degradation
loyal adhesion
lucid treatment
lucrative profession
ludicrous incongruity

lugubrious question
  [lugubrious = mournful, dismal, gloomy]

lukewarm repentance

lumbering gaiety

luminous interpretation

lurid picturesqueness

lurking suspicion

lustrous surface

luxuriant richness

lying equivocations

M

maddening monotony

magic fascination

magisterial emphasis

magnanimous concessions

magnetic fascination

magnificent florescence

magniloquent diction
  [magniloquent = extravagant in speech]

maidenly timidity

main ramifications

majestic dignity

maladjusted marriages

malevolent ingenuity

malicious aspersions

malign influence

malodorous gentility

manageable proportions

mangled arguments

manifest reluctance

manifold functions

manly reticence

mantling smile
  [mantling = cover with a mantle; concealing]

manual dexterity

manufactured melancholy

marked individuality

marketable commodity

marshaled hosts

martial footsteps

marvelous lucidity

masculine power

masked expression

massive strength

master achievement

matchless charm

material misconception

maternal solicitude

mathematical precision

matrimonial alliance

matured reflection

maudlin sentimentalism
  [maudlin = tearfully sentimental]

mawkish insipidity

maximum intensity

meager evidence

mean trickeries

meaningless confusion

measured cadence

mechanical handicraft

meditatively silent

meek ambition

melancholy musing

mellifluous eloquence
   [mellifluous = flowing with sweetness or honey]

mellow refinement

melodious platitudes

melodramatic resource

melting mood

memorable experience

menacing attitude

mendacious tongue
   [mendacious = false; untrue]

mendicant pilgrim
   [mendicant = beggar]

mental metamorphosis

mercenary view

merchantable literature

merciful insensibility

merciless censor

mercurial temperament

mere generalization

meretricious allurements
   [meretricious = plausible but false]

meridian splendor

merited ridicule

merry jest

metallic immobility

metaphysical obscurity

meteoric splendors

methodical regularity

metrical exactness

microscopic minuteness

mighty animosity

mild rejoinder

militant struggles

military autocracy

millennial reign

mimic gestures

minatory shadow
   [minatory = menacing or threatening]

mincing precision

mingled decorousness

miniature imitations

minor impulses

minute consideration

miraculous profusion

mirroring lake

mirthful glance

mischievous effusion

miserable musings

misleading notion

misshapen oddities

misspent strength

mistaken assumption

mistrustful superiority

misty depression

mitigating circumstances

mobile countenance

mock seriousness

modest cheerfulness

modified sentiment

moldy doctrines

mollifying conditions
   [mollifying = calming; soothing]

momentary discomfiture

momentous pause

monarchial institutions

monastic austerity

monotonous sameness

monstrous absurdity

monumental structure

moody silence

moonlight witchery

moral obliquity
   [obliquity = deviation or aberration]

morbid imagination

mordant wit

moribund mediocrities
mortal affront
mortified coldness
motley appearance
mountainous inequalities
mournful magnificence
mouthing amplitude
muddled opinion
muddy inefficiency
muffled detonations
mullioned windows
   [mullioned = vertical member dividing a window]
multifarious activity
multiform truth
multiple needs
multitudinous details
mundane importance
mural decorations
murderous parody
murky recesses
musical diapason
   [diapason = full, rich outpouring of harmonious sound]
mute insensibility
mutinous thoughts
muttered warning
mutual animosity
myriad lights
mysterious potency

mystic meaning
mythical kingdom

N

naive manner

naked eye

nameless fear

narcotic effect

narrowing axioms

nasal drone

nascent intercourse

national shortcomings

native incompetence

natural sluggishness

nauseous dose

nautical venture

neat refutation

nebulous uncertainty

necessary adjuncts

necromantic power
   [necromancy = communicating with the dead to predict the future. Black magic; sorcery.]

needless depression

nefarious scheme

negative approbation
   [approbation = warm approval; praise]

negligible quantity

neighboring mists
nerveless hand
nervous solicitude
nettled opponent
neutral eye
new perplexities
nice discrimination
niggardly allowance
nightmare fantasy
nimble faculty
noble condescension
nocturnal scene
nodding approval
noiseless reverie
noisy platitudes
nomadic life
nominal allegiance
nonchalant manner
non-committal way
nondescript garb
nonsense rhymes
noonday splendor
normal characteristics
notable circumstance
noteworthy friendship
noticeably begrimed
notoriously profligate
novel signification

nugatory cause
  [nugatory = little or no importance; trifling]

numbed stillness

numberless defeats

numerical majority

O

obdurate courage
  [obdurate = hardened in wrongdoing]

obedient compliance

objectionably apologetic

obligatory force

obligingly expressed

oblique tribute

obscure intimation

obsequious homage
  [obsequious = servile compliance; fawning]

observant eye

obsolete phraseology

obstinate defiance

obstreperous summons
  [obstreperous = noisily and stubbornly defiant]

obtrusive neatness

obvious boredom

occasional flights

occult sympathy

ocean depth

odd makeshifts

odious tyranny

odorous spring

offensive hostility

official asperity
   [asperity = harshness; ill temper or irritability]

olfactory sense

olive grayness

ominous rumors

omnipotent decree

omniscient affirmation

oncoming horde

onerous cares

onflaming volume

opalescent sea

opaque mass

openly disseminated

opinionated truculence
   [truculence = ferociously cruel behavior]

opportunely contrived

oppressive emptiness

opprobrious epithet
   [opprobrious = contemptuous reproach; scornful]

oracular utterance
   [oracular = solemnly prophetic; enigmatic; obscure]

oratorical display

ordinary delinquencies

organic assimilation

oriental spicery

originally promulgated

oscillatory movement
ostensible occupation
ostentatious display
outlandish fashion
outrageously vehement
outspoken encouragement
outstanding feature
outstretching sympathies
outward pomp
outworn creed
overbearing style
overestimated importance
overflowing sympathy
overhanging darkness
overmastering potency
overpowering argument
overshadowing dread
overstrained enthusiasm
overt act
overvaulting clouds
overweening sense
   [overweening = presumptuously arrogant; overbearing]
overwhelming solicitude
overworked drudge

P

pacific disposition

painful obstinacy
painstaking reticence
palatable advice
pallidly illumined
palpable originality
palpitating emotion
paltry hypocrisies
pampered darling
panic fear
panting eagerness
parabolic obscureness
paradoxical talker
paralyzing sentimentalism
paramount authority
parasitical magnificence
parental permission
paroxysmal outburst
particularly notable
partizan prejudice
passing panorama
passionate insistence
passive obedience
patchwork manner
patent example
paternal tenderness
pathetic helplessness
patient endurance
patriarchal visage

patriotic enthusiasm

peacefully propagated

peculiar piquancy
  [piquancy = appealingly provocative; charming]

pecuniary privation

pedantic ineptitude
  [pedantic = attention to detail or rules]

pedestrian vigor

peerless raconteur
  [raconteur = skilled storyteller]

peevish ingratitude

pending determination

penetrating warmth

penitential cries

penniless wanderer

pensive reflections

perceptible difference

peremptory punishment
  [peremptory = ending all debate or action]

perennial charm

perfect embodiment

perfunctory inquiries

perilous expedient

permanent significance

pernicious doctrine

perpetual oscillation

perplexing problem

persecuting zeal

persistent adherence

personal predilection
  [predilection = a preference]

persuasive eloquence

pert prig

pertinacious solemnity
  [pertinacious = stubbornly persistent]

pertinent question

perusing earnestness

pervading tendencies

perverse quaintness

pessimistic skepticism

pestiferous career
  [pestiferous = evil or deadly; pernicious]

pet aversion

petrified smile

petticoat diplomacy

pettifogging business

petty pedantries
  [pedantries = attention to detail or rules]

phantom show

philanthropic zeal

philosophical acuteness

phlegmatic temperament
  [phlegmatic = calm, sluggish; unemotional]

phosphorescent shimmer

photographic exactitude

physical convulsion

pictorial embellishments

picturesque details

piercing clearness

pinchbeck dignity
  [pinchbeck = cheap imitation]

pining melancholy

pioneering spirit

pious platitudes

piquant allusions
  [piquant = attracting or delighting]

pitiable frenzy

pitiless precision

pivotal point

placid stupidity

plainly expedient

plainspoken rebuke

plaintive cadence

plastic mind

plausible commonplaces

playful wit

pleasing reveries

pleasurable excitement

plenary argument

plentiful harvest

plighted word
  [plighted = promised by a solemn pledge]

poignant clearness

pointless tale

poisonous counsels

polished ease

polite indifference
political malcontent
polluting taints
pompous platitudes
ponderous research
pontifical manner
popular resentment
populous fertility
portentous gulf
positively deteriorating
posthumous glory
potential energy
powerful stimulant
practical helpfulness
precarious path
precautionary measure
precipitous flight
precise purpose
precocious wisdom
preconceived view
predatory writers
predestined spinster
predominant habit
pregnant hint
preliminary assumption
premature ripening
premonitory symptoms
preoccupied attention

prepossessing appearance

preposterous assertion

prescient reflection
 [prescient = perceiving the significance of events before they occur]

prescribed conditions

presiding genius

pressing necessity

pretended surprise

pretentious dignity

preternatural sagacity
 [preternatural = extraordinary]
 [sagacity = farsighted; wise]

pretty plaintiveness

prevailing misconception

priestly austerity

primal energy

prime factor
 [no integer factors; irreducible; 1,2,3,5,7,11...]

primeval silence

primordial conditions

princely courtesy

prismatic blush

pristine dignity

private contempt

privileged caste

prized possession

problematic age

prodigally lavished

prodigious variety

productive discipline

profane denunciation

professedly imitated

professional garrulity
  [garrulity = excessive talkativeness]

proffered service

profitable adventure

profligate expenditure

profound conviction

profuse generosity

projected visit

prolegomenous babbler
  [prolegomenous = preliminary discussion]

prolific outpouring

prolix narrative
  [prolix = wordy]

prolonged happiness

promiscuous multitude

promising scions
  [scions = descendants]

prompt courage

propagandist literature

propelling impulse

proper punctilio
  [punctilio = fine point of etiquette]

prophetic vision

propitious moment
  [propitious = auspicious, favorable]

proportionately vigilant

proprietary sense

prosaic excellence
  [prosaic = dull and lacking excitement]

prospective success

prosperity revival

prostrate servility

protoplasmic ancestors

protracted agony

proud destiny

proverbial situation

provincial prejudice

provoked hostility

prudential wisdom

prurient desire

prying criticism

psychic processes

public derision

puerile fickleness
  [puerile = immature; childish]

pugnacious defiance

pulsating life

punctilious care
  [punctilious = precise; scrupulous]

pungent epigram

puny dimensions

purblind brutality
  [purblind = partly blind; slow to understanding]

pure coincidence

purgatorial fires

puritanical primness

purplish shadows

purposed attempt

purposeful drama

pursuing fancies

pusillanimous desertion
  [pusillanimous = cowardly]

pyrotechnic outburst

Q

quailing culprit

quaint peculiarities

qualifying service

quavering voice

queer tolerance

quenchless despair

querulous disposition
  [querulous = habitually complaining]

questionable data

questioning gaze

quibbling speech

quick sensibility

quiescent melancholy

quiet cynicism

quivering excitement

quixotic impulse

quizzical expression

quondam foe
  [quondam = former]

R

racial prejudice

racy humor

radiant happiness

radical distinction

raging billows

rambling looseness

rampant wickedness

rancorous animosities

random preconceptions

rank luxuriance

ranting optimism

rapacious speculation
  [rapacious = taking by force; plundering]

rapid transitions

rapturous adoration

rare endowment

rarefied humor

rashly overrated

rational discourse

ravenous eagerness

ravishing spectacle

raw composition

reactionary movement

ready sympathy

realistic portrayal

reanimating ideas

reasonably probable

rebellious thought

reciprocal influence

reckless lavishness

recognized authority

recondite description
   [recondite = not easily understood; abstruse]

reconstructive era

recovered composure

recumbent figure

recurring doubt

reddening dawn

redoubled activity

refining influence

reflective habits

refractory temper

refreshing novelty

regal countenance

regretful melancholy

regular recurrence

relatively mild

relaxed discipline

relentless justice

religious scruples

reluctant tolerance

remarkable sagacity
  [sagacity = wisdom]

remedial measure

remorseless logic

remote epoch

renowned achievement

repeated falsification

repelling vices

repentant sense

reprehensible action

repressed ardor

reproachful misgiving

repulsive spectacle

reputed disposition

requisite expertness

resentful flame

resilient spirit

resistless might

resolute daring

resonant gaiety

resounding blare

resourceful wickedness

respectful condescension

resplendent brightness

responsive throb

restless inquisitiveness

restorative influence

restricted meaning
resultant limitation
retaliating blows
retarding influence
retreating footsteps
revengeful scowl
reverent enthusiasm
revolting cynicism
revolutionary tradition
rhapsodical eulogy
rhetorical amplification
rhythmical movements
richly emblazoned
righteous indignation
rightful distinction
rigid propriety
rigorous reservation
riotous clamor
ripe reflection
rising misgivings
riveted attention
robust sense
rollicking mirth
romantic solitudes
rooted habits
roseate tints
rough brutality
roundabout approach

rousing chorus

royal exultations

rubicund tinge
  [rubicund = healthy rosiness]

rude awakening

rudimentary effort

rueful conclusion

ruffled feelings

rugged austerity

ruling motive

rumbling hoarseness

ruminating mood

rural imagery

rustic simplicity

rustling forest

ruthless commercialism

S

sacerdotal preeminence
  [sacerdotal = priestly]

sacred tenderness

sacrilegious violence

sacrosanct fetish

sadly disconcerted

sagacious mind
  [sagacious = keen discernment, sound judgment]

sage reflections

saintly serenity

salient feature

salutary amusement

sanctimonious hypocrite
  [sanctimonious = feigning piety]

sane observer

sanguinary measures
  [sanguinary = eager for bloodshed; bloodthirsty]

sanguine expectations
  [sanguine = cheerfully confident; optimistic]

sarcastic incredulity

sardonic taciturnity
  [sardonic = cynically mocking]
  [taciturnity = habitually untalkative]

satirical critic

satisfying equipoise
  [equipoise = equilibrium]

savage satirist

scalding jests

scandalous falsehood

scant recognition

scathing satire

scattered distractions

scholarly attainments

scientific curiosity

scintillating wit

scoffing defiance

scorching criticism

scornful negligence

scriptural exegesis
  [exegesis = Critical explanation or analysis]

scrubby foreland

scrupulous fidelity

sculptured sphinx

scurrilous blustering
  [scurrilous = foul-mouthed]

searching eye

secluded byways

secret dismay

sectarian sternness

secure anchorage

sedentary occupation

seditious speaking
  [seditious = arousing to action or rebellion]

seductive whisperings

sedulously fostered
  [sedulously = persevering]

seeming artlessness

seething hate

selective instinct

self-conscious activity

self-deprecating irony

selfish vindictiveness

selfsame strain

senile sensualist

senseless gibberish

sensibly abated

sensitively courteous

sensuous music

sententious wisdom
  [sententious = terse and energetic; pithy]

sentimental twaddle

sepulchral quiet

sequestered nook

seraphic promiscuousness

serene triumph

serious resentment

serpentine curves

servile obedience

sesquipedalian words
  [sesquipedalian = long]

settled dislike

severe censure

shabby imitation

shadowy abstraction

shady retirements

shallow sophistry

sham enthusiasm

shambling gait

shamed demeanor

shameless injustice

shapeless conformations

shaping impulses

sharp rebuke

shattered reason

sheepish look

sheer boredom
sheltering hypocrisy
shifting panorama
shimmering gaiety
shining virtues
shivering soul
shocking rudeness
shoreless sea
shortening days
shrewd suspicion
shrewish look
shrill dissonance
shrunken wisp
shuddering reluctance
shuffling preliminaries
shy obeisance
sibilant oath
   [sibilant = producing a hissing sound]
sickening jealousy
sidelong glance
significant symbol
silent agony
silken filaments
silly escapades
silvery sea
similar amplitude
simple rectitude
simulated rapture

simultaneous acclamation
sincere hospitality
singular sensitiveness
sinister forebodings
sinuous movements
skeptical contempt
skillfully maintained
skulking look
slackened tension
slavish imitation
sledge-hammer blows
sleepless soul
sleepy enchantment
slender resource
slight acceleration
slovenly deportment
slow stupefaction
sluggish resolution
slumbering stream
smacking breeze
small aptitude
smiling repose
smirking commonplace
smoldering resentment
smothered sob
smug hypocrisy
snappish impertinence
sneering jibes

snowy whiteness

snug retreat

soaring ambition

sobbing wail

sober melancholy

social banalities

sociological bearing

soft allurement

solemn emptiness

solid knowledge

solidifying substance

solitary grandeur

somber relations

somewhat scandalized

somnolent state

sonorous simplicity
  [sonorous = full, deep, rich sound; impressive in style of speech]

sophistical argument

soporific emanations
  [soporific = inducing sleep]

sordid selfishness

sorely beset

sorrowful resignation

soulless mechanism

sounding verbiage

sourly ascetic

sovereign panacea

spacious tracklessness

sparkling splendor

specialized skill

specific characteristics

specious artifice
  [specious = having the ring plausibility but actually fallacious]

spectral fears

speculative rubbish

speechless surprise

speedy extinction

spendthrift prodigality

spirited vindication

spiritual dazzlement

splendid irony

splenetic imagination
  [splenetic = ill humor or irritability]

spontaneous challenge

sporadic exception

sportive gaiety

spotless honor

sprightly talk

spurious enthusiasm

squalid distress
  [squalid = Dirty and wretched; morally repulsive; sordid]

squandered talent

squeamish taste

staggering surprise

stainless womanhood

stale sciolism
  [sciolism = superficial knowledge]

stalwart defiance

stammered apology

starched sterility

starlit eminence

startling eccentricity

starving proletariat

stately stride

statesmanlike person

statistical knowledge

statuesque immobility

staunch manhood

steadfast obedience

stentorian voice
  [stentorian = extremely loud]

stereotyped commonness

sterile hatred

sterling sense

stern defiance

stiff conceit

stifled convulsions

still solitudes

stilted bombast

stimulating impression

stinging reproach

stinted endowment

stipulated reward

stock pleasantries
stoic callousness
stolid obstinacy
stony stare
storied traditions
stormy passion
stout assertion
straggling association
straightforward logic
straightway vanished
strained interpretation
straitened circumstance
strange wistfulness
strenuous insistence
striking diversity
stringent statement
strong aversion
stubborn reality
studious reserve
stultified mind
stunning crash
stupendous magnitude
stupid bewilderment
sturdy genuineness
subaltern attitude
  [subaltern = secondary]
subconscious conviction
subduing influence

sublime anticipations

submissive behavior

subordinate pursuit

subsidiary advantage

substantial agreement

subterranean sunlessness

subtle sophistry

subversive accident

successfully dispelled

successive undulations

succinct phrase

sudden perturbation

sullen submission

summary vengeance

sumptuously decorated

superabundant energy

superannuated coquette
  [superannuated = retired]
  [coquette = flirt]

superb command

supercilious discontent
  [supercilious = haughty disdain]

superficial surliness

superfluous precaution

superhuman vigor

superior skill

superlative cleverness

supernatural incident

supine resignation

suppliant posture

suppressed excitement

supreme exaltation

surging multitude

surly tone

surpassing loveliness

surprising intimacy

surreptitious means
   [surreptitious = clandestine; stealthy]

sustained vigor

swaggering bully

swampy flatness

swarming population

sweeping assertion

sweet peaceableness

swelling magnitude

swift transition

swinging cadence

symmetrical brow

sympathetic insight

syncopated tune

synthetic judgment

systematic interaction

T

tacit assumption

taciturn magnanimity
  [taciturn = habitually untalkative]

tactical niceties

tameless energy

tangible realities

tangled network

tardy recognition

tarnished reputation

tart temper

tasteful gratification

tasteless insipidity

tattered mendicant
  [mendicant = beggar]

taunting accusation

tawdry pretentiousness

tearful sensibilities

tearing gallop

teasing persistency

technical precision

tedious formality

teeming population

temerarious assertion
  [temerarious = presumptuous; reckless]

temperamental complacency

tempered pathos

tempestuous breeze

temporary expedient

tenacious memory

tender solicitude

tense attention

tentative moment

tepid conviction

termagant wife
 [termagant = quarrelsome, scolding]

terrible sublimity

terrifying imprecations
 [imprecations = curses]

terse realism

testamentary document

thankless task

thawing laughter

theological complexities

thirsting ear

thorny pathway

thorough uprightness

thoughtful silence

thoughtless whim

threadbare sentiment

threatened wrath

thrilling eloquence

throbbing pride

throneless monarch

thronging images

thundering rage

thwarted impulse

tideless depth

tigerish stealth

tightened ominously

timid acquiescence

tingling expectation

tinkling cymbal

tipsy jocularity
 [jocularity = given to joking]

tip-toe curiosity

tireless egotism

tiresome braggadocio
 [braggadocio = pretentious bragging]

titanic force

toilsome pleasure

tolerably comprehensive

tolerant indifference

tormenting thought

torn asunder

torpid faculties

tortuous labyrinth

tortured innocence

totally engrossed

touching pathos

tousled head

towering pride

traceable consanguinity

trackless forest

traditional type

tragic intensity

trailing sweetness

tranquil grandeur

transcendent power

transfiguring tints

transient emotion

translucent cup

transmuting touch

transparent complement

treacherous intelligence

treasured possessions

trembling anxiety

tremendous domination

tremulous sense
   [tremulous = timid or fearful]

trenchant phrase
   [trenchant = forceful, effective, vigorous]

trifling superfluity

trite remark

triumphant boldness

trivial conventionality

tropical luxuriance

troubled inertness

trudging wayfarer

trustworthy source

tumultuous rapture

tuneful expression

turbulent times

turgid appeal
  [turgid = excessively ornate or complex]
twilight shadow
twittered sleepily
twofold bearing
typical excellence
tyrannical disposition

U

ubiquitous activity
ugly revelation
ulterior purpose
ultimate sanction
ultrafashionable world
unabashed insolence
unabated pleasure
unaccountable protervity
  [protervity = peevishness; petulance]
unaccustomed toil
unadorned style
unaffected pathos
unaffrighted innocence
unagitated abstraction
unalloyed satisfaction
unalterable determination
unanimous acclamation
unanswerable argument

unapologetic air

unappeasable resentment

unapproached supremacy

unassailable position

unassuming dignity

unattainable perfection

unavailing consolation

unavoidable propensities

unballasted eloquence
  [unballasted = unsteady; wavering]

unbeaten track

unbecoming behavior

unbending reserve

unbiased judgment

unblemished character

unblinking observation

unblushing iteration

unbounded hospitality

unbridgeable chasm

unbridled fancy

unbroken continuity

uncanny fears

unceasing variation

unceremonious talk

uncertain tenure

unchallenged supremacy

unchanging affection

uncharitable ambition

uncharted depths
unchastised offense
unclouded splendor
uncomfortable doubt
uncommonly attractive
uncommunicable quality
uncomplaining endurance
uncomprehending smile
uncompromising dogmatism
unconcealed aversion
unconditioned freedom
uncongenial task
unconquerable patience
unconscious serenity
uncontrollable delight
unconventional demeanor
uncounted generations
uncouth gambols
uncritical position
unctuously belaud
   [unctuously = exaggerated, insincere]
   [belaud = praise greatly]
undaunted defender
undazzled eyes
undefined anticipations
undeniable charm
underlying assumption
undeviating consistency

undignified peccadilloes
   [peccadilloes = small sin or fault]

undiluted skepticism

undiminished relish

undimmed luster

undisciplined genius

undisguised amusement

undismayed expression

undisputed ascendency

undistracted attention

undisturbed silence

undivided energies

undoubted authenticity

undue predilection
   [predilection = preference]

undulating hills

unduly troublesome

undying friendship

unearthly gladness

uneasy craving

unembarrassed scrutiny

unembittered sweetness

unending exactions

unenlightened zealot

unenvied insipidity

unequaled skill

unequivocally resented

unerring fidelity

unessential details

unexampled sweetness

unexhausted kindliness

unexpected confidence

unfailing courtesy

unfaltering glance

unfamiliar garb

unfathomable indifference

unfeigned assent

unfettered liberty

unflagging zest

unflattering truth

unflecked confidence

unfledged novice
  [unfledged = young bird without feathers necessary to fly]

unflinching zeal

unfolding consciousness

unforced acquiescence

unforeseen vicissitudes
  [vicissitudes = sudden or unexpected changes]

unforgivable tragedy

unfounded conjecture

unfulfilled longing

ungainly figure

ungarnished reality

ungenerously resolved

ungenial temperament

ungovernable vehemence

ungracious temper
ungrudging tribute
unguessed riches
unhallowed threshold
unhampered expression
unhappy predecessor
unheeded beauties
unheroic measure
unhesitating faith
unhindered flight
unholy triumph
uniform blending
unimaginable bitterness
unimpassioned dignity
unimpeachable sentiment
unimpeded activity
uninstructed critic
uninterrupted process
unique personality
universal reprobation
  [reprobation = condemned to hell; severe disapproval]
unjust depreciation
unknown appellations
  [appellation = name, title, or designation]
unlettered laborer
unlikely contingency
unlimited opulence
unlucky dissembler

unmanly timidity
unmastered possibility.
unmeaning farce
unmeasured hostility
unmellowed dawn
unmelodious echoes
unmerciful plundering
unmingled consent
unmistakably fabulous
unmitigated gloom
unmixed astonishment
unmodified passion
unmurmuring sea
unnecessary platitudes
unnumbered thousands
unobtrusive deference
unostentatious display
unpalatable truth
unparalleled atrocities
unpardonable error
unphilosophical dreamer
unpleasant excrescence
  [excrescence = abnormal enlargement]
unprecedented advance
unprejudiced intelligence
unpretentious character
unprincipled violence
unprofitable craft

unpurchasable luxury
unqualified submission
unquenchable tenderness
unquestionable genius
unquestioning fate
unreasonable pretense
unreasoning distrust
unredeemable forfeit
unrefreshing sameness
unrelaxing emphasis
unrelenting spirit
unremembered winter
unremitting toil
unrepining sadness
unreproved admiration
unrequited love
unresentful disposition
unreserved assent
unresisted authority
unresolved exceptions
unresponsive gloom
unresting speed
unrestrained anger
unrestricted ease
unrivaled distinction
unruffled concord
unsatisfied yearning
unscrupulous adventurer

unseasonable apology

unseemly mirth

unselfish fidelity

unsettled trait

unshakable foundation

unshrinking determination

unslackened volubility
   [volubility = ready flow of speech; fluent]

unsophisticated youth

unsparing abuse

unspeakable delight

unspiritual tone

unspoiled goodness

unstinted praise

unsullied virtue

unsurpassed purity

unswerving integrity

untameable energy

unthinkable hypothesis

untiring energy

untold calamity

untoward circumstances
   [untoward = improper]

untrammeled expression

untrodden woodland

untroubled repose

untuneful phrase

untutored mind

unusual audacity
unutterable sadness
unvarnished feeling
unwarranted limitation
unwasting energies
unwavering allegiance
unwearied diligence
unwelcome alliance
unwieldy bulk
unwilling homage
unwittingly mingled
unwonted kindness
   [unwonted = unusual]
unworldly foolishness
unworthy alliance
unyielding nature
uproarious laughter
upstart pretensions
useless fripperies
   [fripperies = pretentious, showy]
utmost scorn

V

vacant stupidity
vacillating obedience
vacuous ease
vagabondish spirit

vagrant wandering

vaguely discursive

vain contemplation

vainglorious show

valid objection

valuable acquisition

valueless assertion

vampire tongue

vanished centuries

vantage ground

vapid generalities
  [vapid = lacking liveliness, interest; dull]

variable temperament

variegated career
  [variegated = varied]

vast advantage

veering purpose

vehement panting

veiled insolence

velvety lawn

venerable placidity

venomous passion

veracious journals
  [veracious = honest; truthful; accurate; precise]

verbal audacities

verbose manner

verdant hope

verifiable facts

veritable triumph

vernacular expression

vernal charm
  [vernal = resembling spring; fresh; youthful]

versatile grace

vexatious circumstances

vicarious virtue

vigilant sensibility

vigorous invective
  [invective = abusive language]

vile desecrater

villainous inconsistency

vindictive sentiment

violent agitation

virgin grace

virile leadership

virtual surrender

virtuous disdain

virulent prejudice

visible embarrassment

visionary dreamer

vital interpretation

vitiated taste
  [vitiated = reduce the value; corrupt morally]

vitriolic sneer

vivacious excitement

vivid portrayal

vociferous appeal

voiceless multitude

volatile fragrance

volcanic suddenness

voluble prose
  [voluble = ready flow of speech; fluent]

voluminous biography

voluntary relinquishment

voracious animosity

votive wreath

vulgar prosperity

vulnerable foe

W

wabbling enterprise
  [wabbling = wobbling]

waggishly sapient
  [sapient = wise]

wailing winds

wandering fancy

waning popularity

wanton butchery

warbling lute

warlike trappings

warning prophecy

warped purpose

warranted interference

wasteful prodigality

wavering courage
waxwork sex
wayward fancy
weakly imaginative
wearisome wordiness
wedded incompatibility
weighty argument
weird fascination
welcoming host
well-turned period
weltering current
whimsical touch
whirling confusion
whirring loom
whispering breeze
whistling winds
whited sepulcher
wholesome aspirations
wholly commendable
wicked ingratitude
wide signification
widespread acclaim
wild extravagance
willful waywardness
willing allegiance
willowy nothingness
wily antagonist
winding pilgrimage

windowless soul
winged fancies
winking stars
winning plaintiveness
winsome girlhood
wise dissertations
wistful entreaty
withering scorn
witnessing approval
witty expedient
wizard influence
woebegone countenance
woeful weariness
wolfish tendency
womanlike loveliness
wonderful affluence
wonted activity
   [wonted = usual]
wordy warfare
worthy achievement
wounded avarice
wrathful pugnacity
wretched effeminacy
wriggling disputant
writhing opponent

Y

yawning space
yearning tenderness
yielding disposition
youthful ambition

Z

zealous devotion
zigzag method
zoologically considered

SECTION II

SIGNIFICANT PHRASES

A

abashed and ashamed
abhorrence and repulsion
abilities and attainments
abject and hopeless
ably and vigorously
abrupt and perilous
absolute and eternal
absorbed and occupied
abstinence and self-denial
abstract and metaphysical
absurd and impertinent
abundant and sustained
abuse and slander
accentual and rhythmic
accidental and temporary
accomplished and popular
accurate and illuminating
achievement and character

acquisition and possession
active and aggressive
actual and immediate
acute and painful
admirable and accomplished
adorned and amplified
adroitness and judgment
adventurous and prodigal
advice and assistance
affable and courteous
affectation and coquetry
affectionate and warm-hearted
affluent and exuberant
affright and abhorrence
agencies and influences
ages and generations
aggrandizement and plunder
agreeable and ingenuous
aggressive and sullen
aghast and incredulous
agility and briskness
agitate and control
agony and despair
aids and auxiliaries
aim and purpose
airy and frivolous
alarm and uneasiness
alert and unsparing

all and sundry
allegiance and fidelity
alone and undistracted
alterations and additions
amazement and admiration
ambiguity and disagreement
ambition and determination
amiable and unpretending
ample and admirable
amusing and clever
analytical and critical
anarchy and chaos
ancient and venerable
anecdote and reminiscence
anger and fury
anguish and hopelessness
animated and effective
anomalies and absurdities
antagonism and opposition
antipathies and distastes
antiquated and obsolete
anxiety and trepidation
apathy and torpor
apologetic and uneasy
appalling and devastating
apparent and palpable
appearance and surroundings
apprehensive and anxious

appropriate and eloquent

approve and admire

apt and novel

archness and vivacity
  [archness = inappropriate playfulness]

ardent and aspiring

argument and inference

arid and unprofitable

arrangement and combination

arrogant and overbearing

artificial and elaborate

artistic and literary

artlessness and urbanity

ashamed and speechless

aspects and phases

aspiring and triumphal

assiduity and success

assimilated and combined

assuaged and pacified

astonished and curious

astound and perplex

athletic and nimble

atonement and forgiveness

atrocious and abominable

attacks and intrigues

attention and respect

attitudes and expressions

attractiveness and ability

audacity and skill

august and splendid

austere and icy

available and capable

avarice and cruelty

avidity and earnestness
  [avidity = desire; craving]

awake and active

awe and reverence

awkwardness and crudity

B

babel and confusion

backbone and sinew

baffled and disappointed

balanced and forceful

barbarity and wickedness

bards and sages

base and unworthy

beam and blaze

bearing and address

beautiful and majestic

bedraggled and disappointed

befogged and stupefied

beliefs and practises

bellowing and shouting

benevolence and candor

benign and hopeful
bent and disposition
benumbed and powerless
bewildered and stupefied
bigots and blockheads
billing and cooing
birth and breeding
bite and sting
bits and scraps
bitter and disdainful
black and solitary
bland and ingenious
blasphemous and profane
bleak and unrelenting
blend and harmonize
blessing and benediction
blind and unreasoning
blundering and plundering
blurred and confused
bluster and vulgarity
boast and assertion
bold and haughty
bombast and egotism
bone and sinew
boundless and unlimited
bourgeois and snobbish
brag and chatter
bravado and cowardice

brave and chivalrous
breathless and reverential
brevity and condensation
bribery and corruption
brief and pithy
bright and vivacious
brilliancy and grace
brisk and enlivening
broad and deep
brooding and solemn
brutal and degrading
bulks and masses
bungling and trifling
businesslike and practicable
bustle and business

C

cajoled and bullied
calamity and sorrow
callous and impervious
calmness and composure
calumny and exaggeration
   [calumny = maliciously lying to injure a reputation]
candor and kindness
cant and hypocrisy
   [cant = hypocritically pious language]
capable and efficient

capacity and ability
capricious and unreasonable
career and occupation
cares and anxieties
carping and ungenerous
casual and transient
causes and circumstances
cautious and reticent
celebrated and praised
celerity and violence
   [celerity = swiftness of action]
ceremony and splendor
certain and verifiable
chafe and exasperate
chagrin and despondency
chance and opportunity
change and variety
chaos and confusion
character and temperament
characteristic and complete
charges and insinuations
charm and perfection
chaste and refined
cheap and convenient
checked and thwarted
cheerfulness and gaiety
cherish and guard
chief and paramount

chilled and stiffened

choleric and sanguine
  [choleric = easily angered; bad-tempered]
  [sanguine = cheerfully confident; optimistic]

churlishness and violence
  [churlish = boorish or vulgar]

citation and allusion

civility and communicativeness

civilized and cultured

clamorous and wild

claptrap and platitude

clarity and straightforwardness

classical and perspicuous
  [perspicuous = easy to understand]

clatter and clang

clear and decisive

cleverness and acuteness

clogged and dulled

clumsy and smudgy

coarse and grotesque

coaxed and threatened

coexistent and correlative

cogent and conclusive

cohesion and sequence

cold and unemotional

comely and vivacious

comfort and security

command and threaten

common and familiar

commotion and annoyance
compact and complete
comparison and discrimination
compass and power
competent and experienced
complaints and imprecations
  [imprecation = a curse]
complaisance and readiness
complete and permanent
complex and various
composure and gracefulness
comprehensive and accurate
compression and pregnancy
conceal and deny
conceit and impertinence
conceived and consummated
concentrated and intensified
conception and treatment
concern and wonder
concise and emphatic
concrete and definite
condemned and upbraided
conditions and limitations
confession and doubt
confidence and loyalty
confusion and dismay
congratulations and welcomings
connection and interdependence

conquered and transformed
conquest and acquisition
consciously and purposely
consistent and harmonious
conspicuous and impressive
conspired and contrived
constant and intimate
constructive and vital
contemn and decry
   [contemn = despise]
contempt and indignation
contentment and serenity
continuous and undeviating
contorted and fantastic
contradictions and inconsistencies
contrast and comparison
contrivance and disguise
conventional and limited
cool and indifferent
copiousness and vivacity
cordial and cheerful
corruption and decay
costly and gorgeous
counselor and guide
countless and indescribable
courage and endurance
courted and feted
courteous and sympathetic

coveted and deserved
coy and furtive
cramped and distorted
creative and inventive
credulity and ignorance
creeds and dogmas
crime and misdemeanor
crippled and maimed
crises and struggles
crisp and sparkling
critical and skeptical
crowded and jostled
crowned and sceptered
crude and primitive
cruel and rapacious
crumbling and shapeless
crushed and bewildered
cultured and refined
cumbrous and diffuse
  [cumbrous = cumbersome]
cunning and cruelty
curious and inexpressible
curved and channeled
customs and manners
cynical and contemptuous

D

dangers and pitfalls
daring and resolute
dark and starless
dart and quiver
dashing and careless
dates and details
dazzled and confounded
debased and demoralized
debilitating and futile
decencies and restraints
deception and cruelty
decided and definite
declamation and delivery
decline and decay
deductions and inferences
deep and subtle
deface and injure
defame and tarnish
deference and concession
defiant and antagonistic
deficient and unskilled
definite and memorable
deft and offensive
degraded and dishonored
deliberate and effective

delicate and lambent
  [lambent = effortlessly brilliant]

delight and consolation

delusion and trickery

demands and expectations

demeanor and conduct

demoralizing and enfeebling

denial and defense

dense and luminous

denunciations and censures

deplorable and baneful

depravity and frivolity

depressing and discouraging

depth and richness

derision and skepticism

described and classified

desecration and decay

designs and activities

desires and motives

desolation and wretchedness

despatch and resolution

desperation and defiance

despise and satirize

despoiled and destroyed

despondency and melancholy

despotism and coercion

destitution and misery

desultory and slipshod
  [desultory = haphazardly; random]

detached and isolated

determined and courageous

detestable and intolerable

development and culture

devoted and unwavering

dictatorial and insolent

diction and pronunciation

differences and disputes

difficult and arduous

diffidence and constraint

diffuseness and warmth

dignified and austere

digressive and wanton

dilatory and hesitating
  [dilatory = postpone or delay]

diligent and sedulous
  [sedulous = persevering]

dim and distant

din and traffic

directed and controlled

disagreeable and painful

disappointed and abashed

disapprobation and condemnation
  [approbation = warm approval; praise]

disapproval and apprehension

discipline and development

discomfiture and degradation

disconcerted and dismayed
discontent and disquiet
discords and differences
discouraging and distressing
discovery and invention
discretion and moderation
disdain and mockery
disfigured and shapeless
disgrace and ruin
disgust and dismay
dishonor and ruin
disillusioned and ironical
disintegration and decay
disinterested and gracious
disjointed and voluble
  [voluble = fluent]
dislike and disdain
dislocation and chaos
dismay and apprehension
dispirit and discourage
disposition and power
disquietude and uneasiness
dissolute and hateful
dissolve and disappear
distant and diverse
distended and distorted
distinctive and appropriate
distinguishing and differentiating

distress and humiliation
distrust and aversion
disturbed and anxious
diverging and contracting
docile and obedient
dogma and ritual
dominant and permanent
dormant and subdued
doubt and trepidation
dramatic and sensational
drastic and revolutionary
dread and terror
dreams and ambitions
dreariness and desolation
dregs and sediments
drill and discipline
driveling and childish
drollery and ridicule
drooping and disconsolate
dubious and dangerous
dull and spiritless
dumb and nerveless
dupe and victim
duplicity and equivocation
dust and oblivion
duties and difficulties
dwarfed and obscured
dwindle and disappear

E

eagerness and ecstasy
earnestness and animation
ease and lightness
ebb and flow
eclectic and assimilated
edifying and enchanting
education and skill
effective and competent
efficiency and success
egotism and bigotry
elaboration and display
elation and delight
elegance and gentility
elementary and simple
elevate and ennoble
eligibility and suitableness
elongated and narrow
eloquent and expressive
elusive and exquisite
embarrassed and concerned
embittered and despairing
embodiment and actualization
emerged and flowered
eminent and remarkable

emoluments and honors
  [emoluments = compensation]

emotion and passion

emphasize and magnify

employment and profession

encouragement and stimulus

energy and activity

enfeebled and exhausted

enfold and enwrap

engulfed and buried

enjoyment and satisfaction

enlightenment and progress

enraptured and amazed

enriched and ennobled

enslave and dominate

enterprising and intelligent

entertaining and diverting

enthusiasm and zeal

enticing and alluring

entire and complete

environment and training

envy and despair

ephemeral and feeble
  [ephemeral = markedly short-lived]

episodes and interludes

epithet and description

equality and solidarity

equity and justice

erratic and confused

errors and infirmities

essential and predominating

estimable and agreeable

eternal and sublime

ethical and religious

ever and anon

evident and manifest

exactitude and completeness

exaggerate and distort

exaltation and enthusiasm

examination and comparison

examples and models

exasperations and paroxysms
  [paroxysms = outbursts of emotion or action]

excellent and worthy

exceptional and remarkable

excessive and unreasonable

excitable and irritable

exclusive and limited

excusable and justifiable

execration and defiance
  [execration = curse]

exertion and excitement

exhaustion and fatigue

exhibition and display

exhilarating and beneficial

exigency and requirement
  [exigency = urgent situation]
expansive and digressive
expediency and utility
expensive and unprofitable
experience and skill
experiment and explorations
expert and vigorous
explanation and elucidation
explore and examine
expressions and exclamations
expressive and effective
exquisite and powerful
extent and importance
extraordinary and unexpected
extravagant and grotesque
extreme and morbid
exuberant and infectious

F

fabulous and fabricated
facile and brilliant
facts and traditions
faculties and powers
faded and withered
failures and misadventures
faint and obscure

fair and impartial

faith and reverence

fallacy and danger

false and fugitive

fame and fortune

familiar and gracious

famous and foremost

fancies and sentiments

fanciful and chimerical
  [chimerical = highly improbable]

fantastic and meretricious
  [meretricious = plausible but false]

fascination and awe

fashion and frivolity

fastidious and exacting

fatigued and careworn

faults and delusions

favors and kindnesses

fear and bewilderment

feasible and practical

feebleness and folly

feeling and passion

felicitous and exquisite

ferocious and mercenary

fertility and vigor

fervor and simplicity

feverishly and furiously

fickle and uncertain

fidelity and zeal

fierce and menacing

fiery and controversial

final and irreversible

finish and completeness

firm and decisive

first and foremost

fitful and capricious

fitting and appropriate

fixity and finality

flaming and mendacious
  [mendacious = lying; untruthful]

flare and flicker

flatness and insipidity

flattery and toadyism

flexible and spontaneous

flickering and ambiguous

flighty and impetuous

flippant and contemptuous

florid and healthy
  [florid = ornate; flowery]

flotsam and jetsam

flow and fullness

flowery and figurative

fluctuating and transitory

fluency and flippancy

fluttering and restless

focus and concentrate

fogs and complications
foibles and follies
foiled and defeated
folly and indecorum
fools and underlings
force and effectiveness
formal and cold
formidable and profound
formlessness and exaggeration
fortitude and perseverance
foul and ominous
fragile and pale
fragments and morsels
fragrance and beauty
frailties and absurdities
frank and genial
free and independent
frequent and poignant
freshness and fragrance
fretful and timorous
friend and benefactor
frigid and pompous
frivolous and empty
froth and effervescence
frustrated and confounded
fuddled and contradictory
full and sonorous
fumbling and blundering

fuming and bustling
fun and satire
function and aim
fundamental and necessary
furrowed and ragged
furtive and illusive
fury and madness
fussing and fuming
futile and untrustworthy

G

gaiety and grace
gallant and proud
galling and humiliating
gaunt and ghastly
gay and genial
general and universal
generosity and prodigality
generous and humane
genial and refreshing
genius and reputation
gentle and amiable
genuine and infectious
germ and root
gesticulation and emphasis
   [gesticulation = deliberate, vigorous motion or gesture]
ghastly and inconceivable

gifts and graces

gigantic and portentous

glamour and fascination

glare and pretension

glib and loquacious
  [loquacious = very talkative]

glitter and glamour

gloomy and morose

glorious and gorgeous

glowing and exaggerated

glum and grim

goodness and rectitude

goodwill and merriment

gorgeousness and splendor

gossiping and grumbling

govern and overrule

grace and dignity

gracious and generous

gradual and progressive

graft and dishonesty

grand and sublime

grandeur and massiveness

grandiose and oracular
  [oracular = solemnly prophetic; obscure]

graphic and gorgeous

gratification and enjoyment

gratitude and generosity

gratuitous and ungracious

grave and stately
graveyards and solitudes
greatness and stability
greed and covetousness
grief and remorse
grim and sullen
grimaces and gesticulations
grope and fumble
grossness and brutality
grotesque and monstrous
grouped and combined
growth and development
guesses and fancies
guidance and inspiration
gush and hysteria
gusto and effect

H

habits and humors
habitual and intuitive
hackneyed and tawdry
haggard and pale
handsome and amiable
haphazard and dangerous
happiness and pleasantness
harass and pursue
hard and unsparing

hardships and indignities
harmony and beauty
harsh and austere
hasty and unwarranted
hateful and loathsome
haughtiness and arrogance
hauteur and disdain
   [hauteur = arrogance]
hazard and peril
hazy and indefinite
headstrong and foolish
healthy and vigorous
hearth and shrine
heartless and hypocritical
heat and impatience
heaviness and weariness
hecklings and interruptions
hectic and pitiful
heretics and schismatics
heritage and privilege
heroism and wisdom
hesitation and irresolution
hideous and grotesque
high and conscientious
hilarity and mirth
hints and suggestions
history and tradition
hither and thither

hoarse and rumbling
hobbies and eccentricities
hollowness and unreality
holy and prayerful
homeliness and simplicity
honestly and confessedly
honors and emoluments
   [emoluments = compensation]
hooted and mobbed
hopes and prospects
horror and ghastliness
hospitality and magnificence
hubbub and confusion
huge and unwieldy
humane and sympathetic
humility and devoutness
humors and singularities
hurry and bustle
hushed and still
husks and phantoms
hypocrisy and impudence

I

ideas and achievements
idle and presumptuous
ignoble and shabby
ignominy and misfortune

ignorance and superstition

illiterate and unfit

ill-tempered and unjust

illuminative and suggestive

illustrative and typical

images and impressions

imagination and memory

imbitter and exasperate

imitators and disciples

immature and unpromising

immediate and instantaneous

immensity and intricacy

imminent and terrible

immovable and unchangeable

impalpable and spiritual

impassioned and energetic

impatient and restless

imperfection and fallibility

imperil and destroy

imperious and ruthless
  [imperious = arrogantly domineering]

impertinent and personal

impinging and inexorable

implacable and destructive

important and formidable

imposed and enforced

impossibilities and absurdities

impressible and plastic

improvement and progress
imprudent and thoughtless
impulse and indignation
inaccessible and audacious
inactive and supine
inadequate and misleading
inapplicable and alien
inarticulate and confused
inborn and native
incensed and alarmed
inchoate and tentative
  [inchoate = imperfectly formed]
incoherent and inconclusive
incompetence and ignorance
incomplete and erroneous
incongruity and absurdity
inconvenient and troublesome
incorrigible and irrepressible
incredulous and mortified
indefatigable and irresistible
indefinite and vague
independent and democratic
indifference and brevity
indigence and obscurity
indignation and chagrin
indirectly and unconsciously
indispensable and irreplaceable
indistinct and misty

indolence and indifference
indomitable and dogged
indorsed and applauded
indulge and cherish
industrious and vigilant
ineffective and bungling
inert and uncertain
inevitable and assured
inexhaustible and indomitable
inexperienced and timid
infallible and disdainful
inference and suggestion
infinite and eternal
inflexible and unchanging
influence and authority
informed and competent
ingenious and eloquent
ingratitude and cruelty
inharmonious and irregular
injustice and inhumanity
innocence and fidelity
innuendo and suggestion
inopportune and futile
insanely and blindly
inscrutable and perplexing
insecurity and precariousness
insensibly and graciously
insignificant and transitory

insincere and worthless

insipid and silly

insistent and incongruous

insolence and absurdity

inspiring and animating

instant and momentous

instinctive and rational

insulted and thwarted

intangible and indefinable

integral and indestructible

integrity and honor

intelligence and insight

intense and overpowering

intentness and interest

interesting and engrossing

intimate and familiar

intolerant and bumptious
    [bumptious = loudly assertive; pushy]

intractable and untameable

intricate and endless

intrusive and unmannerly

intuitive and axiomatic

invasion and aggression

invective and innuendo
    [invective = abusive language]

investigation and research

invidious and painful
    [invidious = rousing ill will, animosity]

inviolate and unscathed
invisible and silent
involuntary and automatic
irksome and distasteful
irrational and excessive
irregular and intermittent
irreligious and immoral
irremediable and eternal
irrepressible and insistent
irreverence and ingratitude
irritable and churlish
   [churlish = boorish or vulgar]
isolated and detached

J

jabber and chatter
jagged and multifarious
jargon and absurdity
jaundiced and jealous
jeer and scoff
jeopardy and instability
jests and sarcasms
jocular and vivacious
jostle and stumble
joy and felicity
jubilant and boastful
judgment and discretion

judicious and acute

juggled and manipulated

jumble and confuse

juncture and circumstance

jurisdiction and authority

justice and virtue

juvenile and budding

K

keen and pertinacious
   [pertinacious = stubbornly persistent]

kind and forbearing

kindle and intensify

kindred and analogous

kingly and autocratic

knavish and tyrannical

knowledge and conviction

known and recognized

L

labor and drudgery

lame and impotent

lamentable and depressing

languid and indifferent

large and opulent

lassitude and languor
   [languor = dreamy, lazy mood]
latent and lifeless
latitude and scope
laudable and deserving
laughable and grotesque
lavish and wasteful
lawlessness and violence
laxity and forbearance
laziness and profligacy
leafage and fruitage
learning and austerity
legends and traditions
legitimate and logical
leisure and tranquillity
lengthy and diffuse
lenient and sympathetic
lethargy and sloth
levity and gaiety
liberal and ample
liberty and freedom
license and laxity
likely and plausible
limited and abbreviated
listless and inert
literal and exact
literary and artistic
lithe and sinewy

lively and poignant

loathsome and abject

lofty and sonorous
 [sonorous = producing a full, rich sound; impressive speech]

logical and consistent

loquacity and exuberance
 [loquacity = very talkative.]

loss and deterioration

loud and passionate

loving and reverential

low and groveling

loyal and devoted

lucidity and vividness

lucky and propitious
 [propitious = auspicious, favorable; kindly]

lucrative and advantageous

ludicrous and detestable

lugubrious and unfortunate
 [lugubrious = dismal, gloomy]

lukewarm and indifferent

lull and silence

luminous and keen

lure and captivate

lurid and fiery

luscious and lasting

luster and resplendence

lusty and big-sounding

luxury and pomp

M

madness and folly

magical and secret

magnificent and luxurious

majestic and imposing

malice and revenge

malignity and spitefulness

manifold and complex

manly and powerful

manner and conduct

marvels and mysteries

massive and compact

masterly and convincing

materialistic and sordid

maternal and filial

maudlin and grotesque
  [maudlin = tearfully sentimental]

maxims and morals

meager and bare

mean and debasing

meaning and significance

means and materials

mechanical and monotonous

meddling and muddling

meditative and sympathetic

meek and manageable

melody and softness

memorable and glorious

menace and superciliousness
  [superciliousness = haughty disdain]

merciful and chivalrous

merciless and unpitying

merit and virtue

mighty and majestic

mild and virtuous

mince and temporize

minds and memories

minuteness and fidelity

mirth and joviality

misdemeanors and improprieties

misery and degradation

misrepresented and reviled

misty and indefinite

mobile and expressive

mockery and imposture

moderate and cautious

modes and methods

modest and retiring

molding and upbuilding

momentary and languid
  [languid = lacking energy; weak]

momentous and appalling

monopoly and injustice

monotony and indecorum

monstrous and insupportable
moody and brooding
moral and religious
morbid and irritable
motionless and commanding
motives and aims
mud and mire
muddled and incoherent
murmurs and reproaches
muscularity and morality
mutable and fleeting
mute and insensate
mutilated and disfigured
muttering and murmuring
mutual and friendly
mysterious and incomprehensible
mystic and wonderful

N

nagging and squabbling
nameless and obscure
narrow and timorous
natural and spontaneous
nauseous and disgusting
neatness and propriety
necessarily and essentially
needs and demands

nefarious and malevolent

negations and contradictions

neglect and evade

negotiate and bargain

nerve and fiber

neutral and colorless

nicety and precision

nimble and airy

noble and powerful

nodding and blinking

noisy and scurrilous
   [scurrilous = vulgar, coarse, abusive language]

nonsense and absurdity

nooks and corners

notable and conspicuous

noted and distinguished

noteworthy and intelligible

notoriety and prominence

nourish and foster

novelty and freshness

novice and ignoramus

nucleus and beginning

nugatory and ineffectual
   [nugatory = no importance; trifling]

nullify and destroy

number and variety

numerous and important

O

oaths and revilings

obdurate and impenitent
  [obdurate = hardened in wrongdoing]
  [impenitent = without remorse for sins]

obedient and dutious

obeisance and submission

objectionable and inexpedient

obligation and dependence

obliquity and hypocrisy

oblivious and insensible

obloquy and detraction
  [obloquy = abusive language]

obnoxious and odious

obscure and enigmatical

obsequies and panegyrics
  [obsequies = funeral rite]
  [panegyrics = elaborate praise]

obsequious and conciliating
  [obsequious = servile compliance; fawning]

observations and reflections

obstacles and disasters

obstinate and stupid

obstreperous and noisy
  [obstreperous = stubbornly defiant]

obtrusive and vulgar

obtuse and imbecile

obvious and palpable

occasional and contingent

occult and hidden

occupations and habits

odd and dismal

odious and oppressive

offensive and aggressive

official and authoritative

oily and servile

old and decrepit

ominous and untrustworthy

omnivorous and sordid

oneness and unity

onerous and perplexing

open and inviting

opinions and hypotheses

opportunism and inconsistency

opposite and discordant

oppressed and sullen

optimistic and reassuring

opulence and magnitude

oracular and occult
   [oracular = solemnly prophetic; obscure]

order and uniformity

organic and rational

organization and system

origin and discovery

original and attractive
ornate and variegated
ostensible and explicit
ostentatiousness and gaiety
outlines and appearances
outrageous and scandalous
overburdened and confused
overcome and vanquish
overstep and contravene
overt and unmistakable
overwearied and outworn
overworked and fagged
   [fagged = worked to exhaustion]

P

pains and penalties
painstaking and cumbersome
pale and anxious
palpable and plain
paltry and inglorious
pampered and petted
parade and display
parched and dry
partial and provisional
particularly and individually
parties and sects
passion and prejudice

passive and indifferent

pastimes and diversions

patent and pertinent

pathos and terror

patience and perseverance

patriotism and reverence

pattern and exemplar
  [exemplar = worthy of imitation]

peaks and pinnacles

pedagogue and pedant
  [pedant = exhibits learning or scholarship ostentatiously]

pedantries and affectations

pedigree and genealogy

peevishness and spleen

pellucid and crystal
  [pellucid = transparently clear]

penetrating and insidious

penned and planned

peppery and impetuous

perception and recognition

peremptorily and irrevocably
  [peremptorily = not allowing contradiction]

perilous and shifting

permanent and unchangeable

permeate and purify

pernicious and malign

perplexity and confusion

persistent and reiterated

personal and specific

perspicuous and flowing
  [perspicuous = clearly expressed]

perturbed and restless

perverted and prejudicial

pessimistic and disenchanted

pestilence and famine

petted and indulged

pettiness and prudence

petulance and acrimony

pharisaical and bitter
  [pharisaical = hypocritically self-righteous and condemnatory]

pictorial and dramatic

picturesque and illustrative

pilgrim and crusader

pillage and demolish

piquant and palatable
  [piquant = agreeable pungent taste]

pith and brevity

pitiful and destitute

place and power

plagued and persecuted

plainness and severity

plaintive and mournful

plans and projects

plastic and ductile

plausibility and humbug

pleasant and pungent

pleasurable and wholesome

pliant and submissive
plot and verisimilitude
plunder and sacrilege
poetical and pastoral
pointless and ineffective
polite and elegant
political and sociological
pomp and pageantry
ponderous and unwieldy
poor and barren
possession and dominion
potent and prevailing
power and luxury
praise and commend
precedence and usage
precision and efficiency
preference and prejudice
pregnant and suggestive
prejudice and predilection
   [predilection = preference]
presence and address
present and tangible
prestige and authority
presumptuous and futile
pretentious and inept
pretty and enchanting
pride and indignation
primary and essential

priority and predominance

probity and candor
  [probity = integrity; uprightness]

prodigal and careless

profile and outline

profound and philosophical

profuse and tearful

prolix and tedious
  [prolix = prolonged; wordy]

prominence and importance

promise and performance

promptitude and dispatch

proneness and readiness

pronounced and diversified

proof and illustration

propensity and desire

proportion and consistency

propriety and delicacy

prostration and loss

protection and safety

protesting and repelling

protracted and fruitless

provincialism and vulgarity

prudent and sagacious
  [sagacious = keenly discerning]

puerile and sickly
  [puerile = immature; childish]

puffy and dissipated

puissant and vigorous
  [puissant = with power, might]

punctilious and severe
  [punctilious = precise; scrupulous]

purity and simplicity

purpose and intention

pusillanimous and petty
  [pusillanimous = cowardly]

puzzled and affected

Q

quackery and incompetence

quaintness and oddity

qualities and gifts

quarrel and wrangle

queer and affected

querulous and plaintive
  [querulous = complaining; peevish]

quibble and fabricate

quickness and agility

quiet and unobtrusive

quintessential and nuclear
  [quintessential = perfect example]

quips and cranks

quirks and graces

quivering and fearful

quizzical and whimsical

R

racked and oppressed

racy and incisive

rage and apprehension

rank and learning

rant and gush

rapacity and villainy
   [rapacity = plundering]

rapidity and precision

rapt and silent

rapture and enthusiasm

rare and exquisite

rashness and heedlessness

ready and spontaneous

real and positive

realistic and effective

reasonable and practical

rebellion and disloyalty

rebuffs and anxieties

receptive and responsive

recognized and honored

recoil and reaction

reconciliation and peace

recondite and abstruse
   [recondite = concealed; hidden]
   [abstruse = difficult to understand]

reconnoiter and explore
recreation and amusement
rectitude and delicacy
redeeming and transforming
refined and dignified
refreshing and invigorating
regard and esteem
regret and remorse
regular and symmetrical
rejection and scorn
reliable and trustworthy
relief and redress
   [redress = set right; remedy]
remarkable and interesting
remorseful and sullen
remote and distant
rend and devastate
repellent and ungracious
repetition and reiteration
repress and silence
repugnance and aversion
repulsive and loathsome
resentment and indignation
reserve and coyness
resistless and implacable
resolution and effort
resonant and tuneful
resourceful and unscrupulous

respected and obeyed

responsibilities and burdens

restive and bored

restless and impatient

retaliation and revenge

reticence and repose

revered and cherished

reverses and disasters

revised and corrected

revolution and sedition
   [sedition = insurrection; rebellion]

rhapsodies and panegyrics
   [panegyrics = elaborate praise]

richness and fertility

ridicule and censure

right and praiseworthy

rigid and inexpressive

ripeness and plenitude

rivals and antagonists

roar and ring

robust and rugged

rococo and affected
   [rococo = elaborate ornamentation]

romantic and pathetic

rough and barren

roundabout and complicated

roused and stimulated

rude and fiery

rugged and inaccessible
rumors and impressions
rushing and gurgling
rust and disuse

S

sad and melancholy

sagacity and virtue
  [sagacity = farsighted; wise]

sane and simple

sarcastic and cruel

sayings and quibbles

scant and incidental

scattered and desultory
  [desultory = haphazard; random]

scenes and associations

scholastic and erudite
  [erudite = learned]

scientific and exact

scintillating and brilliant

scoffing and unbelief

scope and significance

scorched and shriveled

scorn and loathing

scrupulous and anxious

scrutiny and investigation

searching and irresistible

seared and scorched

secondary and subsidiary

secretive and furtive

sedate and serious

selfish and overbearing

sensational and trivial

senseless and unreasoning

sensibilities and emotions

sensitive and capricious

sententious and tiresome
 [sententious = pompous moralizing; terse and energetic]

sentiment and passion

serene and quiet

serious and studious

severe and saturnine
 [saturnine = melancholy or sullen]

shabbiness and vulgarity

shadowy and confused

shame and mortification

shams and hypocrisies

shaped and sculptured

sharp and vigorous

shelter and safeguard

shifts and compromises

shivering and chattering

shocked and astonished

short and precarious

shreds and tatters

shrewd and diligent

shrill and piercing

shrinking and nervous

shy and subdued

significant and sinister

signs and tokens

silence and obscurity

similarities and resemblances

simple and straightforward

simpletons and nincompoops

sincerity and frankness

sinewy and active

skill and coolness

skulk and shirk

sleek and languid
  [languid = lacking energy or vitality; weak]

slight and precarious

slipshod and untidy

slothfulness and perversity

slow and sluggish

slumbering and unsuspected

small and hampered

smirched and tarnished

smoothness and artifice

sneering and sentimental

soberly and truthfully

softness and effeminacy

solemn and dramatic

solitary and idle

solitude and depression

sonorous and musical

sons and scions
 [scions = descendant or heir]

soporific and sodden
 [soporific = inducing sleep]

sordid and stupid

sorrow and lamentation

soulless and mindless

sovereign and independent

spacious and lofty

sparkling and spontaneous

spasmodic and hysterical

speedy and inevitable

spicy and pungent

spiritual and invisible

spiteful and sordid

splash and dash

splendor and glory

spontaneity and intensity

sportive and playful

sprightly and vigorous

spur and impulse

spurious and misleading

squalid and dismal
 [squalid = wretched, dirty, repulsive]

stare and gasp

stately and ponderous
statesmanship and character
staunch and influential
stay and solace
steadfast and resolute
steadily and patiently
stealthy and hostile
stern and unbending
stiff and cumbersome
stifling and venomous
still and translucent
stimulating and wholesome
stings and stimulants
stir and tumult
stolid and soulless
strain and struggle
strange and incomprehensible
stratagems and plots
strenuous and energetic
strictly and absolutely
strife and contention
striking and picturesque
strong and youthful
structure and organization
struggles and misgivings
studied and artificial
stunned and insensible
stupor and despair

sturdy and manly

style and temperament

suave and winning

sublime and aspiring

submission and patience

subordinate and dependent

substance and basis

subtle and elusive

suddenness and vehemence

suffering and desperation

suffused and transfigured

suggestions and stimulations

sullen and fierce

summarize and epitomize

sumptuous and aromatic

sunshine and smiles

superb and showy

supercilious and obstinate
  [supercilious = haughty disdain]

superficial and obvious

superfluous and impertinent

suppressed and restrained

surmises and suggestions

surprise and wonder

susceptibility and vulnerability

suspense and excitement

suspicion and innuendo
  [innuendo = indirect derogatory implication]

sustained and measured
sweet and wholesome
swelled and bloated
swift and stealthy
swoop and range
symbolism and imagery
sympathetic and consoling

T

taciturn and laconic
  [taciturn = untalkative]
  [laconic = terse]
tactful and conciliatory
talkative and effusive
tame and insipid
tangible and sufficient
tangled and shapeless
tardy and belated
tartness and contradiction
taste and elegance
tattle and babble
taunt and reproach
tawdry and penurious
  [tawdry = gaudy, cheap]
  [penurious = stingy]
tears and lamentations
tedious and trivial
temperament and taste

temperately and judiciously

tempest and violence

temporal and evanescent
 [evanescent = vanishing like vapor]

tenacity and coherence

tender and emotional

tense and straining

tentative and experimental

terrible and satanical

testiness and crabbedness

thankfulness and acknowledgment

theories and speculations

thorough and effective

threatening and formidable

thriftless and unenterprising

thrilling and vitalizing

ties and associations

time and opportunity

timid and vacillating

tiresome and laborious

tolerant and kindly

tone and treatment

topics and instances

tormented and tantalized

tortuous and twisted

tottering and hopeless

touched and thrilled

tractable and gracious

traditions and practises

training and temperament

tranquillity and benevolence

transfuse and irradiate

transitory and temporary

transparent and comprehensible

treacherous and cowardly

tremble and oscillate

trenchant and straightforward
   [trenchant = effective, and vigorous]

trials and tribulations

tricks and stratagems

trifling and doubtful

trite and commonplace

trivial and ridiculous

troublous and menacing

truisms and trivialities

trust and confidence

truth and righteousness

turbid and noise some

turgid and bombastic
   [turgid = excessively complex]
   [bombastic = pompous]

turmoil and shouting

twisted and perverted

type and forerunner

tyrant and oppressor

U

unaccountable and grotesque
unaffected and undaunted
unapproached and unapproachable
unassuming and unpretending
unchangeable and enduring
unconsciously and innocently
uncouth and barbarous
unctuous and irresistible
   [trenchant = insincere earnestness]
undeveloped and ignorant
undignified and futile
uneasiness and apprehension
uneducated and inexperienced
unfamiliar and distant
unfettered and vigorous
unforced and unchecked
unfortunate and unparalleled
unfounded and incredible
ungracious and reluctant
unhappiness and discomfort
unique and original
unity and completeness
unjust and ungrateful
unlimited and absolute
unnatural and harmful

unobserved and unsuspected

unobtrusive and tactful

unparalleled and inexhaustible

unpleasant and bewildering

unpopular and unimpressive

unprecedented and objectionable

unpremeditated and heartfelt

unpromising and scanty

unprotected and friendless

unreal and unsubstantial

unreasoning and uncompromising

unrecognized and unrewarded

unseemly and insufferable

unseen and unsuspected

unsmiling and critical

unswerving and unfaltering

unthinking and careless

untutored and infantine

unusual and unexpected

unuttered and unutterable

unwholesome and vile

upright and credible

uproar and confusion

upstart and braggart

urbanity and unction
  [unction = exaggerated earnestness]

utter and disastrous

V

vacillation and uncertainty
vague and indistinct
vain and profitless
validity and value
vanities and vices
vapory and chaotic
varied and animated
varnish and falsehood
vassals and inferiors
vast and superlative
vehement and clamorous
veiled and unreadable
venality and corruption
venerable and interesting
veracity and fidelity
verbally and literally
versatility and sympathy
vexation and anxiety
vibrating and sonorous
views and experiences
vigilant and inflexible
vigorous and graphic
violent and ill-balanced
virtuous and wise

virulence and invective
  [invective = abusive language]

visible and apparent

visionary and obscure

vistas and backgrounds

vital and vigorous

vitiate and poison
  [vitiate = reduce the value]

vituperation and abuse
  [vituperation = abusive language]

vivacious and agreeable

vivid and varied

void and nothingness

volatile and fiery

volubly and exuberantly
  [volubly = ready flow of speech]

volume and impetus

voluminous and varied

voluntarily and habitually

vulgar and artificial

W

wandering and erratic

wanton and unnecessary

war and revelry

warp and woof
  [warp = lengthwise threads]
  [woof = crosswise threads]

wasteful and circuitous
waxing and waning
weak and perfidious
wealth and distinction
wearisome and dull
weighed and winnowed
weighty and dominant
weird and fantastic
wheezing and puffing
whims and inconsistencies
wholesome and beautiful
wholly and solely
wicked and malicious
widened and amplified
wild and irregular
wily and observant
winking and blinking
winning and unforced
wise and beneficent
wistful and dreamy
wit and jocularity
   [jocularity = given to joking]
withered and wan
woe and lamentation
wonder and delight
work and utility
worldly and ambitious
worth and excellence

wrath and menace
wretched and suppliant

Y

yearning and eagerness
yielding and obedience
yoke and bondage
young and fragile
youthful and callow
  [callow = immature]

Z

zeal and vehemence
zenith and climax
zest and freshness
zigzag and deviating

SECTION III

FELICITOUS PHRASES

A

ability, humor, and perspicacity
  [perspicacity = perceptive]
abrupt, rough, and immoderate
abstruse, metaphysical, and idealistic
abundant, varied, and vigorous
accessible, knowable, and demonstrable
accomplished, inventive, and deft-fingered
accuracy, ease, and grace
acquire, classify, and arrange
action, incident, and interest
active, learned, and liberal
acts, activities, and aims
actual, stern, and pathetic
acuteness, honesty, and, fearlessness
addition, correction, and amplification
adventurous, eager, and afraid
affected, pedantic, and vain
  [pedantic = attention to
  detail or rules]

affluent, genial, and frank
aggressive, envious, and arrogant
agreeable, engaging, and delightful
air, woodland, and water
alarmed, anxious, and uneasy
alert, hopeful, and practical
amazement, resentment, and indignation
ambiguous, strange, and sinister
amiable, genial, and charitable
amusing, sympathetic, and interesting
ancient, subtle, and treacherous
annoyances, shifts, and inconveniences
anxious, fearful, and anticipative
appearance, conversation, and bearing
approbation, wealth, and power
   [approbation = warm
   approval; praise]
apt, explicit, and communicative
ardent, undisciplined, and undirected
arrogance, conceit, and disdain
artificial, rhetorical, and mundane
artistic, progressive, and popular
aspirations, dreams, and devotions
assured, stern, and judicial
astonishment, apprehension, and horror
attainments, possessions, and character
attention, forbearance, and patience
attract, interest, and persuade

augmenting, furthering, and reenforcing
austere, calm, and somber
authority, leadership, and command
avarice, pride, and revenge
awakened, girded, and active
awe, reverence, and adoration
awkwardness, narrowness, and self-consciousness

B

barbarous, shapeless, and irregular
beautiful, graceful, and accomplished
beggar, thief, and impostor
belittling, personal, and selfish
birth, rank, and fortune
bitter, baleful, and venomous
bland, patient, and methodical
blessing, bestowing, and welcoming
blind, partial, and prejudiced
blithe, innocent, and free
bluster, swagger, and might
body, soul, and mind
boisterous, undignified, and vulgar
bold, original, and ingenious
bombastic, incongruous, and unsymmetrical
bountiful, exuberant, and luxurious
brain, energy, and enterprise
brave, authoritative, and confident

breadth, richness, and freshness
breathless, confused, and exhilarated
brief, isolated, and fragmentary
brilliancy, energy, and zeal
broad, spare, and athletic
broken, apologetic, and confused
brotherhood, humanity, and chivalry
brusqueness, rudeness, and self-assertion
brutish, repulsive, and terrible
busy, active, and toiling

C

calculated, logical, and dispassionate
calm, earnest, and genial
candor, integrity, and straightforwardness
capricious, perverse, and prejudiced
careful, reasoned, and courteous
cautious, prudent, and decisive
caviling, petulance, and discontent
    [caviling = finding trivial objections]
censured, slighted, and despised
certain, swift, and final
chance, doubt, and mutability
character, life, and aims
charitable, just, and true
charm, grace, and glory
cheerful, modest, and delicate

childish, discordant, and superfluous
chill, harden, and repel
circumstances, properties, and characteristics
civilized, mild, and humane
clear, cloudless, and serene
cleverness, independence, and originality
coarseness, violence, and cunning
coherent, interdependent, and logical
cold, cynical, and relentless
color, intensity, and vivacity
comfort, virtue, and happiness
comments, criticisms, and judgments
common, dull, and threadbare
compact, determinate, and engaging
conceited, commonplace, and uninspiring
conception, direction, and organization
confident, inflexible, and uncontrollable
conflict, confusion, and disintegration
confused, broken, and fragmentary
conscience, heart, and life
conscientious, clear-headed, and accurate
consistent, thoughtful, and steadfast
consoling, pacifying, and benign
constant, wise, and sympathetic
constitution, temperament, and habits
convince, convert, and reconstruct
copious, redundant, and involved
corroding, venomous, and malignant

corrupt, self-seeking, and dishonest
countenance, voice, and manner
country, lake, and mountain
courage, patience, and honesty
courteous, patient, and indefatigable
covetousness, selfishness, and ignorance
credulous, weak, and superstitious
crimes, follies, and misfortunes
crisp, emphatic, and powerful
crude, warped, and barren
cruelty, violence, and injustice
culture, growth, and progress
cunning, cruelty, and treachery
curious, fantastic, and charming

D

danger, difficulty, and hardship
darkness, doubt, and difficulty
dazzle, amaze, and overpower
deadly, silent, and inaccessible
deceitful, lazy, and dishonest
decent, respectable, and sensible
decisions, affirmations, and denials
deep, flexible, and melodious
defeated, discredited, and despised
deferential, conciliatory, and courteous
definite, tangible, and practicable

deftness, delicacy, and veracity
degraded, defeated, and emasculated
dejected, discouraged, and disappointed
deliberately, coolly, and methodically
delicate, mobile, and complex
delightful, witty, and sensible
denounced, persecuted, and reviled
dependent, subsidiary, and allied
depth, tenderness, and sublimity
desolated, impoverished, and embittered
despair, finality, and hopelessness
detailed, described, and explained
devastating, horrible, and irremediable
devout, gentle, and kindly
difficult, painful, and slow
digestion, circulation, and assimilation
dignity, solemnity, and responsibility
diligent, cautious, and painstaking
dingy, cumbersome, and depressing
directness, spontaneity, and simplicity
disciplined, drilled, and trained
discontent, revolt, and despair
discordant, coarse, and unpleasing
discourses, lectures, and harangues
disheveled, wild, and distracted
disinterested, patient, and exact
dislikes, jealousies, and ambitions
dismal, cold, and dead

dismay, remorse, and anguish
disordered, wild, and incoherent
dispassionate, wise, and intelligent
disposition, taste, and temperament
dissension, discord, and rebellion
distracted, hopeless, and bankrupt
disturbed, shaken, and distressed
diversified, animated, and rapid
division, prejudice, and antagonism
doctrine, life, and destiny
dogmatic, scientific, and philosophic
doubt, cynicism, and indifference
draggled, dirty, and slouching
dramatic, picturesque, and vigorous
dream, speculate, and philosophize
drunkenness, licentiousness, and profanity
dry, inane, and droll
dull, hideous, and arid
dullards, hypocrites, and cowards
dust, turmoil, and smoke
duties, labors, and anxieties
dwarfed, scant, and wretched

E

eagerness, heartiness, and vehemence
earnestness, zeal, and intelligence
ease, power, and self-confidence

easy, natural, and unembarrassed

effluent, radiating, and fructifying
 [fructifying = Make fruitful or productive]

egotistic, disdainful, and proud

elegant, convincing, and irresistible

emotion, affection, and desire

empty, noisy, and blundering

end, aim, and purpose

energies, capacities, and opportunities

enlighten, uplift, and strengthen

enmity, suspicion, and hatred

enrich, discipline, and embellish

enthusiasm, vehemence, and spirit

envy, jealousy, and malice

equable, animated, and alert

erect, elastic, and graceful

error, ignorance, and strife

essence, existence, and identity

esteem, confidence, and affection

evil, disease, and death

exact, logical, and convincing

examine, compare, and decide

excessive, inaccurate, and unliterary

excitements, interests, and responsibilities

experience, knowledge, and conduct

exposure, ruin, and flight

exterior, formal, and imposing

F

faded, dusty, and unread
failures, experiences, and ambitions
fair, proud, and handsome
fairies, sprites, and angels
faith, hope, and love
false, wicked, and disloyal
fantastic, absurd, and impossible
fear, dread, and apprehension
features, form, and height
feeble, illogical, and vicious
feelings, motives, and desires
fertility, ingenuity, and resource
fervently, patiently, and persistently
fibs, myths, and fables
fierce, dogmatic, and bigoted
figure, face, and attitude
fire, force, and passion
flit, change, and vary
flushed, trembling, and unstrung
foibles, tricks, and fads
foliage, color, and symmetry
follies, fashions, and infatuations
foolish, ignorant, and unscrupulous
force, grace, and symmetry
forcible, extraordinary, and sublime

foremost, preeminent, and incomparable

foresight, prudence, and economy

form, color, and distance

formless, silent, and awful

forward, onward, and upward

frank, kindly, and unfaltering

free, equal, and just

freedom, honor, and dignity

fresh, vigorous, and telling

fretfulness, irritability, and petulance

friendly, amiable, and sincere

frigid, austere, and splendid

fruitful, luminous, and progressive

full, animated, and varied

fullness, force, and precision

furious, sanguinary, and disorganizing
  [sanguinary = Accompanied by bloodshed]

fustian, padding, and irrelevancy
  [fustian = pompous, bombastic, and ranting]

G

gaunt, desolate, and despoiled

gay, easy, and cordial

generous, large-hearted, and magnanimous

genial, frank, and confiding

genius, learning, and virtue

gentle, firm, and loving

genuineness, disinterestedness, and strength
germinate, develop, and radiate
gesture, accent, and attitude
ghastly, hateful, and ugly
gibes, sneers, and anger
gifts, graces, and accomplishments
gladness, exaltation, and triumph
glean, gather, and digest
gloomy, silent, and tranquil
glow, grace, and pleasantness
good, gentle, and affectionate
gorgeous, still, and warm
grace, simplicity, and sweetness
gracious, mild, and good
gradual, cautious, and well-reasoned
gratitude, happiness, and affection
grave, disastrous, and wanton
gravity, sweetness, and patience
gray, monotonous, and uninteresting
great, grand, and mighty
greed, lust, and cruelty
grim, lean, and hungry
gross, ignorant, and impudent
growth, progress, and extension
guide, philosopher, and friend

H

habits, tastes, and opinions
hard, stern, and inexorable
harmony, peace, and happiness
harsh, intolerant, and austere
health, character, and efficiency
helpful, suggestive, and inspiring
helpless, hopeless, and downtrodden
high, lofty, and noble
high-spirited, confident, and genial
history, philosophy, and eloquence
homage, ability, and culture
honesty, probity, and justice
  [probity = integrity; uprightness]
honors, riches, and power
hopes, aspirations, and longings
hot, swift, and impatient
humanity, freedom, and justice
humble, submissive, and serviceable
humor, fancy, and susceptibility

I

idle, profuse, and profligate
ignorance, fear, and selfishness
illuminating, chastening, and transforming

images, events, and incidents
imagination, judgment, and reason
immediate, sure, and easy
immethodical, irregular, and inconsecutive
impatient, inconsiderate, and self-willed
impetuous, fierce, and irresistible
impracticable, chimerical, and contemptible
impulse, energy, and activity
inclinations, habits, and interests
incoherent, loud, and confusing
incomparable, matchless, and immortal
inconsiderate, irritable, and insolent
indignation, surprise, and reproach
indirect, obscure, and ambiguous
indolent, dreamy, and frolicsome
inert, torpid, and lethargic
ingenuity, force, and originality
innocence, intelligence, and youth
inordinate, excessive, and extravagant
insight, knowledge, and capacity
insincere, partial, and arbitrary
insipid, commonplace, and chattering
insolence, injustice, and imposture
intelligence, taste, and manners
intense, weighty, and philosophical
inventions, sciences, and discoveries
irksome, painful, and depressing
irresolute, procrastinating, and unenterprising

irritable, sulky, and furious
issues, hopes, and interests

J

jealousy, exclusiveness, and taciturnity
    [taciturnity = habitually untalkative]
jovial, ready-witted, and broad-gaged
joyous, delightful, and gay
justice, mercy, and peace

K

keen, clear, and accurate
knowing, feeling, and willing
knowledge, skill, and foresight

L

labors, anxieties, and trials
large, rhythmical, and pleasing
laughter, ridicule, and sneers
lead, attack, and conquer
learning, profundity, and imagination
legislation, education, and religion
levity, indolence, and procrastination
libelers, reviewers, and rivals
liberating, vitalizing, and cheering

liberty, justice, and humanity
light, easy, and playful
literature, history, and legend
lively, careless, and joyous
lofty, serene, and impregnable
logical, clear, and consistent
loitering, heart-sick, and reluctant
lonely, sad, and enslaved
long, wailing, and passionate
lost, ruined, and deserted
loud, deep, and distinct
love, veneration, and gratitude
lucid, lively, and effective
luxurious, whimsical, and selfish

M

magnificent, sumptuous, and stately
magnitude, duration, and scope
majesty, beauty, and truth
malevolence, vanity, and falsehood
manly, refined, and unaffected
mean, pitiful, and sordid
meek, humane, and temperate
melancholy, grave, and serious
mercy, truth, and righteousness
methodical, sensible, and conscientious
might, majesty, and power

mild, sweet, and peaceable
mischief, cruelty, and futility
moans, shrieks, and curses
mobile, quick, and sensitive
modest, sympathetic, and kind
molding, controlling, and conforming
monstrous, incredible, and inhuman
moral, material, and social
motionless, staring, and appalled
motives, purposes, and intentions
mountains, seas, and vineyards
moved, swayed, and ruled
murder, destruction, and agony
mystery, vagueness, and jargon

N

narrow, precise, and formal
natural, innocent, and laudable
neatness, order, and comfort
necessary, just, and logical
neglect, rashness, and incompetence
new, strange, and unusual
niggardly, sordid, and parsimonious
   [grudging, wretched and frugal]
noble, laudable, and good
noise, clatter, and clamor
null, void, and useless

O

obscure, difficult, and subtle
observation, discrimination, and comparison
obsolete, artificial, and inadequate
obstinacy, stupidity, and wilfulness
officious, fidgety, and talkative
old, absurd, and meaningless
one, individual, and integral
openly, frankly, and legitimately
opposition, bitterness, and defiance
oppressive, grasping, and slanderous
opulent, powerful, and prosperous
organization, monopoly, and pressure
origin, character, and aim
original, terse, and vigorous
overriding, arrogant, and quarrelsome

P

pain, toil, and privation
pale, ugly, and sinister
parable, precept, and practise
partial, false, and disastrous
passion, tenderness, and reverence
patient, gentle, and kind
peace, order, and civilization

pellucid, animated, and varied
  [pellucid = transparently clear]

permanent, true, and real

perplexed, tedious, and obscure

personal, sharp, and pointed

perspicuity, vivacity, and grace
  [perspicuity = clearness and lucidity]

pert, smirking, and conceited

pervading, searching, and saturating

petty, unsuccessful, and unamiable

philosophy, morals, and discoveries

picturesque, daring, and potent

piety, charity, and humility

pillage, arson, and bloodshed

pious, patient, and trustful

pity, sympathy, and compassion

placable, reasonable, and willing
  [placable = easily calmed; tolerant]

place, fame, and fortune

placid, clear, and mellow

plague, pestilence, and famine

plan, purpose, and work

pleasant, friendly, and amiable

pleased, interested, and delighted

pleasure, enjoyment, and satisfaction

plenty, content, and tranquillity

plodding, sedentary, and laborious

poise, dignity, and reserve

polished, elegant, and sumptuous

politics, business, and religion

pompous, affected, and unreal

poor, miserable, and helpless

pose, gesture, and expression

powerful, dazzling, and daring

practical, visible, and tangible

precious, massive, and splendid

precise, formal, and cynical

prejudice, dulness, and spite

prepossessions, opinions, and prejudices

presiding, directing, and controlling

pride, passion, and conceit

princely, picturesque, and pathetic

principles, conduct, and habits

progress, order, and happiness

prolonged, obstinate, and continued

prompt, fiery, and resolute

propriety, perspicacity, and accuracy
  [perspicacity = perceptive]

prosaic, dull, and unattractive

protective, propitiatory, and accommodating
  [propitiatory = conciliatory]

protests, criticisms, and rebukes

proud, reserved, and disagreeable

prudence, mildness, and firmness

puckered, winking, and doddering

pure, honorable, and just

purge, brace, and strengthen
purpose, intention, and meaning
puzzles, tangles, and questionings

Q

quarrels, misunderstandings, and enmities
questions, disputes, and controversies
quicken, sharpen, and intensify
quiet, unaffected, and unostentatious

R

raise, refine, and elevate
rapid, robust, and effective
rapt, emotional, and mystic
raptures, transports, and fancies
rash, violent, and indefinite
readiness, skill, and accuracy
reading, reflection, and observation
reaffirmed, amplified, and maintained
real, earnest, and energetic
regard, esteem, and affection
relaxation, recreation, and pleasure
religion, politics, and literature
reminiscences, associations, and impressions
remote, careless, and indifferent
reparations, restitutions, and guarantees

repress, curb, and correct
reproach, shame, and remorse
reproof, correction, and instruction
resentment, hatred, and despair
resolute, patient, and fervent
resourceful, steadfast, and skilful
respect, admiration, and homage
rest, respite, and peace
restless, discontented, and rebellious
restraint, self-denial, and austerity
reticent, restrained, and reserved
reverie, contemplation, and loneliness
rich, thoughtful, and glowing
ridicule, sarcasm, and invective
   [invective = abusive language]
rights, powers, and privileges
rise, flourish, and decay
robustness, elasticity, and firmness
romance, adventure, and passion
rough, barren, and unsightly
rude, sulky, and overbearing
rush, roar, and shriek

S

sacredness, dignity, and loveliness
sad, gloomy, and suspicious
safe, sensible, and sane

sanguine, impulsive, and irrepressible
  [sanguine = cheerfully confident; optimistic]

sarcasm, satire, and ridicule

satiety, surfeit, and tedium

savage, fierce, and intractable

scheming, contriving, and dishonesty

self-absorbed, conceited, and contemptuous

self-conscious, artificial, and affected

self-exacting, laborious, and inexhaustible

selfishness, coarseness, and mendacity
  [mendacity = untruthfulness]

sense, grace, and good-will

sensibility, harmony, and energy

sensitive, ardent, and conscientious

serene, ineffable, and flawless
  [ineffable = indescribable]

serious, calm, and searching

settled, adjusted, and balanced

shallow, false, and petty

shapes, forms, and artifices

sharpness, bitterness, and sarcasm

shivering, moaning, and weeping

shrewd, artful, and designing

shy, wild, and provocative

sick, ashamed, and disillusioned

silent, cold, and motionless

simple, full, and impressive

sin, selfishness, and luxury

sincere, placable, and generous
  [placable = easily calmed; tolerant]
skill, sagacity, and firmness
  [sagacity = farsighted; wise]
sleekness, stealth, and savagery
slovenly, base, and untrue
slow, reluctant, and unwelcome
smirking, garrulous, and pretentious
  [garrulous = excessive
  and trivial talk]
smooth, sentimental, and harmonious
smug, fat, and complacent
sneers, innuendoes, and insinuations
social, esthetic, and intellectual
solitary, sedentary, and lifeless
sound, human, and healthy
sour, malignant, and envious
spacious, clean, and comfortable
speechless, motionless, and amazed
spirit, vigor, and variety
spitefulness, dishonesty, and cruelty
splendid, powerful, and enduring
startling, alarming, and vehement
statesmen, philosophers, and divines
steadiness, self-control, and serenity
stern, forbidding, and unfeeling
stiff, decorous, and formal
strained, worn, and haggard
strange, dark, and mysterious

strengthen, invigorate, and discipline
strenuous, intelligent, and alive
striking, bold, and magnificent
stripped, swept, and bare
strong, cool, and inflexible
studied, discussed, and debated
sturdy, energetic, and high-minded
style, manner, and disposition
subtle, delicate, and refined
successful, energetic, and ingenious
sudden, vehement, and unfamed
suggestive, stimulating, and inspiring
sullen, silent, and disconsolate
suppliant, gentle, and submissive
 [suppliant = asking humbly]
surprise, admiration, and wonder
suspicious, restive, and untractable
swiftness, mobility, and penetrativeness
sympathy, service, and compassion

T

talent, scholarship, and refinement
tameness, monotony, and reserve
taste, feeling, and sentiment
tedious, painful, and distressing
temper, pride, and sensuality
temperament, character, and circumstance

temperate, sweet, and venerable
tenderness, loyalty, and devotion
terror, remorse, and shame
terseness, simplicity, and quaintness
theatrical, sensational, and demonstrative
thought, utterance, and action
threats, cries, and prayers
thrilling, dramatic, and picturesque
thwart, criticize, and embarrass
time, thought, and consideration
touched, strengthened, and transformed
tradition, prejudice, and stupidity
tragic, tremendous, and horrible
transparent, theatric, and insincere
treachery, envy, and selfishness
tremulous, soft, and bright
   [tremulous = trembling, quivering, shaking]
trial, discipline, and temptation
tricks, shufflings, and frauds
trivial, labored, and wearisome
true, lasting, and beneficial
tyranny, injustice, and extortion

U

ugly, scowling, and offensive
unbending, contemptuous, and scornful

unclean, shameful, and degrading
undecided, wavering, and cautious
unearthly, horrible, and obnoxious
uneasy, overstrained, and melancholy
unity, emphasis, and coherence
unmodulated, cold, and expressionless
unphilosophical, unsystematic, and discursive
unscrupulous, heartless, and hypocritical
unwholesome, bewildering, and unprofitable
unworldly, peaceable, and philosophical
upright, kind-hearted, and blameless
urgent, tumultuous, and incomprehensible

V

vague, impalpable, and incongruous
vanities, stupidities, and falsehoods
venerable, patriotic, and virtuous
verities, certainties, and realities
vigilant, inveterate, and unresting
  [inveterate = long established]
vigorous, subtle, and comprehensive
violent, sinister, and rebellious
virtue, genius, and charm
visionary, fraudulent, and empirical
vital, formidable, and dominant
vivid, comprehensible, and striking
vulgarity, ignorance, and misapprehension

W

waddling, perspiring, and breathless
want, worry, and woe
wasteful, indolent, and evasive
watchful, suspicious, and timid
wealth, position, and influence
wearied, despondent, and bewildered
weight, size, and solidity
well-proportioned, logical, and sane
whimsical, fantastic, and impracticable
wholesome, beautiful, and righteous
wicked, pernicious, and degrading
wild, confused, and dizzy
wilful, wanton, and deliberate
will, energy, and self-control
wisdom, patriotism, and justice
wit, fancy, and imagination
worthless, broken, and defeated
wretchedness, deformity, and malice
wrinkled, careworn, and pale

SECTION IV

IMPRESSIVE PHRASES

A

able, skilful, thorough, and genuine
absolute, complete, unqualified, and final
accurate, precise, exact, and truthful
active, alert, vigorous, and industrious
actual, positive, certain, and genuine
adequate, uniform, proportionate, and equitable
adventurous, fine, active, and gossipy
adverse, antagonistic, unfriendly, and hostile
advisable, advantageous, acceptable, and expedient
affable, diffident, humble, and mild
affectionate, tender, loving, and attached
affluent, opulent, abundant, and ample
allurements, pits, snares, and torments
anger, indignation, resentment, and rage
animate, impel, instigate, and embolden
animosity, malice, enmity, and hatred
annul, frustrate, reverse, and destroy
anxiety, caution, watchfulness, and solicitude

apparent, ostensible, plausible, and specious

appropriate, use, arrogate, and usurp
 [arrogate = claim without right; appropriate]

approval, enthusiasm, sympathy, and applause

aptitude, capacity, efficiency, and power

arbitrary, dictatorial, domineering, and imperious
 [imperious = arrogantly domineering or overbearing]

architecture, sculpture, painting, and poetry

ardent, impatient, keen, and vehement

argue, discuss, dispute, and prove

arrangement, place, time, and circumstance

art, science, knowledge, and culture

artful, wily, insincere, and disingenuous

artificial, soulless, hectic, and unreal

assemble, amass, accumulate, and acquire

assiduity, tenderness, industry, and vigilance
 [assiduity = persistent application]

assurance, persuasion, fidelity, and loyalty

attention, effort, diligence, and assiduity
 [assiduity = persistent application]

august, magnanimous, important, and distinguished

authoritative, independent, arbitrary, and supreme

avaricious, grasping, miserly, and parsimonious
 [parsimonious = excessively frugal]

aversion, dislike, hatred, and repugnance

B

bad, vicious, unwholesome, and distressing

babble, prate, chatter, and prattle
barbarous, brutal, inhuman, and cruel
base, cowardly, abject, and hideous
battle, defeat, frustrate, and ruin
bearing, deportment, manner, and behavior
beg, entreat, implore, and supplicate
beliefs, doctrines, ceremonies, and practices
boorish, clownish, rude, and uncultivated
boundless, immeasurable, unlimited, and infinite
bravery, courage, fearlessness, and confidence
breadth, knowledge, vision, and power
brilliant, beautiful, elegant, and faithful
broaden, enlarge, extend, and augment
business, profession, occupation, and vocation

C

candid, sincere, familiar, and ingenuous
captious, petulant, peevish, and splenetic
  [captious = point out trivial faults]
cautious, discreet, considerate, and provident
certain, confident, positive, and unquestionable
chagrin, vexation, irritation, and mortification
character, disposition, temperament, and reputation
charm, fascinate, bewitch, and captivate
cheap, inexpensive, inferior, and common
cheer, animate, vivify, and exhilarate
  [vivify = bring life to]

chiefly, particularly, principally, and especially
childhood, youth, manhood, and age
circumstance, condition, environment, and surroundings
claim, grab, trick, and compel
clean, fastidious, frugal, and refined
clear, distinct, obvious, and intelligible
clumsy, crawling, snobbish, and comfort-loving
coarse, gross, offensive, and nauseous
coax, flatter, wheedle, and persuade
cogitate, contemplate, meditate, and ponder
cold, frigid, unfeeling, and stoical
commanding, authoritative, imperative, and peremptory
  [peremptory = ending all debate or action]
compassion, goodwill, admiration, and enthusiasm
confirm, establish, sustain, and strengthen
conform, submit, obey, and satisfy
confuse, distort, involve, and misinterpret
consistent, congruous, firm, and harmonious
cool, collected, calm, and self-possessed
copious, commanding, sonorous, and emotional
cowardly, timid, shrinking, and timorous
crazy, absurd, nonsensical, and preposterous
crude, rough, jagged, and pitiless

D

daring, cordial, discerning, and optimistic
darkness, dimness, dulness, and blackness

deadly, destructive, fatal, and implacable
deceit, delusion, treachery, and sham
deep, abstruse, learned, and profound
deficient, inadequate, scanty, and incomplete
define, explain, determine, and circumscribe
degrade, defame, humble, and debase
delicacy, daintiness, tact, and refinement
delicious, sweet, palatable, and delightful
democracy, equality, justice, and freedom
deny, dismiss, exclude, and repudiate
deprive, dispossess, divest, and despoil
describe, delineate, depict, and characterize
designed, contrived, planned, and executed
desperate, extreme, wreckless, and irremediable
despicable, abject, servile, and worthless
destructive, detrimental, deleterious, and subversive
desultory, discursive, loose, and unmethodical
  [desultory = disconnected: haphazard]
detestable, abominable, horrible, and hideous
developed, revealed, measured, and tested
difference, disagreement, discord, and estrangement
difficult, arduous, intricate, and perplexing
diffuse, discursive, rambling, and wordy
diligence, attention, industry, and assiduity
  [assiduity = persistent application]
disagreement, discrepancy, difference, and divergence
disconsolate, desolate, pessimistic, and impossible
discrimination, acuteness, insight, and judgment

disgust, distaste, loathing, and abhorrence
dissatisfied, rebellious, unsettled, and satirical
distinct, definite, clear, and obvious
distinguished, glorious, illustrious, and eminent
disturbed, shaken, distressed, and bewildered
docile, tractable, compliant, and teachable
dogmatic, bigoted, libelous, and unsympathizing
doubt, indecision, suspense, and perplexity
dread, disgust, repugnance, and dreariness
dreary, dispirited, unhappy, and peevish
dry, lifeless, tiresome, and uninteresting
dubious, equivocal, fluctuating, and uncertain
dull, heavy, painstaking, and conscientious

E

earth, air, stars, and sea
efficient, forcible, adequate, and potent
emaciated, scraggy, meager, and attenuated
endless, ceaseless, immutable, and imperishable
energy, eagerness, earnestness, and enthusiasm
enhance, exalt, elevate, and intensify
enormous, base, prodigious, and colossal
enrage, incense, infuriate, and exasperate
enthusiasm, devotion, intensity, and zeal
envy, discontent, deception, and ignorance
equitable, reasonable, just, and honest
equivocal, uncertain, cloudy, and ambiguous

eradicate, extirpate, exterminate, and annihilate
   [extirpate = pull up by the roots]
erroneous, faulty, inaccurate, and inexact
eternal, unchangeable, unerring, and intelligent
evil, misfortune, corruption, and disaster
exacting, suspicious, irritable, and wayward
exalt, dignify, elevate, and extol
examination, inquiry, scrutiny, and research
exceed, outdo, surpass, and transcend
exceptional, uncommon, abnormal, and extraordinary
excitement, distraction, diversion, and stimulation
exhaustive, thorough, radical, and complete
expend, dissipate, waste, and squander

F

facile, showy, cheap, and superficial
faithful, truthful, loyal, and trustworthy
fame, distinction, dignity, and honor
fanatic, enthusiast, visionary, and zealot
fanciful, unreal, fantastic, and grotesque
fancy, humor, vagary, and caprice
   [vagary = extravagant or erratic notion or action]
fashion, practise, habit, and usage
fastidious, proud, gracious, and poised
fate, fortune, contingency, and opportunity
fatuous, dreamy, moony, and impracticable
fear, timidity, cowardice, and pusillanimity

feeble, languid, timid, and irresolute

ferocious, restive, savage, and uncultivated

fervent, enthusiastic, anxious, and zealous

fiction, fancy, falsehood, and fabrication

fine, fragile, delicate, and dainty

firmness, steadfastness, stability, and tenacity

flash, flame, flare, and glare

flat, insipid, tame, and monotonous

fluctuating, hesitating, vacillating, and oscillating

folly, foolishness, imbecility, and fatuity

foolhardy, hasty, adventurous, and reckless

fop, coxcomb, puppy, and jackanapes
   [jackanapes = conceited person]

force, vigor, power, and energy

formal, precise, stiff, and methodical

fortunate, happy, prosperous, and successful

fragile, frail, brittle, and delicate

freedom, familiarity, liberty, and independence

frightful, fearful, direful, and dreadful

frivolous, trifling, petty, and childish

fruitful, fertile, prolific, and productive

fruitless, vain, trivial, and foolish

frustrate, defeat, disappoint, and thwart

fully, completely, abundantly, and perfectly

furious, impetuous, boisterous, and vehement

G

gaiety, merriment, joy, and hilarity
gallant, ardent, fearless, and self-sacrificing
garnish, embellish, beautify, and decorate
generous, candid, easy, and independent
genius, intellect, aptitude, and capacity
genteel, refined, polished, and well-bred
gentle, persuasive, affective, and simple
genuine, true, unaffected, and sincere
ghastly, grim, shocking, and hideous
gibe, mock, taunt, and jeer
giddy, fickle, flighty, and thoughtless
gleam, glimmer, glance, and glitter
gloomy, dismal, dark, and dejected
glorious, noble, exalted, and resplendent
glut, gorge, cloy, and satiate
   [cloy = too filling, rich, or sweet]
good, safe, venerable, and solid
government, law, order, and organization
grand, stately, dignified, and pompous
grave, contemplative, reserved, and profound
great, joyous, strong, and triumphant
greed, avarice, covetousness, and cupidity
gross, academic, vulgar, and indiscriminate

H

habit, custom, method, and fashion
handsome, exquisite, brilliant, and accomplished
harmless, innocent, innocuous, and inoffensive
harmony, order, sublimity, and beauty
harsh, discordant, disagreeable, and ungracious
hasty, superficial, impatient, and desultory
   [desultory = disconnected: haphazard]
healed, soothed, consoled, and assuaged
healthy, hale, sound, and wholesome
heavy, sluggish, dejected, and crushing
high-minded, truthful, honest, and courageous
holy, hallowed, sacred, and consecrated
homely, hideous, horrid, and unsightly
honor, obedience, virtue, and loyalty
hopefulness, peace, sweetness, and strength
hopes, dreams, programs, and ideals
hospitable, generous, tolerant, and kindly
hot, hasty, fervent, and fiery
humane, gentle, kind, and generous
humble, simple, submissive, and unostentatious

I

idea, imagination, conception, and ideal
idleness, recreation, repose, and rest

ignominious, infamous, despicable, and contemptible

illumine, instruct, enlighten, and inform

imaginative, sensitive, nervous, and highly-strung

impatience, indolence, wastefulness, and inconclusiveness

impel, stimulate, animate, and inspirit

imperious, wayward, empirical, and impatient
  [imperious = arrogantly domineering or overbearing]

improvident, incautious, prodigal, and thriftless

impudent, insolent, irrelevant, and officious

inadvertency, carelessness, negligence, and oversight

indecision, doubt, fear, and lassitude

indifference, caution, coldness, and weariness

indolent, passive, sluggish, and slothful

ineffectual, powerless, useless, and unavailing

infamy, shame, dishonor, and disgrace

infantile, childish, boyish, and dutiful

informal, natural, unconventional, and careless

insolent, impudent, impertinent, and flippant

integrity, frankness, sincerity, and truthfulness

intellectual, moral, emotional, and esthetic

intense, earnest, violent, and extreme

invent, discover, design, and contrive

inveterate, confirmed, chronic, and obstinate

invidious, envious, odious, and offensive

invincible, unconquerable, insurmountable, and insuperable

irksome, tiresome, tedious, and annoying

irregular, uncertain, devious, and unsystematic

irritable, choleric, petulant, and susceptible

J

jangle, wrangle, squabble, and quarrel
jealousy, suspicion, envy, and watchfulness
joyful, lively, happy, and hilarious
judgment, discrimination, penetration, and sagacity
  [sagacity = farsighted; wise]
just, impartial, equitable, and unbiased
juvenile, childish, trifling, and puerile
  [puerile = immature; childish]

K

keen, intelligent, penetrating, and severe
keep, protect, support, and sustain
kind, sympathetic, ready, and appreciative
kingly, noble, imperial, and august
knowledge, learning, enlightenment, and understanding

L

lapses, makeshifts, delays, and irregularities
lawful, legitimate, allowable, and just
lazy, listless, drowsy, and indifferent
lightly, freely, unscrupulously, and irresponsibly
lively, vivacious, vigorous, and forcible
loss, deprivation, forfeiture, and waste

loud, noisy, showy, and clamorous

loutish, prankish, selfish, and cunning

love, depth, loyalty, and faithfulness

lucidity, impressiveness, incisiveness, and pungency
  [pungency = to the point]

M

malice, anger, uncharitableness, and indignation

malignity, brutality, malevolence, and inhumanity

manners, morals, habits, and behavior

marvelous, wonderful, extraordinary, and incredible

massive, ponderous, solid, and substantial

mastery, proficiency, dexterity, and superiority

matchless, unrivaled, inimitable, and incomparable

maxim, proverb, truism, and apothegm
  [apothegm = terse, witty, instructive saying]

medley, mixture, jumble, and hodge-podge

meekness, inwardness, patience, and self-denial

merciless, remorseless, relentless, and ruthless

mild, gentle, humble, and submissive

mismanagement, indecision, obstinacy, and hardihood

mixture, medley, variety, and diversification

modesty, fineness, sensitiveness, and fastidiousness

money, position, power, and consequence

mood, temper, humor, and caprice

motive, impulse, incentive, and intimation

mysterious, dark, secret, and enigmatical

N

narrow, limited, selfish, and bigoted

necessary, expedient, indispensable, and unavoidable

necessity, emergency, exigency, and crisis
 [exigency = urgent situation]

neglect, overlook, disregard, and contemn
 [contemn = despise]

nice, finical, effeminate, and silly
 [finical = Finicky]

niggardly, close, miserly, and parsimonious
 [parsimonious = Excessively frugal]

noble, pure, exalted, and worthy

nonsense, trash, twaddle, and rubbish

novel, recent, rare, and unusual

noxious, unwholesome, mischievous, and destructive

O

obdurate, unfeeling, callous, and obstinate

obedient, respectful, dutiful, and submissive

object, propose, protest, and decline

obliging, kind, helpful, and courteous

obscure, shadowy, intricate, and mysterious

obsequious, cringing, fawning, and servile
 [obsequious = fawning.]

observations, sentiments, ideas, and theories

obstinacy, pertinacity, stubbornness, and inflexibility
  [pertinacity = persistent]
offensive, disagreeable, distasteful, and obnoxious
officious, impertinent, insolent, and meddlesome

P

particular, precise, formal, and punctilious
  [punctilious = scrupulous]
passions, weaknesses, uglinesses, and deformities
patient, loyal, hard-working, and true
peace, quiet, tranquillity, and harmony
peculiar, individual, specific, and appropriate
perplex, embarrass, confuse, and mystify
phrases, figures, metaphors, and quotations
piteous, woebegone, dismal, and dolorous
placid, meek, gentle, and moderate
plain, transparent, simple, and obvious
play, diversion, pastime, and amusement
pleasant, jocular, witty, and facetious
pliable, ductile, supple, and yielding
poetry, sentiment, morality, and religion
polished, deft, superficial, and conventional
polite, polished, cultured, and refined
positive, direct, explicit, and dogmatic
powerful, efficient, vivid, and forcible
precise, delicate, discriminating, and fastidious
prejudicial, injurious, noxious, and pernicious

preposterous, irrational, unreasonable, and nonsensical
pretense, subterfuge, simulation, and disguise
prevent, restrain, dissuade, and dishearten
primary, foremost, leading, and principal
probity, directness, simplicity, and sincerity
  [probity = integrity]
profession, business, trade, and vocation
profit, advantage, benefit, and emolument
  [emolument = compensation]
profuse, excessive, copious, and extravagant
progress, prosperity, peace, and happiness
prolix, prosaic, prolonged, and wordy
  [prolix = excessive length]
property, comforts, habits, and conveniences
prudence, judgment, wisdom, and discretion
pulsing, coursing, throbbing, and beating
pure, kind, sweet-tempered, and unselfish
purified, exalted, fortified, and illumined
purpose, meaning, scope, and tendency

Q

quack, imposture, charlatan, and mountebank
  [mountebank = flamboyant charlatan]
qualified, powerful, vigorous, and effective
quality, property, attribute, and character
quarrels, misunderstandings, enmities, and disapprovals
queries, echoes, reactions, and after-thoughts
quick, impetuous, sweeping, and expeditious

quiet, peaceful, sane, and normal

R

racy, smart, spicy, and pungent
rational, sane, sound, and sensible
ravenous, greedy, voracious, and grasping
recreation, sport, pastime, and amusement
relation, work, duty, and pleasure
reliable, accurate, truthful, and duty-loving
reports, stories, rumors, and suspicions
reproach, dishonor, disgrace, and ignominy
restrained, calm, quiet, and placid
reverential, disciplined, self-controlling, and devoted
rigid, inelastic, stiff, and unbending
rough, rude, gruff, and surly
rude, curt, insolent, and unpleasant

S

sad, despondent, melancholy, and depressed
sane, sober, sound, and rational
scandalize, vilify, traduce, and offend
　[traduce = humiliate with false statements]
scanty, pinched, slender, and insufficient
science, art, religion, and philosophy
scope, design, purpose, and judgment
sensual, cruel, selfish, and unscrupulous

sentence, judgment, verdict, and doom

serene, composed, conservative, and orderly

several, sundry, many, and various

severe, stern, stiff, and stringent

shameless, corrupt, depraved, and vicious

shock, surprise, terror, and forlornness

simple, hearty, joyous, and affectionate

sin, injustice, grievance, and crime

skill, courage, prowess, and attractiveness

sleepy, soporific, sluggish, and dull
  [soporific = induces sleep]

slim, slender, slight, and scraggy

slow, dilatory, slack, and procrastinating
  [dilatory = postpone]

solemn, profound, serious, and difficult

solicit, urge, implore, and importune
  [importune = insistent requests]

sorrow, disaster, unhappiness, and bereavement

spontaneity, freedom, ease, and adequacy

stately, stern, august, and implacable

steady, reliable, dependable, and well-balanced

stern, severe, abrupt, and unreasonable

stories, pictures, shows and representations

strength, agility, violence, and activity

strong, inventive, daring, and resourceful

sublime, consoling, inspiring, and beautiful

substantial, solid, strong, and durable

suffering, regret, bitterness, and fatigue

superficial, shallow, flimsy, and untrustworthy
superfluous, excessive, unnecessary, and redundant
suspicious, cynical, crafty, and timid
symmetry, proportion, harmony, and regularity

T

tact, courtesy, adroitness, and skill
talents, opportunities, influence, and power
talkative, selfish, superstitious, and inquisitive
tastes, appetites, passions, and desires
tease, tantalize, worry, and provoke
tenacious, stubborn, pertinacious, and obstinate
  [pertinacious = perversely persistent]
tendency, drift, scope, and disposition
tests, trials, temptations, and toils
theatrical, ceremonious, meretricious, and ostentatious
  [meretricious = plausible but insincere]
theory, assumption, speculation, and conjecture
think, reflect, weigh, and ponder
tortuous, twisted, sinuous, and circuitous
tractable, gentle, pliant, and submissive
traditional, uncertain, legendary, and unverified
traffic, trade, commerce, and intercourse
tricky, insincere, wily, and shifty
trite, ordinary, commonplace, and hackneyed
trivial, petty, frivolous, and insignificant
true, upright, real, and authentic

tumultuous, riotous, disorderly, and turbulent

U

ugly, evil, hateful, and base
uncertain, questionable, erroneous, and mistaken
unctuous, shrill, brisk, and demonstrative
  [unctuous = exaggerated, insincere]
unhappy, unfortunate, distressed, and disastrous
uninteresting, lifeless, obscure, and commonplace
unity, aggressiveness, efficiency, and force
unkind, severe, oppressive, and callous
unpractical, childish, slipshod, and silly
unreasonable, foolish, excessive, and absurd
unrivaled, unequaled, incomparable, and matchless
upright, high-minded, brave, and liberal
urgent, important, immediate, and imperative
usage, custom, habit, and practise

V

vain, useless, unproductive, and unavailing
vanities, envies, devices, and jealousies
vast, scattered, various, and incalculable
versatile, eloquent, sagacious, and talented
  [sagacious = wise]
vigorous, upright, dignified, and imperative
vile, mean, debased, and sordid

violent, impetuous, intense, and ungovernable
virtuous, upright, honest, and moral
visionary, dreamy, pensive, and sensitive
vulgar, heavy, narrow, and obtuse

W

want, lack, poverty, and paucity
warm, soft, clear, and serene
waste, devastate, pillage, and destroy
watched, tendered, fostered, and pruned
weak, inefficient, stupid, and futile
wealth, position, influence, and reputation
well-being, happiness, prosperity, and distress
wild, restless, aimless, and erring
wisdom, judgment, understanding, and far-sightedness
wit, purity, energy, and simplicity
wonderful, interesting, active, and delightful
works, sorrows, visions, and experiences
worry, annoyance, awkwardness, and difficulty

SECTION V

PREPOSITIONAL PHRASES

Preposition "of"

A

abandon of spontaneity
abatement of misery
aberrations of judgment
abhorrence of meanness
absence of vainglory
abyss of ignominy
accent of conviction
accretions of time
accumulation of ages
accuracy of aim
acquisition of knowledge
activity of attention
acuteness of sensibility
admixture of fear
affectation of content

affinity of events
age of ignorance
agility of brain
agony of despair
air of assumption
ambitious of success
amiability of disposition
amplitude of space
anachronisms of thought
anchor of moderation
angle of vision
annulment of influence
aping of manners
apostle of culture
ardor of life
arrogance of opinion
aspect of grandeur
assumption of sternness
atmosphere of obscurity
attitude of mind
attribute of weakness
austerities of fanaticism
authority of manner
avalanche of scorn
avenues of dissemination

B

babel of tongues
ban of exclusion
barren of enthusiasm
barriers of reticence
bars of sunlight
basis of fact
beam of moonlight
beast of prey
beauty of imagery
beggared of faith
bent of mind
betrayal of trust
bevy of maidens
bewilderment of feeling
birds of prey
bit of portraiture
bitterness of anguish
blackness of spirit
blandishments of society
blast of adversity
blaze of fury
blend of dignity
bliss of solitude
bloom of earth
blow of fate

boldness of conception
bond of alliance
bone of contention
bouts of civility
breach of law
breath of life
breeze of anxiety
brilliancy of wit
brimful of fun
broil of politics
brood of emotions
brow of expectation
brunt of disgrace
bulk of mankind
bundle of conceptions
buoyancy of youth
burden of proof
burst of confidence
business of life

C

cadences of delirium
calmness of manner
calumny of passion
   [calumny = maliciously lying to injure a reputation]
caprice of inclination
careless of opinion

catholicity of spirit
  [catholicity = universality]

cause of solicitude

celerity of movement
  [celerity = swiftness; speed]

chain of evidence

change of habitude

chaos of confusion

chill of indifference

chimera of superstition
  [chimera = fanciful illusion]

chorus of approbation
  [approbation = warm approval; praise]

circle of hills

clamor of envy

clap of thunder

clarity of thinking

clash of arms

cloak of ecclesiasticism

code of morals

cogency of argument

combination of calamities

command of wit

community of interest

compass of imagination

complexity of life

confidence of genius

conflict of will

conquest of difficulty

consciousness of peril
constellation of luminaries
contagion of conflict
continuity of life
contradiction of terms
contrariety of opinion
convulsion of laughter
copiousness of diction
cord of sympathy
countenance of authority
courage of conviction
course of existence
courtliness of manner
cover of hospitality
crash of thunder
creature of circumstance
criteria of feeling
crown of civilization
crudity of thought
cry of despair
curl of contempt
current of thought

D

darkness of calamity
dash of eccentricity
dawning of recognition

day of reckoning

daylight of faith

decay of authority

declaration of indifference

deeds of prowess

defects of temper

degree of hostility

delicacy of thought

delirium of wonder

depth of despair

dereliction of duty

derogation of character

despoiled of riches

destitute of power

desultoriness of detail
  [desultoriness = haphazard; random]

device of secrecy

devoid of merit

devoutness of faith

dexterity of phrase

diapason of motives
  [diapason = full, rich, harmonious sound]

dictates of conscience

difference of opinion

difficult of attainment

dignity of thought

dilapidations of time

diminution of brutality

disabilities of age
display of prowess
distinctness of vision
distortion of symmetry
diversity of aspect
divinity of tradition
domain of imagination
drama of action
dream of vengeance
drop of comfort
ductility of expression
dull of comprehension
duplicities of might
dust of defeat

E

earnestness of enthusiasm
easy of access
ebullitions of anger
   [ebullitions = sudden, violent outpouring; boiling]
eccentricity of judgment
ecstasy of despair
effect of loveliness
efficacy of change
effusion of sentiment
elasticity of mind
element of compulsion

elevation of sentiment

eloquence of passion

emotions of joy

emulous of truth
   [emulous = prompted by a spirit of rivalry]

encroachments of time

encumbrance of mystery

energy of youth

enigma of life

equanimity of mind

era of fads

error of judgment

essence of eloquence

excellence of vision

excess of candor

excitation of purpose

excursiveness of thought

exhibition of joy

exhilaration of spirits

expenditure of energy

explosion of rage

expression of sternness

extension of experience

extravagance of eulogy

extremity of fortune

exuberance of wit

F

fabric of fact
facility of expression
faculty of perception
failure of coordination
feast of reason
feats of strength
feebleness of purpose
feeling of uneasiness
felicities of expression
fertility of invention
fervor of devotion
fickleness of fortune
field of activity
fierceness of jealousy
fineness of vision
fire of imagination
firmament of literature
firmness of purpose
fit of laughter
fitness of circumstance
fixity of purpose
flag of truce
flash of humor
flashlight of introspection
fleetness of foot

flexibility of spirit

flicker of recognition

flight of fancy

flood of hatred

flourish of manner

flower of life

fluctuation of fortune

flush of youth

flutter of expectation

fog of sentimentalism

force of conviction

forest of faces

form of captiousness
  [captiousness = point out trivial faults]

fountain of learning

fragment of conversation

frame of mind

frankness of manner

freak of fancy

freedom of enterprise

frenzy of pursuit

freshness of feeling

frigidity of address

frivolity of tone

frown of meditation

fulfilment of purpose

fulness of time

fury of resentment

futility of pride

G

gaiety of spirit
gales of laughter
garb of thought
garlands of roses
gateway of fancy
gem of truth
genuineness of sentiment
gesture of despair
gift of repartee
glamor of sensationalism
glare of scrutiny
gleam of light
glib of speech
glimmer of suspicion
glory of salvation
glow of enthusiasm
gorgeousness of coloring
grace of simplicity
gradations of outrage
grandeur of outline
grasp of comprehension
gravity of manner
greatness of nature
greed of office

grimace of disappointment
grimness of spirit
grip of attention
groundwork of melancholy
growth of experience
guide of aspiration
gulf of incongruity
gust of laughter

H

harbor of refuge
harvest of regrets
haven of rest
haze of distance
heat of enthusiasm
height of absurdity
hint of bitterness
hopeful of success
horizon of life
horror of solitude
hubbub of talk
hue of divinity
hum of pleasure
hush of suspense

I

ideals of excellence
idol of society
illusion of youth
immensity of extent
immolation of genius
impatient of restraint
impetuosity of youth
implacability of resentment
impotent of ideas
impress of individuality
impulse of enthusiasm
imputation of eccentricity
incapable of veracity
independence of mind
index of character
indolence of temperament
indulgence of vanity
inequality of treatment
infinity of height
infirmity of temper
infusion of hatred
inheritance of honor
insensibility of danger
insolence of office
inspiration of genius

instability of purpose
instrument of expression
integrity of mind
intensity of faith
interchange of ideas
interval of leisure
intoxication of vanity
intrepidity of youth
intuition of immortality
invasion of thought
irony of life

J

jangle of sounds
jargon of philosophy
jumble of facts
justness of decision

K

keenness of intellect
kernel of truth
key of knowledge
keynote of success
king of finance
kinship of humanity

L

lack of restraint
languor of nature
  [languor = dreamy, lazy mood]
lapse of time
laws of decorum
laxity of mind
legacy of thought
liberty of conscience
light of experience
limit of endurance
link of sequence
loftiness of spirit
look of dominance
loophole of escape
love of approbation
  [approbation = warm approval; praise]
lust of conquest
lustihood of youth
luxuriance of expression

M

magnanimity of mind
majesty of despair
man of iron

mantle of verdure
  [verdure = lush greenness of flourishing vegetation]

martyrdom of ambition

marvel of competency

mask of flippancy

mass of mediocrity

master of phrasing

maze of words

measure of absurdity

minister of vengeance

minuteness of description

miracle of miracles

mists of criticism

modesty of reserve

moment of lassitude

monster of ingratitude

monstrosities of character

mood of tranquillity

muddle of motives

multitude of details

mummery of words
  [mummery = meaningless ceremonies and flattery]

murmur of satisfaction

mutations of time

myriads of stars

mysteries of taste

N

narrowness of range
nebulae of romance
nectar of enjoyment
neglect of duty
niceties of difference
nightingale of affection
nobility of purpose
note of triumph

O

obduracy of mind
  [obduracy = intractable; hardened]
object of contempt
obligation of loyalty
obliquity of vision
  [obliquity = mental deviation or aberration]
obscurity of twilight
ocean of eloquence
omission of fact
onrush of life
onsets of temptation
openness of mind
opulence of detail
orgy of lying

ornaments of eloquence
outbreak of hostilities
outburst of tears
outflow of sympathy
outposts of morality
overflow of vitality

P

page of desolation
pageant of life
pang of regret
parade of erudition
  [erudition = extensive learning]
passion of patriotism
passivity of mind
pattern of virtue
peals of laughter
pendulum of opinion
pensiveness of feeling
perils of fortune
period of lassitude
perturbation of mind
perversity of chance
pests of society
petrifaction of egoism
  [petrifaction = fossilization; paralyzed with fear]
phantom of delight

phase of belief

physiognomy of nature

piece of pedantry
  [pedantry = attention to detail]

pinions of eloquence
  [pinions = primary feather of a bird]

pinnacle of favor

pit of oblivion

plainness of speech

play of fancy

plea of urgency

plenitude of power

point of view

poise of mind

policy of severity

portent of danger

power of imagination

precipice of stupefaction

precision of phrase

prerogative of age

presence of mind

pressure of expediency

presumption of doubt

prey of fancy

pride of life

process of effacement

profundity of thought

profusion of argument

progress of events
promptings of reason
propriety of action
provocative of scorn
puff of applause
pulse of life
purity of diction
pursuit of knowledge
puzzledom of life

Q

quagmire of distrust
qualities of leadership
qualm of conscience
question of honor
quickness of apprehension
quivering of pain

R

radiance of morning
range of experience
rashness of intention
ravages of time
ray of hope
reaches of achievement
realities of life

realm of peace
rebound of fascination
rectitude of soul
redress of grievances
redundance of words
refinement of style
reins of life
relish of beauty
remorse of guilt
residue of truth
resoluteness of conviction
resource of expression
restraint of speech
revel of imagination
revulsion of feeling
richness of outline
riddle of existence
ridicule of ignorance
riot of words
ripeness of wisdom
roars of exultation
robe of humility
robustness of mind
root of individuality
round of platitudes
rush of agony
rust of neglect
ruts of conventionality

S

sadness of soul

sanguine of success
  [sanguine = cheerfully confident; optimistic]

sanity of judgment

savoring of quackery

scantiness of resources

scarves of smoke

school of adversity

scrap of knowledge

scruple of conscience

searchlight of truth

semblance of composure

sensation of pity

sense of urgency

sentiment of disapprobation
  [approbation = warm approval; praise]

sequence of events

serenity of mind

severity of style

shackles of civilization

shade of doubt

shadow of truth

shallowness of thought

shock of apprehension

shouts of approval

shower of abuse

shriek of wrath

shuttle of life

sigh of wind

singleness of purpose

slave of malice

slough of ignorance

slumber of death

smile of raillery
   [raillery = good-natured teasing; banter]

solace of adversity

soul of generosity

source of renown

spark of perception

species of despotism

spell of emotion

sphere of influence

spice of caricature

splendor of imagination

spur of necessity

start of uneasiness

stateliness of movement

sting of satire

stolidity of sensation

storehouse of facts

storm of criticism

stream of humanity

stress of life

string of episodes
stroke of fate
substratum of belief
subtlety of intellect
succession of events
suggestion of fancy
sum of happiness
summit of misery
sunshine of life
supremacy of good
surface of events
surfeit of verbiage
  [surfeit = supply to excess]
surge of pathos
suspense of judgment
suspicion of flattery
sweep of landscape
symbol of admiration
system of aspersion

T

taint of megalomania
tardiness of speech
task of conciliation
tempest of passion
tenacity of execution
tenderness of sentiment

term of reproach
threshold of consciousness
thrift of time
thrill of delight
throb of compunction
throng of sensations
tide of humanitarianism
timid of innovation
tincture of depreciation
tinge of mockery
tissue of misrepresentations
tolerant of folly
tone of severity
top of ambition
torrent of fervor
totality of effect
touch of severity
touchstone of genius
trace of bitterness
tradition of mankind
train of disasters
trait of cynicism
trance of delight
transport of enthusiasm
trappings of wisdom
trend of consciousness
tribute of admiration
trick of fancy

tumult of applause
turmoil of controversy
turn of events
twilight of elderliness
twinge of envy

U

unity of purpose
universality of experience

V

vagrancy of thought
valley of misfortune
vanguard of progress
vehemence of manner
vehicle of intercourse
veil of futurity
vein of snobbishness
velocity of movement
vestige of regard
vicissitudes of life
   [vicissitudes = sudden or unexpected changes]
vision of splendor
vividness of memory
voice of ambition
void of authority

volume of trade
vow of allegiance

W

warmth of temperament
waste of opportunity
wave of depression
wealth of meaning
weariness of sorrow
web of villainy
weight of argument
whiff of irritation
whirl of delight
whirligig of life
whirlwind of words
wilderness of perplexities
wiles of innocence
word of opprobrium
    [opprobrium = disgrace from shameful conduct]
work of supererogation
    [supererogation = to do more than is required]
world of fantasy
worthy of mention

Y

yoke of convention

Z

zest of enjoyment
zone of delusion
Preposition "by"

Preposition "by"

A

affected by externals
allayed by sympathy
animated by victory
appraised by fashion
assailed by conscience
attained by effort
avert by prayer

B

ballasted by brains
beset by difficulties
bound by opinion
branded by defeat

C

characterized by discretion
chastened by sorrow
cheek by jowl
circulated by malice
clogged by insincerity
colored by environment
condemned by posterity
confirmed by habit
consoled by prayer
convinced by argument
convulsed by divisions

D

darkened by shadows
dazzled by fame
depraved by pain
devoured by curiosity
disgusted by servility
driven by remorse

E

embarrassed by timidity
encouraged by success

enfeebled by age
enforced by action
enjoined by religion
enriched by gifts
established by convention
evoked by shame

F

fascinated, by mystery
favored by fortune
fettered by systems
fired by wrath
forbid by authority
fortified by faith

G

governed by precedent
guided by instinct

H

haunted by visions
hushed by denial

I

impelled by duty
inculcated by practise
induced by misrepresentation
influenced by caution
inspired by love

L

learned by rote

M

marked by acuteness
measured by years

N

narrowed by custom

O

occasioned by irritation
oppressed by destiny

P

parched by disuse
persuaded by appeal
portray by words
prescribed by custom
prevented by chance
prompted by coquetry
purged by sorrow

R

racked by suffering
refuted by reason
repelled by censure
restrained by violence
rising by industry

S

sanctioned by experience
shaped by tradition
soured by misfortune
stung by derision
supplanted by others
supported by evidence

T

thwarted by fortune
tempered by charity
tormented by jealousy
tortured by doubt

U

unadorned by artifice
undaunted by failure
undetermined by sorrow
undone by treachery
unfettered by fear
urged by curiosity

V

vitalized by thought

W

won by aggression
worn by time
wrenched by emotions
Preposition "in"

A

absorbed in meditation

affable in manner
  [affable = gentle and gracious]

atone in measure

B

barren in intellect

basking in sunshine

buried in solitude

C

call in question

clothed in truth

cloying in sweetness
  [cloying = too filling, rich, or sweet]

confident in opinion

confute in argument

contemplative in aspect

cumbrous in style
  [cumbrous = cumbersome; difficult to use]

D

deficient in insight
delight in learning
deterioration in quality
difference in detail
diligent in application
diminish in respect
dwarfed in numbers

E

end in smoke
enumerate in detail
experienced in duplicity

F

feeble in influence
fertile in consequence
flourish in luxuriance
founded in truth

G

gaze in astonishment
go in pursuit

graceful in proportion
grievously in error

H

hold in bondage

I

immersed in thought
indulge in reverie
inferior in character
influential in society
ingenuity in planning
instance in point
involved in obscurity

K

kept in abeyance

L

landmarks in memory
languish in obscurity
lie in wait
limited in scope
linger in expectation

listen in amazement
lost in awe
lower in estimation
luxuriant in fancy

M

monstrous in dulness
mysterious in origin

N

noble in amplitude
nursed in luxury

O

organized in thought

P

petulant in expression
plead in vain
pleasing in outline
plunged in darkness
positive in judgment
practical in application
pride in success

protest in vain
pursued in leisure

Q

quick in suggestion

R

ready in resource
recoiling in terror
remote in character
revel in danger
rich in variety
rooted in prejudice

S

schooled in self-restraint
scrupulous in conduct
set in motion
skilled in controversy
sound in theory
stammer in confusion
stricken in years
strides in civilization
striking in character
stunted in growth

T

tender in sentiment

U

unique in literature
unity in diversity
unprecedented in kind

V

versed in knowledge

W

wallow in idolatry
wanting in dignity
waver in purpose
weak in conception
Preposition "into"

Preposition "in"

A

abashed into silence

B

beguile into reading
betray into speech
blending into harmony
bring into disrepute
bullied into silence
burn into memory
burst into view

C

call into question
carry into conflict
chill into apathy
coming into vogue
cringe into favor
crumbled into dust
crystallized into action

D

dash into fragments
deepen into confusion
degenerate into monotony
deluded into believing
descent into death
dissolve into nothingness
dragged into pursuit
drawn into controversy
dribbling into words
driven into servitude
dulled into acquiescence

E

electrify into activity
elevated into importance
enquire into precedents
enter into controversy
expand into weakness

F

fade into insignificance
fall into decay
fashion into festoons

flame into war
flower into sympathy
forced into action
frozen into form
fuse into unity

G

galvanize into life
go into raptures
goaded into action

H

hushed into silence

I

incursions into controversy
insight into truth
inveigled into dispute
  [inveigled = convince by coaxing, flattery]

K

kindle into action

L

lapse into pedantry
  [pedantries = attention to detail or rules]
lash into silence
launch into disapproval
lead into captivity
leap into currency
lulled into indifference

M

melt into space
merge into character

P

pass into oblivion
plunge into despair
pour into print

Q

quicken into life

R

relapse into savagery
rendered into music
resolve into nothingness
retreat into silence
ripened into love
rush into print

S

shocked into attention
sink into insignificance
smitten into ice
snubbed into quiescence
stricken into silence
summoned into being
swollen into torrents

T

take into account
thrown into disorder
transform into beauty
translated into fact

U

usher into society

V

vanish into mystery

W

wander into digression
wheedled into acquiescence
withdraw into solitude
Preposition "to"

Preposition "into"

A

addicted to flattery
adherence to principle
affect to believe
akin to truth
alive to opportunity
allied to virtue
amenable to reason

aspire to rule
attempt to suppress
aversion to publicity

B

blind to demonstration
brought to repentance

C

claim to perpetuity
come to nothing
committed to righteousness
common to humanity
conducive to happiness
conformable to fact
consigned to oblivion
constrained to speak
contribution to knowledge

D

deaf to entreaty
dedicated to friendship
deference to custom
devoted to ideals

disposed to cavil
  [cavil = raise trivial objections]
doomed to destruction
driven to despair
dwarf to unimportance

E

empowered to act
endeared to all
excite to pity
exposed to derision

F

fly to platitudes
foredoomed to failure

G

given to extravagance
ground to atoms

H

harassed to death
hostile to progress

I

impervious to suggestion
impossible to reconcile
impotent to save
incentive to devotion
incitement to anger
inclined to vascillate
indifference to truth
intent to deceive
intolerable to society
inured to fatigue
   [inured = habituate to something undesirable]
invocation to sleep

L

laugh to scorn
left to conjecture
lost to remembrance

O

obedience to conscience
oblivious to criticism
offensive to modesty
open to reason

opposed to innovation

P

pander to prejudice
pertaining to fashion
prone to melancholy
propose to undertake
provoke to laughter
put to confusion

R

recourse to falsehood
reduced to impotence
related to eternity
repeat to satiety
repugnant to justice
requisite to success
resort to violence
run to seed

S

seek to overawe
serve to embitter
spur to action
stimulus to ambition

stirred to remonstrance
subject to scrutiny
succumb to fascination
superior to circumstances
susceptible to argument

T

temptation to doubt
tend to frustrate
trust to chance

U

utilize to advantage

V

venture to say
vital to success

W

wedded to antiquity

Y

yield to reason

Preposition "with"

A

abounding with plenty
accord with nature
act with deliberation
adorn with beauty
afflict with ugliness
aflame with life
allied with economy
anticipate with delight
ascertain with exactness
attended with danger

B

beam with self-approval
behave with servility
big with fate
blinded with tears
blush with shame
branded with cowardice
bubbling with laughter
burn with indignation

C

cling with tenacity
clothe with authority
compatible with freedom
comply with tradition
conceal with difficulty
consistent with facts
covered with ignominy
crush with sorrow

D

deny with emphasis
depressed with fear
dispense with formality
distort with passion

E

echo with merriment
endow with intelligence
endued with faith
  [endued = provide with a quality; put on]
endure with fortitude
examine with curiosity

F

face with indifference
flushed with pride
fraught with peril
furious with indignation

G

glowing with delight

I

imbued with courage
incompatible with reason
inconsistent with beauty
inflamed with rage
inspired with patriotism
intoxicated with joy

K

kindle with enthusiasm

L

laugh with glee

M

meet with rebuke
mingled with curiosity
move with alacrity

O

oppressed with hardship
overcome with shyness
overflowing with love
overhung with gloom

P

performed with regularity
pervaded with grandeur
proceed with alertness
punish with severity

Q

quicken with pride
quiver with anxiety

R

radiant with victory
regard with loathing
relate with zest
repel with indignation

S

saddle with responsibility
scream with terror
scrutinize with care
seething with sedition
  [sedition = conduct or language inciting rebellion]
sick with dread
sob with anguish
squirm with delight
suffuse with spirituality

T

tainted with fraud
teeming with life
tense with expectancy
thrill with excitement
throb with vitality
tinged with romance

touched with feeling
treat with contempt
tremble with fear

U

unmixed with emotion
utter with sarcasm

V

vibrant with feeling
view with awe

W

wield with power
work with zeal

SECTION VI

BUSINESS PHRASES

A

A request for further particulars will not involve any obligation
A telegram is enclosed for your use, as this matter is urgent
Accept our thanks for your recent remittance
Acknowledging the receipt of your recent inquiry
After examination we can confidently say
After very carefully considering
Again thanking you for the inquiry
Agreeable to our conversation
An addressed envelope is enclosed for your convenience
An early reply will greatly oblige
Answering your recent inquiry
Any information you may give us will be appreciated
Any time that may suit your convenience
As a matter of convenience and economy
As a special favor we ask
As directed in your letter, we are shipping to you
As explained in our previous letter
As it will give us an opportunity to demonstrate our ability

As stated in our previous letter

As we have received no response from you

As you, doubtless, are aware

As you probably have been told

As your experience has probably shown you

Assuring you of every courtesy

Assuring you of our entire willingness to comply with your request

Assuring you of prompt and careful cooperation

At the present writing

At the suggestion of one of our patrons

At your earliest opportunity

Awaiting the favor of your prompt attention

Awaiting the pleasure of serving you

Awaiting your early communication

Awaiting your further commands

Awaiting your pleasure

B

Believing you will answer this promptly

C

Complying with your request

Conditions make it obligatory for us

D

Do not hesitate to let us know
Do not overlook this opportunity
Do you realize that you can

E

Enclosed please find a memorandum
Enclosed we beg to hand you
Enclosed you will find a circular which will fully explain

F

For some years past
For your convenience we enclose a stamped envelope
For your further information we take pleasure in sending to you
Frankly, we believe it is extremely worth while for you
From the standpoint of serviceability

H

Here is a complete answer to
Here is your opportunity
Hoping for a continuance of your interest
Hoping for a definite reply

Hoping that our relations may prove mutually satisfactory
Hoping to be favored with your order
How may we serve you further?
However, because of the special circumstances attached

I

I am compelled to inform you
I am confident that you will be thoroughly satisfied
I am directed to say to you
I am, gentlemen, yours faithfully
I am giving the matter my personal attention
I am, my dear sir, yours faithfully
I am still holding this offer open to you
I ask that you be good enough
I beg to request that you give me some information
I believe I understand perfectly just how you feel about
I have been favorably impressed by your
I have now much pleasure in confirming
I have pleasure in acknowledging
I have the honor to acknowledge the receipt
I have the honor to remain
I herewith submit my application
I highly appreciate this mark of confidence
I look forward to pleasant personal relations in the future
I regret exceedingly to inform you
I remain, my dear sir, yours faithfully
I shall be pleased to forward descriptive circulars

I shall esteem it a personal favor

I should welcome an interview at your convenience

I sincerely hope that you will give the subject your earnest consideration

I take pleasure in replying to your inquiry concerning

I trust I shall hear from you soon

I want to express the hope that our pleasant business relations will continue

I want to interest you

I want to thank you for your reply

I wish to confirm my letter

If I can be of further service, please address me

If it is not convenient for you

If there is any valid reason why you are unable

If we can be of service to you

If we can help you in any way

If we have not made everything perfectly clear, please let us know

If you accommodate us, the favor will be greatly appreciated

If you are interested, please let us hear from you

If you are thinking about ordering

If you desire, our representative will call

If you have any cause for dissatisfaction

If you give this matter your prompt attention

In accordance with the terms of our offer

In accordance with your request

In answering your inquiry regarding

In any event, a reply to this will be very much appreciated

In closing we can only assure you

In compliance with your favor

In compliance with your request, we are pleased to send to you

In conclusion, we can assure you

In order to facilitate our future transactions

In reference to your application

In regard to your proposition

In reply thereto, we wish to inform you

In reply to your valued favor

In response to your recent request

In spite of our best efforts it is not probable

In thanking you for the patronage with which you have favored us

In view of all these facts, we feel justified in claiming

Information has just reached me

It gives us pleasure to recommend

It has consistently been our aim to help our customers

It is a matter of great regret to us

It is a pleasure for me to answer your inquiry

It is a well known fact

It is interesting to note

It is our very great pleasure to advise you

It is the policy of our house

It seems clear that our letter must have miscarried

It was purely an oversight on our part

It will be entirely satisfactory to us

It will be our aim to interest you

It will be readily appreciated

It will be to your advantage
It will doubtless be more convenient for you
It will interest you to know
It will receive the same careful attention

J

Just mail the enclosed card

K

Kindly endorse your reply on the enclosed sheet
Kindly let us have your confirmation at your earliest convenience
Kindly let us know your pleasure concerning
Kindly read the enclosed list

L

Let me thank you for the opportunity to give this matter my personal attention
Let us assure you of our desire to cooperate with you
Let us assure you that we are very much pleased
Let us know if there is any further attention
Let us thank you again for opening an account with us
Looking forward to the early receipt of some of your orders

M

May I ask you to do us a great favor by
May we be favored with a reply
Meantime soliciting your forbearance
Meanwhile permit me to thank you for your kind attention

O

On referring to your account we notice
Our letter must have gone astray
Our relations with your house must have hitherto been very pleasant
Our services are at your command
Our stock has been temporarily exhausted
Owing to our inability to collect out-standing debts

P

Permit me to add
Permit us to express our sincere appreciation
Please accept the thanks of the writer
Please consider this letter an acknowledgment
Please favor us with a personal communication
Please feel assured that we shall use every endeavor
Possibly the enclosure may suggest to you
Promptly on receipt of your telegram

Pursuant to your letter

R

Recently we had occasion
Referring to your esteemed favor
Regretting our inability to serve you in the present instance
Reluctant as we are to believe
Requesting your kind attention to this matter

S

Should you decide to act upon this latter suggestion
So many requests of a similar nature come to us
Soliciting a continuance of your patronage

T

Thank you for your expression of confidence
Thanking you for your inquiry
Thanking you for your past patronage
Thanking you for your promptness.
Thanking you in advance for an early reply
Thanking you in anticipation
The causes for the delay were beyond our control
The margin of profit which we allow ourselves
The proof is in this fact
The proposition appeals to us as a good one

Therefore we are able to make you this offer
Therefore we trust you will write to us promptly
These points should be most carefully considered
This arrangement will help us over the present difficulty
This is according to our discussion
This matter has been considered very seriously
This personal guarantee I look upon as a service to you
This privileged communication is for the exclusive use
This will amply repay you
Trusting that we may have the pleasure of serving you
Trusting to receive your best consideration

U

Under no circumstances can we entertain such an arrangement
Under separate cover we are mailing to you
Under these circumstances we are willing to extend the terms
Unfortunately we are compelled at certain times
Unless you can give us reasonable assurance
Upon being advised that these terms are satisfactory
Upon receiving your letter of

W

We acknowledge with pleasure the receipt of your order
We admit that you are justified in your complaint
We again solicit an opportunity
We again thank you for your inquiry

We always endeavor to please
We appreciate the order you were kind enough to send to us
We appreciate your patronage very much
We are always glad to furnish information
We are anxious to make satisfactory adjustment
We are at a loss to understand why
We are at your service at all times
We are confident that you will have no further trouble
We are extremely desirous of pleasing our patrons
We are in a position to give you considerable help
We are in receipt of your communication regarding
We are indeed sorry to learn
We are perfectly willing to make concessions
We are pleased to receive your request for information
We are pleased to send you descriptive circulars
We are reluctant to adopt such severe measures
We are satisfied regarding your statement
We are sending to you by mail
We are sorry to learn from your letter
We are thoroughly convinced of the need
We are totally at a loss to understand
We are very anxious to have you try
We are very glad to testify to the merit of
We ask for a continuance of your confidence
We ask that you kindly let us hear from you
We assume that you are considering
We assure you of our confidence in the reliability
We assure you of our desire to be of service

We await an early, and we trust, a favorable reply

We await the courtesy of an early answer

We beg a moment of your attention and serious consideration

We believe that if you will carefully consider the matter

We believe you will readily understand our position

We can assure you that any order with which you favor us

We desire information pertaining to your financial condition

We desire to effect a settlement

We desire to express our appreciation of your patronage

We desire to impress upon you

We expect to be in the market soon

We feel assured that you will appreciate

We feel sure that you will approve of our action in this matter

We frankly apologize to you

We hasten to acknowledge the receipt

We have anticipated a heavy demand

We have, as yet, no definite understanding

We have come to the conclusion

We have endeavored to serve the needs of your organization

We have found it impossible

We have much pleasure in answering your inquiry

We have no desire to adopt harsh measures

We have not had the pleasure of placing your name on our ledgers

We have not, however, had the pleasure of hearing from you

We have not yet had time to sift the matter thoroughly

We have the honor to be, gentlemen

We have the honor to inform you

We have thought it best to forward

We have your request for information regarding

We hesitated for a while to pursue the matter

We hope that an understanding can be reached

We hope that we shall have many opportunities to demonstrate our ability

We hope that you will find the enclosed booklet very interesting

We hope to hear favorably from you

We hope you will appreciate

We hope you will excuse the unavoidable delay

We invite your attention to

We must insist upon a prompt settlement

We must, therefore, insist on the terms of the agreement

We note that the time is at hand

We offer you the services of an expert

We particularly want to interest you

We realize that this matter has escaped your attention

We realize that this is simply an oversight on your part

We regret exceedingly that you have been inconvenienced

We regret our inability to meet your wishes

We regret that owing to the press of business

We regret that this misunderstanding has occurred

We regret that we are not in a position

We regret that we are unable to grant your request

We regret the necessity of calling your attention

We regret to be compelled for this reason to withdraw the privilege

We regret to learn that you are disappointed

We remain, dear sir, yours faithfully

We remain, gentlemen, with thanks

We shall await your early commands with interest

We shall await your reply with interest

We shall be glad to fill your order

We shall be glad to have you tell us frankly

We shall be glad to render you any assistance in our power

We shall be happy to meet your requirements

We shall be indebted to you for your courtesy

We shall be pleased to receive the remittance

We shall be pleased to take the matter up further

We shall do everything in our power

We shall do our best to correct the mistake

We shall feel compelled

We shall heartily appreciate any information

We shall use every endeavor

We suggest that this is an opportune time

We suggest that you consider

We take pleasure in enclosing herewith

We take pleasure in explaining the matter you asked about

We take the liberty of deviating from your instructions

We take the liberty of writing to you.

We thank you for calling our attention

We thank you for your courteous letter

We thank you for your kind inquiry of recent date

We thank you very gratefully for your polite and friendly letter

We thank you very much for the frank statement of your affairs

We thank you very sincerely for your assistance

We think you will agree

We trust our explanation will meet with your approval

We trust that we may hear favorably from you

We trust that you will give this matter your immediate attention

We trust you may secure some of the exceptional values

We trust you will find it correct

We trust you will not consider us unduly strict

We trust you will promptly comply with our previous suggestions

We understand your position

We urge that you write to us by early mail

We venture to enclose herewith

We very much wish you to examine

We want every opportunity to demonstrate our willingness

We want particularly to impress upon you this fact

We want to please you in every respect

We want to remind you again

We want you to read the booklet carefully

We will at once enter your order

We will be compelled to take the necessary steps

We will be glad to lay before you the fullest details

We will be pleased to give it careful consideration

We will gladly accommodate you

We will gladly extend to you similar courtesies whenever we can do so

We will make it a point to give your correspondence close attention

We would appreciate a remittance

We would consider it a great favor
We would draw your attention to the fact
We would request, as a special favor
We write to suggest to you
We write to urge upon you the necessity
We wrote to you at length
While we appreciate the peculiar circumstances
While we feel that we are in no way responsible
Why not allow us this opportunity to satisfy you
Will you give us, in confidence, your opinion
Will you give us the benefit of your experience
Will you kindly advise us in order that we may adjust our records
Will you please give us your immediate attention
With our best respects and hoping to hear from you
With reference to your favor of yesterday
With regard to your inquiry
With the fullest assurance that we are considering
With the greatest esteem and respect

Y

You are certainly justified in complaining
You are evidently aware that there is a growing demand
You are quite right in your statement
You cannot regret more than I the necessity
You undoubtedly are aware

You will find interest, we believe, in this advance announcement

You will get the benefit of this liberal offer

You will have particular interest in the new and attractive policy

Your early attention to this matter will oblige

Your further orders will be esteemed

Your inquiry has just been received, and we are glad to send to you

Your orders and commands will always have our prompt and best attention

Your satisfaction will dictate our course

Your trial order is respectfully solicited

Your usual attention will oblige

SECTION VII

LITERARY EXPRESSIONS

A

A bitterness crept into her face

A blazing blue sky poured down torrents of light

A book to beguile the tedious hours

A brave but turbulent aristocracy

A broad, complacent, admiring imbecility breathed from his nose and lips

A burlesque feint of evading a blow

A callous and conscienceless brute

A calm and premeditated prudence

A calmness settled on his spirit

A campaign of unbridled ferocity

A carefully appraising eye

A ceaselessly fleeting sky

A certain implication of admiring confidence

A charming air of vigor and vitality

A childish belief in his own impeccability

A cold, hard, frosty penuriousness was his prevalent characteristic
    [penuriousness = stingy; barren; poverty-stricken]

A compassion perfectly angelic

A constant stream of rhythmic memories

A covertly triumphant voice

A creature of the most delicate and rapid responses

A crop of disappointments

A cunning intellect patiently diverting every circumstance to its design

A curious and inexplicable uneasiness

A curious vexation fretted her

A daily avalanche of vituperation
[vituperation = harshly abusive language]

A dandified, pretty-boy-looking sort of figure

A dark and relentless fate

A day monotonous and colorless

A dazzling completeness of beauty

A deep and brooding resentment

A delicious throng of sensations

A deliciously tantalizing sense

A detached segment of life

A dire monotony of bookish idiom

A disheveled and distraught figure

A face singularly acute and intelligent

A faint accent of reproach

A faint sense of compunction moved her

A faint, transient, wistful smile lightened her brooding face

A faint tremor of amusement was on his lips

A faintly quizzical look came into his incisive stare

A fawn-colored sea streaked here and there with tints of deepest orange

A fever of enthusiasm

A few tears came to soften her seared vision

A fiery exclamation of wrath and disdain

A figure full of decision and dignity

A firm and balanced manhood

A first faint trace of irritation

A fitful boy full of dreams and hopes

A flame of scarlet crept in a swift diagonal across his cheeks

A fleeting and furtive air of triumph

A flood of pride rose in him

A foreboding of some destined change

A fortuitous series of happy thoughts

A frigid touch of the hand

A fugitive intangible charm

A gay exuberance of ambition

A generation of men lavishly endowed with genius

A gentle sarcasm ruffled her anger

A ghastly whiteness overspread the cheek

A glance of extraordinary meaning

A glassy expression of inattention

A glassy stare of deprecating horror

A glittering infectious smile

A gloom overcame him

A golden haze of pensive light

A golden summer of marvelous fertility

A graceful readiness and vigor

A grave man of pretending exterior

A great pang gripped her heart

A great process of searching and shifting

A great sickness of heart smote him

A great soul smitten and scourged, but still invested with the dignity of immortality

A grim and shuddering fascination

A gush of entrancing melody

A gusty breeze blew her hair about unheeded

A half-breathless murmur of amazement and incredulity

A half-uneasy, half-laughing compunction

A harassing anxiety of sorrow

A harvest of barren regrets

A haunting and horrible sense of insecurity

A heavy oppression seemed to brood upon the air

A helpless anger simmered in him

A hint of death in the icy breath of the gale

A hot and virulent skirmish

A hot uprush of hatred and loathing

A kind of ineffable splendor crowns the day

A lapse from the well-ordered decencies of civilization

A large, rich, copious human endowment

A late star lingered, remotely burning

A laugh of jovial significance

A light of unwonted pleasure in her eyes
[unwonted = unusual]

A little jaded by gastronomical exertions

A lukewarm and selfish love

A man of imperious will
  [imperious = arrogantly domineering]

A man of matchless modesty and refinement

A manner bright with interest and interrogation

A manner nervously anxious to please

A melancholy monotone beat on one's heart

A mere exhibition of fussy diffuseness

A mere figment of a poet's fancy

A mien and aspect singularly majestic
  [mien = bearing or manner]

A mild and deprecating air

A mind singularly practical and sagacious
  [sagacious = wise]

A mouth of inflexible decision

A murmur of complacency

A mystery everlastingly impenetrable

A nameless sadness which is always born of moonlight

A new and overmastering impulse

A new doubt assailed her

A new marvel of the sky

A new trouble was dawning on his thickening mental horizon

A nimble-witted opponent

A painful thought was flooding his mind

A pang of jealousy not unmingled with scorn

A patience worthy of admiration

A perfect carnival of fun

A perfect crime of clumsiness

A piteous aspect of woe

A portent full of possible danger
A potion to be delicately supped at leisure
A powerful agitation oppressed him
A prevailing sentiment of uneasy discontent
A prey to listless uneasiness
A profound and absorbing interest
A profound and eager hopefulness
A profound and rather irritating egotist by nature
A prop for my faint heart
A propitious sky, marbled with pearly white
    [propitious = favorable; kindly; gracious]
A protest wavered on her lip
A puissant and brilliant family
    [puissant = powerful; mighty]
A queer, uncomfortable perplexity began to invade her
A quick flame leaped in his eyes
A quick shiver ruffled the brooding stillness of the water
A quiver of resistance ran through her
A remarkable fusion of morality and art
A random gleam of light
A rare and dazzling order of beauty
A rhythmical torrent of eloquent prophecy
A river of shame swept over him
A sad inquiry seemed to dwell in her gaze
A satisfied sense of completeness
A secret sweeter than the sea or sky can whisper
A sensation of golden sweetness and delight
A sense of desolation and disillusionment overwhelmed me

A sense of infinite peace brooded over the place
A sense of meditative content
A sense of repression was upon her
A sentiment of distrust in its worth had crept into her thoughts
A sheaf of letters
A shimmer of golden sun shaking through the trees
A shiver of apprehension crisped her skin
A shuffling compromise between defiance and prostration
A sigh of large contentment
A sight for the angels to weep over
A skepticism which prompted rebellion
A slight movement of incredulous dissent
A smile full of subtle charm
A smile of exquisite urbanity
A soft insidious plea
A soft intonation of profound sorrow
A soft suspicion of ulterior motives
A solemn glee possessed my mind
A solemn gray expanse that lost itself far away in the gray of the sea
A solemn utterance of destiny
A somber and breathless calm hung over the deepening eve
A somewhat melancholy indolence
A somewhat sharp and incisive voice
A sonorous voice bade me enter
A soothing and quieting touch was gently laid upon her soul
A sort of eager, almost appealing amiability
A sort of stolid despairing acquiescence

A sort of stunned incredulity

A soundless breeze that was little more than a whisper

A spacious sense of the amplitude of life's possibilities

A staccato cough interrupted the flow of speech

A state of sullen self-absorption

A steady babble of talk and laughter

A step was at her heels

A stifling sensation of pain and suspense

A stinging wind swept the woods

A strange compound of contradictory elements

A stream of easy talk

A strong convulsion shook the vague indefinite form

A strong susceptibility to the ridiculous

A subtle emphasis of scorn

A sudden and stinging delight

A sudden gleam of insight

A sudden uncontrollable outburst of feeling

A super-abundance of boisterous animal spirits

A supercilious scorn and pity
 [supercilious = haughty disdain]

A super-refinement of taste

A swaggering air of braggadocio
 [braggadocio = pretentious bragging]

A sweet bewilderment of tremulous apprehension
 [tremulous = fearful]

A sweet, quiet, sacred, stately seclusion

A swift knowledge came to her

A swift unformulated fear

A swiftly unrolling panorama of dreams

A tangle of ugly words

A thousand evanescent memories of happy days
  [evanescent = vanishing like vapor]

A thousand unutterable fears bore irresistible despotism over her thoughts

A time of disillusion followed

A tiny stream meandering amiably

A tone of arduous admiration

A torn and tumultuous sky

A total impression ineffable and indescribable

A tragic futility

A treacherous throb of her voice

A true similitude of what befalls many men and women

A tumult of vehement feeling

A tumultuous rush of sensations

A twinge of embarrassment

A vague and wistful melancholy

A vast sweet silence crept through the trees

A veritable spring-cleaning of the soul

A very practised and somewhat fastidious critic

A violent and mendacious tongue
  [mendacious = false; untrue]

A vivid and arresting presentation

A waking dream overshadowed her

A weird world of morbid horrors

A well-bred mixture of boldness and courtesy

A wild vivacity was in her face and manner

A wile of the devil's
  [wile = trick intended to deceive or ensnare]

A wind strayed through the gardens

A withering sensation of ineffable boredom

A wordless farewell

Absolutely vulgarized by too perpetual a parroting

Absorbed in a stream of thoughts and reminiscences

Absorbed in the scent and murmur of the night

Accidents which perpetually deflect our vagrant attention

Across the gulf of years

Administering a little deft though veiled castigation

Affected an ironic incredulity

Affecting a tone of gayety

After a first moment of reluctance

After an eternity of resolutions, doubts, and indecisions

Aghast at his own helplessness

Agitated and enthralled by day-dreams

Agitated with violent and contending emotions

Alien paths and irrelevant junketings

All embrowned and mossed with age

All her gift of serene immobility brought into play

All hope of discreet reticence was ripped to shreds

All the lesser lights paled into insignificance

All the magic of youth and joy of life was there

All the place is peopled with sweet airs

All the sky was mother-of-pearl and tender

All the unknown of the night and of the universe was pressing upon him

All the world was flooded with a soft golden light

All was a vague jumble of chaotic impressions

All was incomprehensible

All was instinctive and spontaneous

Aloof from the motley throng

Ambition shivered into fragments

Amid distress and humiliation

Amid the direful calamities of the time

An acute note of distress in her voice

An agreeably grave vacuity

An air half quizzical and half deferential

An air of affected civility

An air of being meticulously explicit

An air of inimitable, scrutinizing, superb impertinence

An air of stern, deep, and irredeemable gloom hung over and pervaded all

An air of uncanny familiarity

An air which was distinctly critical

An almost pathetic appearance of ephemeral fragility
[ephemeral = markedly short-lived]

An almost riotous prodigality of energy

An answering glow of gratitude

An antagonist worth her steel

An artful stroke of policy

An assumption of hostile intent

An assurance of good-nature that forestalled hostility

An atmosphere of extraordinary languor
[languor = dreamy, lazy mood]

An atmosphere thick with flattery and toadyism
An attack of peculiar virulence and malevolence
An audacious challenge of ridicule
An avidity that bespoke at once the restlessness, [avidity = eagerness] and the genius of her mind
An awe crept over me
An eager and thirsty ear
An easy prey to the powers of folly
An effusive air of welcome
An equal degree of well-bred worldly cynicism
An erect, martial, majestic, and imposing personage
An eternity of silence oppressed him
An expression of mildly humorous surprise
An expression of rare and inexplicable personal energy
An exquisite perception of things beautiful and rare
An iciness, a sinking, a sickening of the heart
An ignoring eye
An impenetrable screen of foliage
An impersonal and slightly ironic interest
An impervious beckoning motion
An inarticulate echo of his longing
An increased gentleness of aspect
An incursion of the loud, the vulgar and meretricious [meretricious = plausible but false]
An inexplicable and uselessly cruel caprice of fate
An inexpressible fervor of serenity
An ingratiating, awkward and, wistful grace
An inspired ray was in his eyes

An instant she stared unbelievingly

An intense and insatiable hunger for light and truth

An intense travail of mind

An obscure thrill of alarm

An odd little air of penitent self-depreciation

An open wit and recklessness of bearing

An oppressive sense of strange sweet odor

An optimistic after-dinner mood

An overburdening sense of the inexpressible

An uncomfortable premonition of fear

An unfailing sweetness and unerring perception

An unpleasant and heavy sensation sat at his heart

An unredeemed dreariness of thought

An unsuspected moral obtuseness

An utter depression of soul

And day peers forth with her blank eyes

And what is all this pother about?
   [pother = commotion; disturbance]

Animated by noble pride

Anticipation painted the world in rose

Appalled in speechless disgust

Appealing to the urgent temper of youth

Apprehensive solicitude about the future

Ardent words of admiration

Armed all over with subtle antagonisms

Artless and unquestioning devotion

As if smitten by a sudden spasm

As the long train sweeps away into the golden distance

August and imperial names in the kingdom of thought
Awaiting his summons to the eternal silence

B

Bandied about from mouth to mouth
Barricade the road to truth
Bartering the higher aspirations of life
Beaming with pleasurable anticipation
Before was the open malignant sea
Beguiled the weary soul of man
Beneath the cold glare of the desolate night
Bent on the lofty ends of her destiny
Beset by agreeable hallucinations
Beset with smiling hills
Beside himself in an ecstasy of pleasure
Betokening an impulsive character
Beyond the farthest edge of night
Birds were fluting in the tulip-trees
Biting sentences flew about
Black inky night
Blithe with the bliss of the morning
Blown about by every wind of doctrine
Bookish precision and professional peculiarity
Borne from lip to lip
Borne onward by slow-footed time
Borne with a faculty of willing compromise
Bowed with a certain frigid and deferential surprise

Broke in a stupendous roar upon the shuddering air
Browsing at will on all the uplands of knowledge and thought
Buffeted by all the winds of passion
Buried hopes rose from their sepulchers
Buried in the quicksands of ignorance
But none the less peremptorily
  [peremptorily = ending all debate or action]
By a curious irony of fate
By a happy turn of thinking
By virtue of his impassioned curiosity

C

Carried the holiday in his eye
Chafed at the restraints imposed on him
Cheeks furrowed by strong purpose and feeling
Childlike contour of the body
Cleansed of prejudice and self-interest
Cloaked in prim pretense
Clothed with the witchery of fiction
Clutch at the very heart of the usurping mediocrity
Cold gaze of curiosity
Collapse into a dreary and hysterical depression
Comment of rare and delightful flavor
Conjuring up scenes of incredible beauty and terror
Conscious of unchallenged supremacy
Constant indulgence of wily stratagem and ambitious craft
Contemptuously indifferent to the tyranny of public opinion

Covered with vegetation in wild luxuriance

Crisp sparkle of the sea

Crystallize about a common nucleus

Cultivated with a commensurate zeal

Current play of light gossip

Curtains of opaque rain

D

Dallying in maudlin regret over the past
  [maudlin = tearfully sentimental]

Dark with unutterable sorrows

Darkness oozed out from between the trees

Dawn had broken

Day stood distinct in the sky

Days of vague and fantastic melancholy

Days that are brief and shadowed

Deep shame and rankling remorse

Deficient in affectionate or tender impulses

Delicately emerging stars

Delicious throng of sensations

Despite her pretty insolence

Dignity and sweet patience were in her look

Dim opalescence of the moon

Dimly foreshadowed on the horizon

Dimmed by the cold touch of unjust suspicion

Disfigured by passages of solemn and pompous monotony.

Disguised itself as chill critical impartiality

Dismal march of death
Distinguished by hereditary rank or social position
Distract and beguile the soul
Distressing in their fatuous ugliness
Diverted into alien channels
Diverting her eyes, she pondered
Dogs the footsteps
Doled out in miserly measure
Doubt tortured him
Doubts beset her lonely and daring soul
Down the steep of disenchantment
Dreams and visions were surpassed
Dreams that fade and die in the dim west
Drear twilight of realities
Drift along the stream of fancy
Drowned in the deep reticence of the sea
Drowsiness coiled insidiously about him
Dull black eyes under their precipice of brows

E

Earth danced under a heat haze
Easily moved to gaiety and pleasure
Either way her fate was cruel
Embrace with ardor the prospect of serene leisure
Endearing sweetness and manner
Endeavoring to smile away his chagrin
Endlessly shifting moods

Endowed with all those faculties that can make the world a garden of enchantment

Endowed with life and emphasis

Enduring with smiling composure the near presence of people who are distasteful

Enjoyed with astonishing unscrupulousness

Enticed irresistibly by the freedom of an open horizon

Essay a flight of folly

Evanescent shades of feeling
  [evanescent = vanishing like vapor]

Events took an unexpected sinister turn

Every curve of her features seemed to express a fine arrogant acrimony and harsh truculence

Everywhere the fragrance of a bountiful earth

Exasperated by what seemed a wilful pretense of ignorance

Exhibits itself in fastidious crotchets

Expectation darkened into anxiety

Experience and instinct warred within her

Exquisite graciousness of manner

Exquisitely stung by the thought

F

Familiar and endearing intimacy

Fatally and indissolubly united

Fathomless depths of suffering

Fear held him in a vice

Feeding his scholarly curiosity

Feeling humiliated by the avowal

Felicitousness in the choice and exquisiteness in the collocation of words

Fettered by poverty and toil

Feverish tide of life

Fine precision of intent

Fitful tumults of noble passion

Fleeting touches of something alien and intrusive

Floating in the clouds of reverie

Fluctuations of prosperity and adversity

Flushed with a suffusion that crimsoned her whole countenance

Forebodings possessed her

Foreshadowing summer's end

Forever echo in the heart

Forever sings itself in memory

Formless verbosity and a passionate rhetoric

Fragments of most touching melody

Free from rigid or traditional fetters

Freedom and integrity of soul

Freighted with strange, vague longings

Frosty thraldom of winter
 [thraldom = servitude; bondage]

Fugitive felicities of thought and sensation

Full of dreams and refinements and intense abstractions

Full of majestic tenderness

G

Gathering all her scattered impulses into a passionate act of courage

Gaze dimly through a maze of traditions

Generosity pushed to prudence

Gleams of sunlight, bewildered like ourselves, struggled, surprised, through the mist and disappeared

Glowing with haste and happiness

Go straight, as if by magic, to the inner meaning

Goaded on by his sense of strange importance

Graceful length of limb and fall of shoulders

Great shuddering seized on her

Green hills pile themselves upon each other's shoulders

Grim and sullen after the flush of the morning

Guilty of girlish sentimentality

H

Half choked by a rising paroxysm of rage

Half-suffocated by his triumph

Hardened into convictions and resolves

Haughtiness and arrogance were largely attributed to him

Haunt the recesses of the memory

Haunted with a chill and unearthly foreboding

He accosted me with trepidation

He adroitly shifted his ground

He airily lampooned their most cherished prejudices

He bowed submission

He braced himself to the exquisite burden of life

He condescended to intimate speech with her

He conversed with a colorless fluency

He could detect the hollow ring of fundamental nothingness

He could do absolutely naught

He drank of the spirit of the universe

He drew near to a desperate resolve

He evinced his displeasure by a contemptuous sneer or a grim scowl

He felt an unaccountable loathing

He felt the ironic rebound of her words

He flung diffidence to the winds

He flushed crimson

He found the silence intolerably irksome

He frowned perplexedly

He gave her a baffled stare

He gave himself to a sudden day-dream

He gave his ear to this demon of false glory

He grew wanton with success

He had acted with chivalrous delicacy of honor

He had the eye of an eagle in his trade

He had the gift of deep, dark silences

He held his breath in admiring silence

He laughed away my protestations

He lent no countenance to the insensate prattle

He listened greedily and gazed intent

He made a loathsome object

He made the politest of monosyllabic replies

He murmured a civil rejoinder

He murmured a vague acceptance

He mused a little while in grave thought

He never wears an argument to tatters

He only smiled with fatuous superiority

He paused, stunned and comprehending

He perceived the iron hand within the velvet glove

He raised a silencing hand

He ruled autocratically

He sacrificed the vulgar prizes of life

He sat on thorns

He set his imagination adrift

He shambled away with speed

He sighed deeply, from a kind of mental depletion

He smote her quickening sensibilities

He submitted in brooding silence

He suppressed every sign of surprise

He surrendered himself to gloomy thought

He threaded a labyrinth of obscure streets

He threw a ton's weight of resolve upon his muscles

He threw out phrases of ill-humor

He threw round a measuring eye

He treads the primrose path of dalliance

He used an unguarded adjective

He was a tall, dark, saturnine youth, sparing of speech
 [saturnine = melancholy; sullen]

He was aware of emotion

He was born to a lively and intelligent patriotism

He was dimly mistrustful of it

He was discreetly silent

He was empty of thought

He was entangled in a paradox

He was giving his youth away by handfuls

He was haunted and begirt by presences

He was measured and urbane

He was most profoundly skeptical

He was nothing if not grandiloquent

He was quaking on the precipice of a bad bilious attack

He was utterly detached from life

He went hot and cold

He would fall into the blackest melancholies

He writhed in the grip of a definite apprehension

He writhed with impotent humiliation

Her blank gaze chilled you

Her bright eyes were triumphant

Her eyes danced with malice

Her eyes dilated with pain and fear

Her eyes were full of wondering interest

Her eyes were limpid and her beauty was softened by an air of indolence and languor
 [languor = dreamy, lazy mood]

Her face stiffened anew into a gray obstinacy

Her face was lit up by a glow of inspiration and resolve

Her haughty step waxed timorous and vigilant

Her head throbbed dangerously
Her heart appeared to abdicate its duties
Her heart fluttered with a vague terror
Her heart pounded in her throat
Her heart was full of speechless sorrow
Her hurrying thoughts clamored for utterance
Her imagination recoiled
Her interest flagged
Her life had dwarfed her ambitions
Her limbs ran to marble
Her lips hardened
Her lips parted in a keen expectancy
Her mind was a store-house of innocuous anecdote
Her mind was beaten to the ground by the catastrophe
Her mood was unaccountably chilled
Her musings took a sudden and arbitrary twist
Her scarlet lip curled cruelly
Her smile was faintly depreciatory
Her smile was linked with a sigh
Her solicitude thrilled him
Her stare dissolved
Her step seemed to pity the grass it prest
Her strength was scattered in fits of agitation
Her stumbling ignorance which sought the road of wisdom
Her thoughts outstripped her erring feet
Her tone was gathering remonstrance
Her tongue on the subject was sharpness itself
Her tongue stumbled and was silent

Her voice had the coaxing inflections of a child
Her voice trailed off vaguely
Her voice was full of temper, hard-held
Her voice, with a tentative question in it, rested in air
Her wariness seemed put to rout
His accents breathed profound relief
His agitation increased
His brow grew knit and gloomy
His brow was in his hand
His conscience leapt to the light
His constraint was excruciating
His curiosity is quenched
His dignity counseled him to be silent
His ears sang with the vibrating intensity of his secret existence
His eyes had a twinkle of reminiscent pleasantry
His eyes literally blazed with savage fire
His eyes shone with the pure fire of a great purpose
His eyes stared unseeingly
His face caught the full strength of the rising wind
His face dismissed its shadow
His face fell abruptly into stern lines
His face lit with a fire of decision
His face showed a pleased bewilderment
His face torn with conflict
His face was gravely authoritative
His gaze faltered and fell
His gaze searched her face
His gaze seemed full of unconquerable hopefulness

His hand supported his chin

His hands were small and prehensible
  [prehensible = capable of being seized]

His heart asserted itself again, thunderously beating

His heart rebuked him

His heart was full of enterprise

His impatient scorn expired

His last illusions crumbled

His lips loosened in a furtively exultant smile

His lips seemed to be permanently parted in a good-humored smile

His mind echoed with words

His mind leaped gladly to meet new issues and fresh tides of thought

His mind was dazed and wandering in a mist of memories

His mood yielded

His mouth quivered with pleasure

His passions vented themselves with sneers

His pulses leaped anew

His reputation had withered

His sensibilities were offended

His shrewd gaze fixed appraisingly upon her

His soul full of fire and eagle-winged

His soul was compressed into a single agony of prayer

His soul was wrung with a sudden wild homesickness

His speech faltered

His swift and caustic satire

His temper was dark and explosive

His thoughts galloped

His thoughts were in clamoring confusion

His tone assumed a certain asperity
 [asperity = roughness; harshness]

His torpid ideas awoke again

His troubled spirit shifted its load

His vagrant thoughts were in full career

His voice insensibly grew inquisitorial

His voice was thick with resentment and futile protest

His whole face was lighted with a fierce enthusiasm

His whole frame seemed collapsed and shrinking

His whole tone was flippant and bumptious

His words trailed off brokenly

His youthful zeal was contagious

Hope was far and dim

How sweet and reasonable the pale shadows of those who smile from some dim corner of our memories

Humiliating paltriness of revenge

I

I capitulated by inadvertence

I cut my reflections adrift

I felt a qualm of apprehension

I suffered agonies of shyness

I took the good day from the hands of God as a perfect gift

I was in a somber mood

I was overshadowed by a deep boding

I was piqued
  [piqued = resentment; indignation]

I yielded to the ingratiating mood of the day

Ill-bred insolence was his only weapon

Ill-dissimulated fits of ambition

Imbued with a vernal freshness
  [vernal = resembling spring; fresh]

Immense and careless prodigality

Immense objects which dwarf us

Immersed in secret schemes

Immured in a trivial round of duty
  [immured = confine within]

Impassioned and earnest language

Impatient and authoritative tones

Impervious to the lessons of experience

Implying an immense melancholy

Imprisoned within an enchanted circle

In a deprecating tone of apology

In a flash of revelation

In a gale of teasing merriment

In a misery of annoyance and mortification

In a musing ecstasy of contemplation

In a sky stained with purple, the moon slowly rose

In a spirit of indulgent irony

In a strain of exaggerated gallantry

In a tone of after-dinner perfunctoriness
  [perfunctoriness = with little interest]

In a tone of musing surprise

In a tumult of self-approval and towering exultation

In a vague and fragmentary way
In a wise, superior, slightly scornful manner
In accents of menace and wrath
In its whole unwieldy compass
In moments of swift and momentous decision
In quest of something to amuse
In requital for various acts of rudeness
In the air was the tang of spring
In the dusky path of a dream
In the face of smarting disillusions
In the flush and heyday of youth and gaiety and loveliness
In the heyday of friendship
In the mild and mellow maturity of age
In the perpetual presence of everlasting verities
In this breathless chase of pleasure
In this chastened mood I left him
Incapable of initiative or boldness
Inconceivable perversion of reasoning
Indolently handsome eyes
Indulge in pleasing discursiveness
Ineffable sensation of irritability
Infantile insensibility to the solemnity of his bereavement
Infantine simplicity and lavish waste
Innumerable starlings clove the air
   [clove = split]
Insensible to its subtle influence
Inspired by the immortal flame of youth
Intangible and indescribable essence

Intense love of excitement and adventure
Intimations of unpenetrated mysteries
Into her eyes had come a hostile challenge
Into the purple sea the orange hues of heaven sunk silently
Into the very vestibule of death
Involuntarily she sighed
Involuntary awkwardness and reserve
Involved in a labyrinth of perplexities
It came to him with a stab of enlightenment
It elicited a remarkably clear and coherent statement
It is a flight beyond the reach of human magnanimity
It is a thing infinitely subtle
It is not every wind that can blow you from your anchorage
It lends no dazzling tints to fancy
It moved me to a strange exhilaration
It parted to a liquid horizon and showed the gray rim of the sea
It proved a bitter disillusion
It seemed intolerably tragic
It seemed to exhale a silent and calm authority
It was a breathless night of suspense
It was a desolating vision
It was a night of little ease to his toiling mind
It was a night of stupefying surprises
It was all infinitely soft and refreshing to the eye
It was an evening of great silences and spaces, wholly tranquil
It was sheer, exuberant, instinctive, unreasoning, careless joy
It was the ecstasy and festival of summer
It was torture of the most exquisite kind

J

Jealousies and animosities which pricked their sluggish blood to tingling

Joy rioted in his large dark eyes

Judging without waiting to ponder over bulky tomes

K

Kind of unscrupulous contempt for gravity

Kiss-provoking lips

L

Laden with the poignant scent of the garden honeysuckle

Language of excessive flattery and adulation

Lapped in soft music of adulation

Lapse into pathos and absurdity

Large, dark, luminous eyes that behold everything about them

Latent vein of whimsical humor

Lead to the strangest aberrations

Leaping from lambent flame into eager and passionate fire [lambent = effortlessly brilliant]

Leave to the imagination the endless vista of possibilities

Life flowed in its accustomed stream

Lights and shadows of reviving memory crossed her face

Lionized by fashionable society

Long intertangled lines of silver streamlets
Lost in a delirious wonder
Lost in irritable reflection
Love hovered in her gaze
Ludicrous attempts of clumsy playfulness and tawdry eloquence
Luke-warm assurance of continued love
Lulled by dreamy musings
Luminous with great thoughts

M

Magnanimous indifference to meticulous niceties
Making the ear greedy to remark offense
Marching down to posterity with divine honors
Marked out for some strange and preternatural doom
Mawkishly effeminate sentiment
Memories plucked from wood and field
Memory was busy at his heart
Merged in a sentiment of unutterable sadness and compassion
Microscopic minuteness of eye
Misgivings of grave kinds
Mockery crept into her tone
Molded by the austere hand of adversity
Moments of utter idleness and insipidity
Moods of malicious reaction and vindictive recoil
Morn, in yellow and white, came broadening out of the mountains
Mumble only jargon of dotage

My body is too frail for its moods

N

Nature seemed to revel in unwonted contrasts
  [unwonted = unusual]

New ambitions pressed upon his fancy

New dreams began to take wing in his imagination

Night after night the skies were wine-blue and bubbling with stars

Night passes lightly in the open world, with its stars and dews and perfumes

Nights of fathomless blackness

No mark of trick or artifice

Noble and sublime patience

Nursed by brooding thought

O

Obsessed with the modishness of the hour

Occasional flashes of tenderness and love

Oddly disappointing and fickle

One gracious fact emerges here

One long torture of soul

One of the golden twilights which transfigure the world

Oppressed and disheartened by an all-pervading desolation

Oppressed with a confused sense of cumbrous material
  [cumbrous = cumbersome]

Outweighing years of sorrow and bitterness

Over and over the paroxysms of grief and longing submerged her
Overhung and overspread with ivy
Overshadowed by a vague depression

P

Pale and vague desolation
Pallor of reflected glories
Palpitating with rage and wounded sensibility
Panting after distinction
Peace brooded over all
Pelted with an interminable torrent of words
Penetrate beneath the surface to the core
Peopled the night with thoughts
Perpetual gloom and seclusion of life
Pertinent to the thread of the discussion
Pervasive silence which wraps us in a mantle of content
Piles of golden clouds just peering above the horizon
Platitudinous and pompously sentimental
Plaudits of the unlettered mob
Pleasant and flower-strewn vistas of airy fancy
Pledged with enthusiastic fervor
Plumbing the depth of my own fears
Poignant doubts and misgivings
Power of intellectual metamorphosis
Power to assuage the thirst of the soul
Precipitated into mysterious depths of nothingness

Preening its wings for a skyward flight
Pressing cares absorbed him
Pride working busily within her
Proclaimed with joyous defiance
Prodigal of discriminating epithets
Prodigious boldness and energy of intellect
Products of dreaming indolence
Profound and chilling solitude of the spot
Proof of his imperturbability and indifference
Provocative of bitter hostility
Pulling the strings of many enterprises
Purge the soul of nonsense

Q

Quickened and enriched by new contacts with life and truth
Quivering with restrained grief

R

Radiant with the beautiful glamor of youth
Ransack the vocabulary
Red tape of officialdom
Redolent of the night lamp
Reflecting the solemn and unfathomable stars
Regarded with an exulting pride
Rehabilitated and restored to dignity
Remorselessly swept into oblivion

Resounding generalities and conventional rhetoric
Respect forbade downright contradiction
Restless and sore and haughty feelings were busy within
Retort leaped to his lips
Rigid adherence to conventionalities
Rudely disconcerting in her behavior
Rudely reminded of life's serious issues

S

Sacrificed to a futile sort of treadmill
Sadness prevailed among her moods
Scorched with the lightning of momentary indignation
Scorning such paltry devices
Scotched but not slain
Scrupulous morality of conduct
Seem to swim in a sort of blurred mist before the eyes
Seething with suppressed wrath
Seize on greedily
Sensuous enjoyment of the outward show of life
Serenity beamed from his look
Serenity of paralysis and death
Seriousness lurked in the depths of her eyes
Served to recruit his own jaded ideas
Set anew in some fresh and appealing form
Setting all the sane traditions at defiance
Shadowy vistas of sylvan beauty
She affected disdain

She assented in precisely the right terms

She bandies adjectives with the best

She challenged his dissent

She cherished no petty resentments

She curled her fastidious lip

She curled her lip with defiant scorn

She did her best to mask her agitation

She disarmed anger and softened asperity
  [asperity = harshness]

She disclaimed fatigue

She fell into a dreamy silence

She fell into abstracted reverie

She felt herself carried off her feet by the rush of incoherent impressions

She flushed an agitated pink

She forced a faint quivering smile

She frowned incomprehension

She had an air of restrained fury

She had an undercurrent of acidity

She hugged the thought of her own unknown and unapplauded integrity

She lingered a few leisurely seconds

She nodded mutely

She nourished a dream of ambition

She permitted herself a delicate little smile

She poured out on him the full opulence of a proud recognition

She questioned inimically
  [inimically = unfriendly; hostile]

She recaptured herself with difficulty

She regarded him stonily out of flint-blue eyes
She sat eyeing him with frosty calm
She seemed the embodiment of dauntless resolution
She seemed wrapped in a veil of lassitude
She shook hands grudgingly
She softened her frown to a quivering smile
She spoke with hurried eagerness
She spoke with sweet severity
She stilled and trampled on the inward protest
She stood her ground with the most perfect dignity
She strangled a fierce tide of feeling that welled up within her
She swept away all opposing opinion with the swift rush of her enthusiasm
She thrived on insincerity
She twitted him merrily
She was both weary and placated
She was conscious of a tumultuous rush of sensations
She was demure and dimly appealing
She was exquisitely simple
She was gripped with a sense of suffocation and panic
She was in an anguish of sharp and penetrating remorse
She was oppressed by a dead melancholy
She was stricken to the soul
She wore an air of wistful questioning
Sheer superfluity of happiness
Sickening contrasts and diabolic ironies of life
Silence fell
Singing lustily as if to exorcise the demon of gloom

Skirmishes and retreats of conscience
Slender experience of the facts of life
Slope towards extinction
Slow the movement was and tortuous
Slowly disengaging its significance from the thicket of words
So innocent in her exuberant happiness
Soar into a rosy zone of contemplation
Softened by the solicitude of untiring and anxious love
Solitary and sorely smitten souls
Some dim-remembered and dream-like images
Some exquisite refinement in the architecture of the brain
Some flash of witty irrelevance
Something curiously suggestive and engaging
Something eminently human beaconed from his eyes
Something full of urgent haste
Something indescribably reckless and desperate in such a picture
Something that seizes tyrannously upon the soul
Sore beset by the pressure of temptation
Specious show of impeccability
Spectacular display of wrath
Spur and whip the tired mind into action
Stale and facile platitudes
Stamped with unutterable and solemn woe
Startled into perilous activity
Startling leaps over vast gulfs of time
Stem the tide of opinion
Stern emptying of the soul

Stimulated to an ever deepening subtlety
Stirred into a true access of enthusiasm
Stony insensibility to the small pricks and frictions of daily life
Strange capacities and suggestions both of vehemence and pride
Strange laughings and glitterings of silver streamlets
Stripped to its bare skeleton
Strode forth imperiously
   [imperious = arrogantly overbearing]
Struck by a sudden curiosity
Struck dumb with strange surprise
Stung by his thoughts, and impatient of rest
Stung by the splendor of the prospect
Subdued passages of unobtrusive majesty
Sublime indifference to contemporary usage and taste
Submission to an implied rebuke
Subtle indications of great mental agitation
Subtle suggestions of remoteness
Such things as the eye of history sees
Such was the petty chronicle
Suddenly a thought shook him
Suddenly overawed by a strange, delicious shyness
Suddenly smitten with unreality
Suddenly snuffed out in the middle of ambitious schemes
Suffered to languish in obscurity
Sugared remonstrances and cajoleries
Suggestions of veiled and vibrant feeling
Summer clouds floating feathery overhead
Sunk in a phraseological quagmire

Sunk into a gloomy reverie

Sunny silence broods over the realm of little cottages

Supreme arbiter of conduct

Susceptibility to fleeting impressions

Sweet smoke of burning twigs hovered in the autumn day

Swift summer into the autumn flowed

T

Taking the larger sweeps in the march of mind

Tears of outraged vanity blurred her vision

Teased with impertinent questions

Tenderness breathed from her

Tense with the anguish of spiritual struggle

Terror filled the more remote chambers of his brain with riot

Tethered to earth

That which flutters the brain for a moment

The accelerated beat of his thoughts

The affluent splendor of the summer day

The afternoon was filled with sound and sunshine

The afternoon was waning

The air and sky belonged to midsummer

The air darkened swiftly

The air is touched with a lazy fragrance, as of hidden flowers

The air was caressed with song

The air was full of fugitive strains of old songs

The air was raw and pointed

The allurements of a coquette

The ambition and rivalship of men
The angry blood burned in his face
The anguish of a spiritual conflict tore his heart
The artificial smile of languor
The awful and implacable approach of doom
The babble of brooks grown audible
The babbledom that dogs the heels of fame
The bait proved incredibly successful
The balm of solitary musing
The beauty straightway vanished
The beckonings of alien appeals
The benign look of a father
The blandishments of pleasure and pomp of power
The blinding mist came down and hid the land
The blue bowl of the sky, all glorious with the blaze of a million worlds
The bound of the pulse of spring
The buzz of idolizing admiration
The caressing peace of bright soft sunshine
The chaotic sound of the sea
The chill of forlorn old age
The chill of night crept in from the street
The chivalric sentiment of honor
The chivalrous homage of respect
The clamorous agitation of rebellious passions
The clouded, restless, jaded mood
The constant iteration of the sea's wail
The contagion of extravagant luxury

The conversation became desultory
  [desultory = haphazardly; random]

The crowning touch of pathos

The current of his ideas flowed full and strong

The dance whizzed on with cumulative fury

The dawn is singing at the door

The day sang itself into evening

The day was at once redolent and vociferous
  [redolent = emitting fragrance; aromatic; suggestive; reminiscent]
  [vociferous = conspicuously and offensively loud]

The day was blind with fog

The day was gracious

The days passed in a stately procession

The days when you dared to dream

The debilitating fears of alluring fate

The deep and solemn purple of the summer night

The deep flush ebbed out of his face

The deep tranquillity of the shaded solitude

The deepening twilight filled with shadowy visions

The deepest wants and aspirations of his soul

The delicatest reproof of imagined distrust

The demerit of an unworthy alliance

The desire of the moth for the star

The dimness of the sealed eye and soul

The dreamy solicitations of indescribable afterthoughts

The dying day lies beautiful in the tender glow of the evening

The early morning of the Indian summer day was tinged with blue mistiness

The earth looked despoiled

The east alone frowned with clouds

The easy grace of an unpremeditated agreeable talker

The easy-going indolence of a sedentary life

The echo of its wrathful roar surged and boomed among the hills

The empurpled hills standing up, solemn and sharp, out of the green-gold air

The enchanting days of youth

The eternal questioning of inscrutable fate

The evening comes with slow steps

The evening star silvery and solitary on the girdle of the early night

The exaggerations of morbid hallucinations

The excitement of rival issues

The extraordinary wistful look of innocence and simplicity

The eye of a scrutinizing observer

The eyes burnt with an amazing fire

The eyes filled with playfulness and vivacity

The father's vigil of questioning sorrow

The fine flower of culture

The first recoil from her disillusionment

The flawless triumph of art

The flight of the autumnal days

The flower of courtesy

The fluttering of untried wings

The foreground was incredibly shabby

The fragrance of a dear and honored name

The freshening breeze struck his brow with a cooling hand
The freshness of some pulse of air from an invisible sea
The fruit of vast and heroic labors
The general effect was of extraordinary lavish profusion
The give and take was delicious
The gloom of the afternoon deepened
The gloom of winter dwelt on everything
The gloomy insolence of self-conceit
The glow of the ambitious fire
The golden gloom of the past and the bright-hued hope of the future
The golden riot of the autumn leaves
The golden sunlight of a great summer day
The gray air rang and rippled with lark music
The grimaces and caperings of buffoonery
The grotesque nightmare of a haunting fear
The hand of time sweeps them into oblivion
The haunting melody of some familiar line of verse
The haunting phrase leaped to my brain
The headlong vigor of sheer improvisation
The heights of magnanimity and love
The high-bred pride of an oriental
The hills were clad in rose and amethyst
The hill-tops gleam in morning's spring
The hinted sweetness of the challenge aroused him
The hot humiliation of it overwhelmed her
The hungry curiosity of the mind
The idiosyncratic peculiarities of thought

The idle chatter of the crowd

The immediate tyranny of a present emotion

The inaccessible solitude of the sky

The incarnation of all loveliness

The incoherent loquacity of a nervous patient
    [loquacity = very talkative]

The indefinable air of good-breeding

The indefinable yearning for days that were dead

The indefinite atmosphere of an opulent nature

The intercepted glances of wondering eyes

The intrusive question faded

The invidious stigma of selfishness
    [invidious = rousing ill will]

The iron hand of oppression

The irresistible and ceaseless onflow of time

The irrevocable past and the uncertain future

The landscape ran, laughing, downhill to the sea

The leaden sky rests heavily on the earth

The leaves of time drop stealthily

The leaves syllabled her name in cautious whispers

The lights winked

The little incident seemed to throb with significance

The lofty grace of a prince

The loud and urgent pageantry of the day

The low hills on the horizon wore a haze of living blue

The machinations of a relentless mountebank
    [mountebank = flamboyant charlatan]

The machinations of an unscrupulous enemy

The magical lights of the horizon

The majestic solemnity of the moment yielded to the persuasive warmth of day

The marvelous beauty of her womanhood

The maximum of attainable and communicable truth

The melancholy day weeps in monotonous despair

The melodies of birds and bees

The memory of the night grew fantastic and remote

The meticulous observation of facts

The mind freezes at the thought

The mind was filled with a formless dread

The mocking echoes of long-departed youth

The moment marked an epoch

The moon is waning below the horizon

The more's the pity

The morning beckons

The morning droned along peacefully

The most servile acquiescence

The multiplicity of odors competing for your attention

The murmur of soft winds in the tree-tops

The murmur of the surf boomed in melancholy mockery

The murmuring of summer seas

The music and mystery of the sea

The music of her delicious voice

The music of her presence was singing a swift melody in his blood

The music of unforgotten years sounded again in his soul

The mute melancholy landscape

The mystery obsessed him

The naked fact of death

The nameless and inexpressible fascination of midnight music

The narrow glen was full of the brooding power of one universal spirit

The nascent spirit of chivalry

The night was drowned in stars

The old ruddy conviction deserted me

The onrush and vividness of life

The opulent sunset

The orange pomp of the setting sun

The oscillations of human genius

The outpourings of a tenderness reawakened by remorse

The pageantry of sea and sky

The palest abstractions of thought

The palpitating silence lengthened

The panorama of life was unrolled before him

The paraphernalia of power and prosperity

The parting crimson glory of the ripening summer sun

The past slowly drifted out of his thought

The pendulous eyelids of old age

The penetrating odors assailed his memory as something unforgettable

The pent-up intolerance of years of repression

The perfume of the mounting sea saturated the night with wild fragrance

The piquancy of the pageant of life
  [piquancy = tart spiciness]

The pith and sinew of mature manhood

The plenitude of her piquant ways
  [piquant = engagingly stimulating]

The presage of disaster was in the air

The pressure of accumulated misgivings

The preternatural pomposities of the pulpit

The pristine freshness of spring

The pull of soul on body

The pulse of the rebounding sea

The purging sunlight of clear poetry

The purple vaulted night

The question drummed in head and heart day and night

The question irresistibly emerged

The quick pulse of gain

The radiant serenity of the sky

The radiant stars brooded over the stainless fields, white with freshly fallen snow

The restlessness of offended vanity

The retreating splendor of autumn

The rising storm of words

The river ran darkly, mysteriously by

The river sang with its lips to the pebbles

The roar of the traffic rose to thunder

The romantic ardor of a generous mind

The room had caught a solemn and awful quietude

The rosy-hued sky went widening off into the distance

The rosy twilight of boyhood

The royal arrogance of youth

The sadness in him deepened inexplicably

The scars of rancor and remorse
The scent of roses stole in with every breath of air
The sea heaved silvery, far into the night
The sea slept under a haze of golden winter sun
The sea-sweep enfolds you, satisfying eye and mind
The sea-wind buffeted their faces
The secret and subduing charm of the woods
The see-saw of a wavering courage
The sentimental tourist will be tempted to tarry
The shadows of the night seemed to retreat
The shadows rested quietly under the breezeless sky
The shafts of ridicule
The sheer weight of unbearable loneliness
The shiver of the dusk passed fragrantly down the valley
The silence grew stolid
The silence was uncomfortable and ominous
The silent day perfumed with the hidden flowers
The silver silence of the night
The sinking sun made mellow gold of all the air
The sky grew brighter with the imminent day
The sky grew ensaffroned with the indescribable hue that heralds day
The sky put on the panoply of evening
The sky was a relentless, changeless blue
The sky was dull and brooding
The sky was heavily sprinkled with stars
The sky was turning to the pearly gray of dawn
The smiling incarnation of loveliness

The song of hurrying rivers

The sound of the sea waxed

The spacious leisure of the forest

The spell of a deathless dream was upon them

The star-strewn spaces of the night

The stars looked down in their silent splendor

The stars seemed attentive

The steadfast mind kept its hope

The steady thunder of the sea accented the silence

The still voice of the poet

The stillness of a forced composure

The stillness of the star-hung night

The strangest thought shimmered through her

The stream forgot to smile

The streams laughed to themselves

The strident discord seemed to mock his mood

The stunning crash of the ocean saluted her

The subtle emanation of other influences seemed to arrest and chill him

The sudden rush of the awakened mind

The summit of human attainment

The sun blazed torridly

The sun goes down in flame on the far horizon

The sun lay golden-soft over the huddled hills

The sunlight spread at a gallop along the hillside

The sunset was rushing to its height through every possible phase of violence and splendor

The suspicion of secret malevolence

The swelling tide of memory

The swing of the pendulum through an arch of centuries

The tempered daylight of an olive garden

The tender grace of a day that is fled

The tension of struggling tears which strove for an outlet

The thought leaped

The timely effusion of tearful sentiment

The tone betrayed a curious irritation

The torture of his love and terror crushed him

The trees rustled and whispered to the streams

The tumult in her heart subsided

The tumult in her mind found sudden speech

The tumult of pride and pleasure

The tune of moving feet in the lamplit city

The tyranny of nipping winds and early frosts

The unmasked batteries of her glorious gray eyes

The vacant fields looked blankly irresponsive

The vast and shadowy stream of time

The vast cathedral of the world

The vast unexplored land of dreams

The velvet of the cloudless sky grew darker, and the stars more luminous

The veneer of a spurious civilization

The very pulsation and throbbing of his intellect

The very silence of the place appeared a source of peril

The vision fled him

The vivifying touch of humor

The web of lies is rent in pieces

The wheel of her thought turned in the same desolate groove

The whispering rumble of the ocean

The white seething surf fell exhausted along the shore

The whole exquisite night was his

The whole sea of foliage is shaken and broken up with little momentary shiverings and shadows

The wide horizon forever flames with summer

The wild whirl of nameless regret and passionate sorrow

The wild winds flew round, sobbing in their dismay

The wind charged furiously through it, panting towards the downs

The wind piped drearily

The wind was in high frolic with the rain

The winnowed tastes of the ages

The woods were silent with adoration

The youth of the soul

The zenith turned shell pink

Their ephemeral but enchanting beauty had expired forever [ephemeral = markedly short-lived]

Their eyes met glancingly

Their troth had been plighted

There was a kind of exhilaration in this subtle baiting

There was a mild triumph in her tone

There was a mournful and dim haze around the moon

There was a strange massing and curving of the clouds

There was a thrill in the air

There was a time I might have trod the sunlit heights

There was no glint of hope anywhere

There was no menace in the night's silvern calmness

There was something so kindly in its easy candor

There was spendthrift grandeur

These qualities were raised to the white heat of enthusiasm

They became increasingly turbid and phantasmagorical [phantasmagorical = fantastic imagery]

They escaped the baffled eye

They sit heavy on the soul

They were vastly dissimilar

This exquisite conjunction and balance

This little independent thread of inquiry ran through the texture of his mind and died away

This shadowy and chilling sentiment unaccountably creeps over me

Thought shook through her in poignant pictures

Thoughts came thronging in panic haste

Thrilled by fresh and indescribable odors

Thrilled with a sense of strange adventure

Through a cycle of many ages

Through endless and labyrinthine sentences

Thrilled to the depths of her being

Time had passed unseen

Tinsel glitter of empty titles

Tired with a dull listless fatigue

To all intents and purposes

To speak with entire candor

To stay his tottering constancy

To the scourging he submitted with a good grace

Tossed disdainfully off from young and ardent lips
Touched every moment with shifting and enchanting beauty
Touched with a bewildering and elusive beauty
Transcendental contempt for money
Transformed with an overmastering passion
Trouble gathered on his brow
Turning the world topsy-turvey
Twilight creeps upon the darkening mind

U

Unapproachable grandeur and simplicity
Unaware of her bitter taunt
Under the vivifying touch of genius
Unearthly in its malignant glee
Unfathomed depths and impossibilities
Unforced and unstudied depth of feeling
Unspoiled by praise or blame
Unspoken messages from some vaster world
Unstable moral equilibrium of boyhood
Until sleep overtakes us at a stride
Untouched by the ruthless spirit of improvement
Upon the mountain-tops of meditation
Urbanely plastic and versatile
Uttering grandiose puerilities
   [puerilities = childishness, silly]

V

Vain allurements of folly and fashion

Variously ramified and delicately minute channels of expression

Varnished over with a cold repellent cynicism

Vast sweep of mellow distances

Veiled by some equivocation

Vibrant with the surge of human passions

Vicissitudes of wind and weather
 [vicissitudes = sudden or unexpected changes]

Vigor and richness of resource

Visible and palpable pains and penalties

Voices that charm the ear and echo with a subtle resonance in the soul

Volcanic upheavings of imprisoned passions

W

Wantonly and detestably unkind

Waylay Destiny and bid him stand and deliver

Wayward and strangely playful responses

Wearing the white flower of a blameless life

What sorry and pitiful quibbling

When a pleasant countryside tunes the spirit to a serene harmony of mood

When music is allied to words

When the frame and the mind alike seem unstrung and listless

When the profane voices are hushed
When the waves show their teeth in the flying breeze
Whilst the morn kissed the sleep from her eyes
Whistled life away in perfect contentment
Wholly alien to his spirit
With a vanquished and weary sigh
Womanly fickleness and caprice
Words and acts easily wrenched from their true significance
Worn to shreds by anxiety
Wrapped in a sudden intensity of reflection
Wrapped in an inaccessible mood
Wrapped in scudding rain
Wrapt in his odorous and many-colored robe
Wrapt in inward contemplation
Wrought of an emotion infectious and splendidly dangerous
Wrought out of intense and tragic experience

Y

Yielding to a wave of pity
Your mind enthroned in the seventh circle of content

SECTION VIII

STRIKING SIMILES

A

A blind rage like a fire swept over him

A book that rends and tears like a broken saw

A breath of melancholy made itself felt like a chill and sudden gust from some unknown sea

A cloud in the west like a pall creeps upward

A cloud like a flag from the sky

A cluster of stars hangs like fruit in the tree

A confused mass of impressions, like an old rubbish-heap

A cry as of a sea-bird in the wind

A dead leaf might as reasonably demand to return to the tree

A drowsy murmur floats into the air like thistledown

A face as imperturbable as fate

A face as pale as wax

A face tempered like steel

A fatigued, faded, lusterless air, as of a caged creature

A few pens parched by long disuse

A figure like a carving on a spire

A fluttering as of blind bewildered moths

A giant galleon overhead, looked like some misty monster of the deep

A glacial pang of pain like the stab of a dagger of ice frozen from a poisoned well

A glance that flitted like a bird

A great moon like a red lamp in the sycamore

A grim face like a carved mask

A hand icily cold and clammy as death

A heart from which noble sentiments sprang like sparks from an anvil

A jeweler that glittered like his shop

A lady that lean'd on his arm like a queen in a fable of old fairy days

A life, a Presence, like the air

A life as common and brown and bare as the box of earth in the window there

A light wind outside the lattice swayed a branch of roses to and fro,

shaking out their perfume as from a swung censer

A lightning-phrase, as if shot from the quiver of infallible wisdom

A list of our unread books torments some of us like a list of murders

A little breeze ran through the corn like a swift serpent

A little weed-clogged ship, gray as a ghost

A long slit of daylight like a pointing finger

A memory like a well-ordered cupboard

A mighty wind, like a leviathan, plowed the brine

A mind very like a bookcase

- A mystery, soft, soothing and gentle, like the whisper of a child murmuring its happiness in its sleep
- A name which sounds even now like the call of a trumpet
- A note of despairing appeal which fell like a cold hand upon one's living soul
- A purpose as the steady flame
- A question deep almost as the mystery of life
- A quibbling mouth that snapped at verbal errors like a lizard catching flies
- A radiant look came over her face, like a sudden burst of sunshine on a cloudy day
- A reputation that swelled like a sponge
- A ruby like a drop of blood
- A shadow of melancholy touched her lithe fancies, as a cloud dims the waving of golden grain
- A silver moon, like a new-stamped coin, rode triumphant in the sky
- A slow thought that crept like a cold worm through all his brain
- A smile flashed over her face, like sunshine over a flower
- A soft and purple mist like a vaporous amethyst
- A soft haze, like a fairy dream, is floating over wood and stream
- A soul as white as heaven
- A sound like the throb of a bell
- A stooping girl as pale as a pearl
- A sudden sense of fear ran through her nerves like the chill of an icy wind
- A sweet voice caroling like a gold-caged nightingale
- A thin shrill voice like the cry of an expiring mouse
- A thing of as frail enchantment as the gleam of stars upon snow

A vague thought, as elusive as the smell of a primrose

A vanishing loveliness as tender as the flush of the rose leaf and as ethereal as the light of a solitary star

A voice as low as the sea

A voice soft and sweet as a tune that one knows

A white bird floats there, like a drifting leaf

Against a sky as clear as sapphire

Age, like winter weather

Agile as a leopard

Agitated like a storm-tossed ship

Air like wine

All around them like a forest swept the deep and empurpled masses of her tangled hair

All like an icicle it seemed, so tapering and cold

All my life broke up, like some great river's ice at touch of spring

All silent as the sheeted dead

All sounds were lost in the whistle of air humming by like the flight of a million arrows

All that's beautiful drifts away like the waters

All the world lay stretched before him like the open palm of his hand

All unconscious as a flower

Alone, like a storm-tossed wreck, on this night of the glad New Year

An anxiety hung like a dark impenetrable cloud

An ardent face out-looking like a star

An ecstasy which suddenly overwhelms your mind like an unexpected and exquisite thought

An envious wind crept by like an unwelcome thought

An ideal as sublime and comprehensive as the horizon

An immortal spirit dwelt in that frail body, like a bird in an outworn cage

An impudent trick as hackneyed as conjuring rabbits out of a hat

An indefinable resemblance to a goat

An isle of Paradise, fair as a gem

An old nodding negress whose sable head shined in the sun like a polished cocoanut

An omnibus across the bridge crawls like a yellow butterfly

An undefined sadness seemed to have fallen about her like a cloud

An unknown world, wild as primeval chaos

An unpleasing strain, like the vibration of a rope drawn out too fast

And a pinnace like a flutter'd bird came flying from afar

And a tear like silver, glistened in the corner of her eye

And all our thoughts ran into tears like sunshine into rain

And at first the road comes moving toward me, like a bride waving palms

And Dusk, with breast as of a dove, brooded

And eyes as bright as the day

And fell as cold as a lump of clay

And her cheek was like a rose

And here were forests ancient as the hills

And many a fountain, rivulet, and pond, as clear as elemental diamond, or serene morning air

And melting like the stars in June

And night, as welcome as a friend

And silence like a poultice comes to heal the blows of sound

And spangled o'er with twinkling points, like stars

And the smile she softly uses fills the silence like a speech

As a child in play scatters the heaps of sand that he has piled on the seashore

As a cloud that gathers her robe like drifted snow

As a flower after a drought drinks in the steady plunging rain

As a leaf that beats on a mountain

As a lion grieves at the loss of her whelps

As a man plowing all day longs for supper and welcomes sunset

As a sea disturbed by opposing winds

As amusing as a litter of likely young pigs

As arbitrary as a cyclone and as killing as a pestilence

As austere as a Roman matron

As beautiful as the purple flush of dawn

As blind as a mole

As brief as sunset clouds in heaven

As bright as sunlight on a stream

As busy as a bee

As cattle driven by a gadfly

As chimney sweepers come to dust

As clear as a whistle

As clear as the parts of a tree in the morning sun

As close as oak and ivy stand

As delicate and as fair as a lily

As delightful to the mind as cool well-water to thirsty lip

As diamond cuts diamond

As direct and unvarying as the course of a homing bird

As distinct as night and morning
As dry as desert dust
As dumb as a fish
As easily as the sun shines
As easy as a turn of the hand
As elastic as a steel spring
As extinct as the dodo
As faint as the memory of a sound
As familiar to him as his alphabet
As fatal as the fang of the most venomous snake
As fleeting and elusive as our dreams
As foam from a ship's swiftness
As fresh and invigorating as a sea-breeze
As full of eager vigor as a mountain stream
As full of spirit as a gray squirrel
As gay and busy as a brook
As gently as the flower gives forth its perfume
As gently as withered leaves float from a tree
As graceful as a bough
As grave as a judge
As great as the first day of creation
As high as heaven
As I dropped like a bolt from the blue
As I dwelt like a sparrow among the spires
As if a door were suddenly left ajar into some world unseen before
As impossible as to count the stars in illimitable space
As in the footsteps of a god

As inaccessible to his feet as the clefts and gorges of the clouds

As inexorable as the flight of time

As innocent as a new laid egg

As iridescent as a soap bubble

As locusts gather to a stream before a fire

As mellow and deep as a psalm

As men strip for a race, so must an author strip for the race with time

As merry as bees in clover

As nimble as water

As one who has climbed above the earth's eternal snowline and sees only white peaks and pinnacles

As pale as any ghost

As patient as the trees

As quick as the movement of some wild animal

As quiet as a nun breathless with adoration

As radiant as the rose

As readily and naturally as ducklings take to water

As reticent as a well-bred stockbroker

As ruthlessly as the hoof of a horse tramples on a rose

As shallow streams run dimpling all the way

As simple as the intercourse of a child with its mother

As sleep falls upon the eyes of a child tired with a long summer day of eager pleasure and delight

As some vast river of unfailing source

As stars that shoot along the sky

As still as a stone

As stupid as a sheep

As sudden as a dislocated joint slipping back into place
As summer winds that creep from flower to flower
As supple as a step-ladder
As swaggering and sentimental as a penny novellete [novellete = short novel]
As swift as thought
As the accumulation of snowflakes makes the avalanche
As the bubble is extinguished in the ocean
As the dew upon the roses warms and melts the morning light
As the fair cedar, fallen before the breeze, lies self-embalmed amidst the moldering trees
As the light straw flies in dark'ning whirlwinds
As the lightning cleaves the night
As the loud blast that tears the skies
As the slow shadows of the pointed grass mark the eternal periods
As those move easiest who have learn'd to dance
As though a rose should shut, and be a bud again
As though Pharaoh should set the Israelites to make a pin instead of a pyramid
As unapproachable as a star
As weird as the elfin lights
As well try to photograph the other side of the moon
At extreme tension, like a drawn bow
Away he rushed like a cyclone
Awkward as a cart-horse

B

Babbling like a child

Balmy in manner as a bland southern morning

Be like the granite of thy rock-ribbed land

Beauteous she looks as a water-lily

Beautiful as the dawn, dominant as the sun

Beauty maddens the soul like wine

Beheld great Babel, wrathful, beautiful, burn like a blood-red cloud upon the plain

Beneath a sky as fair as summer flowers

Bent like a wand of willow

Black as a foam-swept rock

Black his hair as the wintry night

Blithe as a bird
  [blithe = carefree and lighthearted]

Bounded by the narrow fences of life

Bowed like a mountain

Breaking his oath and resolution like a twist of rotten silk

Breathed like a sea at rest

Bright as a diamond in the sun

Bright as a fallen fragment of the sky

Bright as the coming forth of the morning, in the cloud of an early shower

Bright as the sunbeams

Bright as the tear of an angel, glittered a lonely star

Brilliant and gay as a Greek

Brisk as a wasp in the sunshine

Brittle and bent like a bow

Bronze-green beetles tumbled over stones, and lay helpless on their backs with the air of an elderly clergyman knocked down by an omnibus

Brown as the sweet smelling loam

Brute terrors like the scurrying of rats in a deserted attic

Buried in his library like a mouse in a cheese

Burns like a living coal in the soul

But across it, like a mob's menace, fell the thunder

But thou art fled, like some frail exhalation

Butterflies like gems

C

Calm as the night

Calm like a flowing river

Calm like a mountain brooding o'er the sea

Calmly dropping care like a mantle from her shoulders

Cast thy voice abroad like thunder

Charm upon charm in her was packed, like rose-leaves in a costly vase

Chaste as the icicle

Cheeks as soft as July peaches

Chill breath of winter

Choked by the thorns and brambles of early adversity

Cities scattered over the world like ant-hills

Cities that rise and sink like bubbles

Clear and definite like the glance of a child or the voice of a girl

Clear as a forest pool

Clear as crystal

Clenched little hands like rumpled roses, dimpled and dear

Cloud-like that island hung afar

Clouds like the petals of a rose

Cloudy mirror of opinion

Cold and hard as steel

Cold as the white rose waking at daybreak

Cold, glittering monotony like frosting around a cake

Collapsed like a concertina

Colored like a fairy tale

Companionless as the last cloud of an expiring storm whose thunder is its knell

Consecration that like a golden thread runs through the warp and woof of one's life
[warp = lengthwise threads]
[woof = crosswise threads]

Constant as gliding waters

Contending like ants for little molehill realms

Continuous as the stars that shine

Cowslips, like chance-found gold

Creeds like robes are laid aside

Creeping like a snail, unwillingly to school

Cruel as death

Curious as a lynx

Cuts into the matter as with a pen of fire

D

Dainty as flowers

Dance like a wave of the sea

Dark and deep as night

Dark as pitch

Dark trees bending together as though whispering secrets

Dazzling white as snow in sunshine

Deafening and implacable as some elemental force

Dear as remembered kisses after death

Dear as the light that visits these sad eyes

Dearer than night to the thief

Debasing fancies gather like foul birds

Deep as the fathomless sea

Deep dark well of sorrow

Delicate as nymphs

Delicate as the flush on a rose or the sculptured line on a Grecian urn

Denominational lines like stone walls

Dependency had dropped from her like a cast-off cloak

Despondency clung to him like a garment that is wet

Destructive as the lightning flash

Die like flies

Dip and surge lightly to and fro, like the red harbor-buoy

Disappearing into distance like a hazy sea

Dissatisfaction had settled on his mind like a shadow

Dissolve like some unsubstantial vision faded

Do make a music like to rustling satin

Dogging them like their own shadow

Dost thou not hear the murmuring nightingale like water bubbling from a silver jar?

Drop like a feather, softly to the ground

Drowned like rats

Dull as champagne

E

Each like a corpse within its grave

Each moment was an iridescent bubble fresh-blown from the lips of fancy

Eager-hearted as a boy

Eager with the headlong zest of a hunter for the game

Ears that seemed as deaf as dead man's ears

Easy as a poet's dream

Emotions flashed across her face like the sweep of sun-rent clouds over a quiet landscape

Eternal as the skies

Evanescent as bubbles
 [evanescent = vanishing like vapor]

Every flake that fell from heaven was like an angel's kiss

Every lineament was clear as in the sculptor's thought
 [lineament = characteristic feature]

Everyone on the watch, like a falcon on its nest

Every phrase is like the flash of a scimitar

Exploded like a penny squib

Eyes as deeply dark as are the desert skies

Eyes as luminous and bright and brown as waters of a woodland river
Eyes half veiled by slumberous tears, like bluest water seen through mists of rain
Eyes like a very dark topaz
Eyes like deep wells of compassionate gloom
Eyes like limpid pools in shadow
Eyes like mountain water that o'erflowing on a rock

F

Faces pale with bliss, like evening stars
Fade away like a cloud in the horizon
Faint and distant as the light of a sun that has long set
Faintly, like a falling dew
Fair and fleet as a fawn
Fair as a star when only one is shining in the sky
Fallen like dead leaves on the highway
Falling away like a speck in space
Fanciful and extravagant as a caliph's dream
Fawning like dumb neglected lap-dogs
Felt her breath upon his cheek like a perfumed air
Fields of young grain and verdured pastures like crushed velvet
Fierce as a bear in defeat
Fierce as the flames
Fills life up like a cup with bubbling and sparkling liquor
Fit closely together as the close-set stones of a building
Fix'd like a beacon-tower above the waves of a tempest

Flame like a flag unfurled

Flap loose and slack like a drooping sail

Flashed with the brilliancy of a well-cut jewel

Fled like sweet dreams

Fleet as an arrow

Flitted like a sylph on wings

Flowers as soft as thoughts of budding love

Fluent as a rill, that wanders silver-footed down a hill

Fluid as thought

Fluttered like gilded butterflies in giddy mazes

Fragile as a spider's web

Free as the air, from zone to zone I flew

Free as the winds that caress

Fresh and unworn as the sea that breaks languidly beside them

Fresh as a jewel found but yesterday

Fresh as the first beam glittering on a sail

Frightened like a child in the dark

Full-throated as the sea

Furious as eagles

G

Gazed like a star into the morning light

Glaring like noontide

Gleam like a diamond on a dancing girl

Glistening like threads of gold

Glitter like a swarm of fire-flies tangled in a silver braid

Glittering like an aigrette of stars
  [aigrette = ornamental tuft of upright plumes]

Gone astray as a sheep that is lost

Gone like a glow on the cloud at the close of day

Gone like tenants that quit without warning

Gorgeous as the hues of heaven

Grazing through a circulating library as contentedly as cattle in a fresh meadow

Great scarlet poppies lay in drifts and heaps, like bodies fallen there in vain assault

H

Hair as harsh as tropical grass and gray as ashes

Hangs like a blue thread loosen'd from the sky

Hard, sharp, and glittering as a sword

Harnessed men, like beasts of burden, drew it to the river-side

Haunts you like the memory of some former happiness

He began to laugh with that sibilant laugh which resembles the hiss of a serpent
  [sibilant = producing a hissing sound]

He bent upon the lightning page like some rapt poet o'er his rhyme

He bolted down the stairs like a hare

He clatters like a windmill

He danced like a man in a swarm of hornets

He fell as falls some forest lion, fighting well

He fell down on my threshold like a wounded stag

He had acted exactly like an automaton

He lay as straight as a mummy

He lay like a warrior taking his rest

He lived as modestly as a hermit

He looked fagged and sallow, like the day [fagged = worked to exhaustion]

He looked with the bland, expressionless stare of an overgrown baby

He played with grave questions as a cat plays with a mouse

He radiated vigor and abundance like a happy child

He sat down quaking like a jelly

He saw disaster like a ghostly figure following her

He snatched furiously at breath like a tiger snatching at meat

He spoke with a uniformity of emphasis that made his words stand out like the raised type for the blind

He swayed in the sudden grip of anger

He sweeps the field of battle like a monsoon

He that wavereth is like a wave of the sea, driven with the wind and tossed

He turned on me like a thunder-cloud

He turned white as chalk

He wandered restlessly through the house, like a prowling animal

He was as splendidly serious as a reformer

He was as steady as a clock

He was as wax in those clever hands

He was bold as the hawk

He was so weak now, like a shrunk cedar white with the hoar-frost

Hearts unfold like flowers before thee

Heavy was my heart as stone

Heeled like an avalanche to leeward

Her arms like slumber o'er my shoulders crept

Her banners like a thousand sunsets glow

Her beauty broke on him like some rare flower

Her beauty fervent as a fiery moon

Her breath is like a cloud

Her cheeks are like the blushing cloud

Her cheeks were wan and her eyes like coals

Her dusky cheek would burn like a poppy

Her expression changed with the rapidity of a kaleidoscope

Her eyes as bright as a blazing star

Her eyes as stars of twilight fair

Her eyes, glimmering star-like in her pale face

Her eyes were as a dove that sickeneth

Her face changed with each turn of their talk, like a wheat-field under a summer breeze

Her face collapsed as if it were a pricked balloon

Her face was as solemn as a mask

Her face was dull as lead

Her face was like a light

Her face was passionless, like those by sculptor graved for niches in a temple

Her hair dropped on her pallid cheeks, like sea-weed on a clam

Her hair hung down like summer twilight

Her hair shone like a nimbus

Her hair was like a coronet

Her hands are white as the virgin rose that she wore on her wedding day

Her hands like moonlight brush the keys

Her head dropped into her hands like a storm-broken flower

Her heart has grown icy as a fountain in the fall

Her holy love that like a vestal flame had burned

Her impulse came and went like fireflies in the dusk

Her lashes like fans upon her cheek

Her laugh is like a rainbow-tinted spray

Her lips are like two budded roses

Her lips like a lovely song that ripples as it flows

Her lips like twilight water

Her little lips are tremulous as brook-water is [tremulous = timid or fearful]

Her long black hair danced round her like a snake

Her mouth as sweet as a ripe fig

Her neck is like a stately tower

Her pale robe clinging to the grass seemed like a snake

Her pulses flutter'd like a dove

Her skin was as the bark of birches

Her sweetness halting like a tardy May

Her two white hands like swans on a frozen lake

Her voice cut like a knife

Her voice like mournful bells crying on the wind

Her voice was like the voice the stars had when they sang together

Her voice was rich and vibrant, like the middle notes of a 'cello

Her words sounding like wavelets on a summer shore

Herding his thoughts as a collie dog herds sheep

Here and there a solitary volume greeted him like a friend in a crowd of strange faces

Here in statue-like repose, an old wrinkled mountain rose

Hers was the loveliness of some tall white lily cut in marble, splendid but chill

His bashfulness melted like a spring frost

His brow bent like a cliff o'er his thoughts

His cheeks were furrowed and writhen like rain-washed crags [writhen = twisted]

His eyes blazed like deep forests

His eyes glowed like blue coals

His eyes were hollows of madness, his hair like moldy hay

His face burnt like a brand

His face was glad as dawn to me

His face was often lit up by a smile like pale wintry sunshine

His fingers were knotted like a cord

His formal kiss fell chill as a flake of snow on the cheek

His fortune melted away like snow in a thaw

His glorious moments were strung like pearls upon a string

His indifference fell from him like a garment

His invectives and vituperations bite and flay like steel whips
[invective = abusive language]
[vituperation = abusive language]

His mind murmurs like a harp among the trees

His mind was like a lonely wild

His mind was like a summer sky

His nerves thrilled like throbbing violins

His retort was like a knife-cut across the sinews

His revenge descends perfect, sudden, like a curse from heaven

His spirits sank like a stone

His talk is like an incessant play of fireworks

His voice is as the thin faint song when the wind wearily sighs in the grass

His voice rose like a stream of rich distilled perfumes

His voice was like the clap of thunder which interrupts the warbling birds among the leaves

His whole soul wavered and shook like a wind-swept leaf

His words gave a curious satisfaction, as when a coin, tested, rings true gold

Hopeful as the break of day

How like a saint she sleeps

How like a winter hath my absence been

How like the sky she bends over her child

Howling in the wilderness like beasts

Huge as a hippopotamus

Humming-birds like lake of purple fire

Hushed as the grave

Hushed like a breathless lyre

I

I had grown pure as the dawn and the dew

I have heard the Hiddon People like the hum of swarming bees

I have seen the ravens flying, like banners of old wars

I saw a face bloom like a flower

I saw a river of men marching like a tide

I saw his senses swim dizzy as clouds
I wander'd lonely as a cloud
I was as sensitive as a barometer
I was no more than a straw on the torrent of his will
I will face thy wrath though it bite as a sword
Ideas which spread with the speed of light
Idle hopes, like empty shadows
Impassive as a statue
Impatient as the wind
Impregnable as Gibraltar
Impressive as a warrant of arrest for high treason
Incredible little white teeth, like snow shut in a rose
Infrequent carriages sped like mechanical toys guided by manikins
In honor spotless as unfallen snow
In that head of his a flame burnt that was like an altar-fire
In yonder cottage shines a light, far-gleaming like a gem
Instantly she revived like flowers in water
Intangible as a dream
It came and faded like a wreath of mist at eve
It cuts like knives, this air so chill
It drops away like water from a smooth statue
It pealed through her brain like a muffled bell
It poured upon her like a trembling flood
It racked his ears like an explosion of steam-whistles
It ran as clear as a trout-brook
It seems as motionless and still as the zenith in the skies
It set his memories humming like a hive of bees

It staggered the eye, like the sight of water running up hill

It stung like a frozen lash

It was as futile as to oppose an earthquake with argument

It was as if a door had been opened into a furnace, so the eyes blazed

It would collapse as if by enchantment

Its temples and its palaces did seem like fabrics of enchantment piled to Heaven

J

Jealousy, fierce as the fires

K

Kindle like an angel's wings the western skies in flame

Kindly mornings when autumn and winter seemed to go hand in hand like a happy aged couple

Kingdoms melt away like snow

L

Laboring like a giant

Languid streams that cross softly, slowly, with a sound like smothered weeping

Laughter like a beautiful bubble from the rosebud of baby-hood

Laughter like the sudden outburst of the glad bird in the tree-top

Lazy merchantmen that crawled like flies over the blue enamel of the sea

Leapt like a hunted stag

Let his frolic fancy play, like a happy child

Let in confusion like a whirling flood

Let thy mouth murmur like the doves

Life had been arrested, as the horologist, with interjected finger, arrests the beating of the clock
   [horologist = one who repairs watches]

Life stretched before him alluring and various as the open road

Life sweet as perfume and pure as prayer

Light as a snowflake

Lights gleamed there like stars in a still sky

Like a ball of ice it glittered in a frozen sea of sky

Like a blade sent home to its scabbard

Like a blast from a horn

Like a blast from the suddenly opened door of a furnace

Like a blossom blown before a breeze, a white moon drifts before a shimmering sky

Like a bright window in a distant view

Like a caged lion shaking the bars of his prison

Like a calm flock of silver-fleeced sheep

Like a cloud of fire

Like a cold wind his words went through their flesh

Like a crowd of frightened porpoises a shoal of sharks pursue

Like a damp-handed auctioneer

Like a deaf and dumb man wondering what it was all about

Like a dew-drop, ill-fitted to sustain unkindly shocks

Like a dipping swallow the stout ship dashed through the storm

Like a distant star glimmering steadily in the darkness

Like a dream she vanished

Like a festooned girdle encircling the waist of a bride

Like a flower her red lips parted

Like a game in which the important part is to keep from laughing

Like a glow-worm golden

Like a golden-shielded army

Like a great express train, roaring, flashing, dashing head-long

Like a great fragment of the dawn it lay

Like a great ring of pure and endless light

Like a great tune to which the planets roll

Like a high and radiant ocean

Like a high-born maiden

Like a jewel every cottage casement showed

Like a joyless eye that finds no object worth its constancy

Like a knight worn out by conflict

Like a knot of daisies lay the hamlets on the hill

Like a lily in bloom

Like a living meteor

Like a locomotive-engine with unsound lungs

Like a long arrow through the dark the train is darting

Like a mirage, vague, dimly seen at first

Like a miser who spoils his coat with scanting a little cloth [scanting = short]

Like a mist the music drifted from the silvery strings

Like a moral lighthouse in the midst of a dark and troubled sea

Like a murmur of the wind came a gentle sound of stillness

Like a noisy argument in a drawing-room

Like a pageant of the Golden Year, in rich memorial pomp the hours go by

Like a pale flower by some sad maiden cherished

Like a poet hidden

Like a river of molten amethyst

Like a rocket discharging a shower of golden stars

Like a rose embower'd in its own green leaves

Like a sea of upturned faces

Like a shadow never to be overtaken

Like a shadow on a fair sunlit landscape

Like a sheeted ghost

Like a ship tossed to and fro on the waves of life's sea

Like a slim bronze statue of Despair

Like a snow-flake lost in the ocean

Like a soul that wavers in the Valley of the Shadow

Like a stalled horse that breaks loose and goes at a gallop through the plain

Like a star, his love's pure face looked down

Like a star that dwelt apart

Like a star, unhasting, unresting

Like a stone thrown at random

Like a summer cloud, youth indeed has crept away

Like a summer-dried fountain

Like a swift eagle in the morning glare breasting the whirlwind with impetuous flight

Like a thing at rest

Like a thing read in a book or remembered out of the faraway past

Like a tide of triumph through their veins, the red, rejoicing blood began to race

Like a triumphing fire the news was borne

Like a troop of boys let loose from school, the adventurers went by

Like a vaporous amethyst

Like a vision of the morning air

Like a voice from the unknown regions

Like a wandering star I fell through the deeps of desire

Like a watch-worn and weary sentinel

Like a wave of the sea driven with the wind and tossed

Like a whirlwind they went past

Like a withered leaf the moon is blown across the bay

Like a world of sunshine

Like a yellow silken scarf the thick fog hangs

Like an alien ghost I stole away

Like an eagle clutching his prey, his arm swooped down

Like an eagle dallying with the wind

Like an engine of dread war, he set his shoulder to the mountain-side

Like an enraged tiger

Like an enthusiast leading about with him an indifferent tourist

Like an icy wave, a swift and tragic impression swept through him

Like an unbidden guest

Like an unbodied joy whose race is just begun

Like an unseen star of birth

Like an unwelcome thought

Like apparitions seen and gone

Like attempting to number the waves on the snore of a limitless sea

Like bells that waste the moments with their loudness

Like blasts of trumpets blown in wars

Like bright Apollo

Like bright lamps, the fabled apples glow

Like building castles in the air

Like bursting waves from the ocean

Like cliffs which have been rent asunder

Like clouds of gnats with perfect lineaments [lineaments = distinctive shape]

Like cobwebs woven round the limbs of an infant giant

Like crystals of snow

Like dead lovers who died true

Like Death, who rides upon a thought, and makes his way through temple, tower, and palace

Like dew upon a sleeping flower

Like dining with a ghost

Like drawing nectar in a sieve

Like earth's decaying leaves

Like echoes from a hidden lyre

Like echoes from an antenatal dream

Like fixed eyes, whence the dear light of sense and thought has fled

Like footsteps upon wool

Like fragrance from dead flowers

Like ghosts, from an enchanter fleeing

Like ghosts the sentries come and go

Like golden boats on a sunny sea

Like great black birds, the demons haunt the woods
Like green waves on the sea
Like having to taste a hundred exquisite dishes in a single meal
Like Heaven's free breath, which he who grasps can hold not
Like helpless birds in the warm nest
Like iridescent bubbles floating on a foul stream
Like kindred drops mingled into one
Like laying a burden on the back of a moth
Like lead his feet were
Like leaves in wintry weather
Like leviathans afloat
Like lighting a candle to the sun
Like making a mountain out of a mole-hill
Like mariners pulling the life-boat
Like mice that steal in and out as if they feared the light
Like mountain over mountain huddled
Like mountain streams we meet and part
Like music on the water
Like notes which die when born, but still haunt the echoes of the hill
Like oceans of liquid silver
Like one pale star against the dusk, a single diamond on her brow gleamed with imprisoned fire
Like one who halts with tired wings
Like one who talks of what he loves in dream
Like organ music came the deep reply
Like pageantry of mist on an autumnal stream
Like phantoms gathered by the sick imagination

Like planets in the sky

Like pouring oil on troubled waters

Like roses that in deserts bloom and die

Like rowing upstream against a strong downward current

Like scents from a twilight garden

Like separated souls

Like serpents struggling in a vulture's grasp

Like sheep from out the fold of the sky, stars leapt

Like ships that have gone down at sea

Like shy elves hiding from the traveler's eye

Like skeletons, the sycamores uplift their wasted hands

Like some grave night thought threading a dream

Like some new-gathered snowy hyacinth, so white and cold and delicate it was

Like some poor nigh-related guest, that may not rudely be dismist

Like some suppressed and hideous thought which flits athwart our musings, but can find no rest within a pure and gentle mind

Like some unshriven churchyard thing, the friar crawled

Like something fashioned in a dream

Like sounds of wind and flood

Like splendor-winged moths about a taper

Like stepping out on summer evenings from the glaring ball-room upon the cool and still piazza

Like straws in a gust of wind

Like summer's beam and summer's stream

Like sunlight, in and out the leaves, the robins went

Like sweet thoughts in a dream

Like the awful shadow of some unseen power

Like the bellowing of bulls

Like the boar encircled by hunters and hounds

Like the bubbles on a river sparkling, bursting, borne away

Like the cold breath of the grave

Like the creaking of doors held stealthily ajar

Like the cry of an itinerant vendor in a quiet and picturesque town

Like the dance of some gay sunbeam

Like the dawn of the morn

Like the detestable and spidery araucaria
[araucaria = evergreen trees of South America and Australia]

Like the dew on the mountain

Like the dim scent in violets

Like the drifting foam of a restless sea when the waves show their teeth in the flying breeze

Like the embodiment of a perfect rose, complete in form and fragrance

Like the faint cry of unassisted woe

Like the faint exquisite music of a dream

Like the fair flower dishevel'd in the wind

Like the fair sun, when in his fresh array he cheers the morn, and all the earth revealeth

Like the falling thud of the blade of a murderous ax

Like the fierce fiend of a distempered dream

Like the fitting of an old glove to a hand

Like the foam on the river

Like the great thunder sounding

Like the jangling of all the strings of some musical instrument
Like the jewels that gleam in baby eyes
Like the kiss of maiden love the breeze is sweet and bland
Like the long wandering love, the weary heart may faint for rest
Like the moon in water seen by night
Like the music in the patter of small feet
Like the prodigal whom wealth softens into imbecility
Like the quivering image of a landscape in a flowing stream
Like the rainbow, thou didst fade
Like the rustling of grain moved by the west-wind
Like the sap that turns to nectar, in the velvet of the peach
Like the sea whose waves are set in motion by the winds
Like the sea-worm, that perforates the shell of the mussel, which straightway closes the wound with a pearl
Like the setting of a tropical sun
Like the shadow of a great hill that reaches far out over the plain
Like the shadows of the stars in the upheaved sea
Like the shudder of a doomed soul
Like the silver gleam when the poplar trees rustle their pale leaves listlessly
Like the soft light of an autumnal day
Like the Spring-time, fresh and green
Like the stern-lights of a ship at sea, illuminating only the path which has been passed over
Like the sudden impulse of a madman
Like the swell of Summer's ocean
Like the tattered effigy in a cornfield
Like the vase in which roses have once been distill'd

Like the visits of angels, short and far between

Like the whole sky when to the east the morning doth return

Like thistles of the wilderness, fit neither for food nor fuel

Like those great rivers, whose course everyone beholds, but their springs have been seen by but few

Like thoughts whose very sweetness yielded proof that they were born for immortality

Like to diamonds her white teeth shone between the parted lips

Like torrents from a mountain source, we rushed into each other's arms

Like troops of ghosts on the dry wind past

Like two doves with silvery wings, let our souls fly

Like two flaming stars were his eyes

Like vaporous shapes half seen

Like village curs that bark when their fellows do

Like wasted hours of youth

Like winds that bear sweet music, when they breathe through some dim latticed chamber

Like wine-stain to a flask the old distrust still clings

Like winged stars the fire-flies flash and glance

Like young lovers whom youth and love make dear

Lingering like an unloved guest

Lithe as a panther

Little white hands like pearls

Lofty as a queen

Loneliness struck him like a blow

Looked back with faithful eyes like a great mastiff to his master's face

Looking as sulky as the weather itself

Looking like a snarling beast baulked of its prey
  [baulked = checked, thwarted]
Loose clouds like earth's decaying leaves are shed
Lost like the lightning in the sullen clod
Love as clean as starlight
Love brilliant as the morning
Love had like the canker-worm consumed her early prime
Love is a changing lord as the light on a turning sword
Love like a child around the world doth run
Love like a miser in the dark his joys would hide
Love shakes like a windy reed your heart
Love smiled like an unclouded sun
Love that sings and has wings as a bird
Lovely as starry water
Lovely the land unknown and like a river flowing

M

March on my soul nor like the laggard stay
Me on whose heart as a worm she trod
Meaningless as the syllables of an unknown tongue
Men moved hither and thither like insects in their crevices
Mentality as hard as bronze
Mentally round-shouldered and decrepit
Merge imperceptibly into one another like the hues of the prism
Meteors that dart like screaming birds
Milk-white pavements, clear and richly pale, like alabaster
More variegated than the skin of a serpent

Motion like the spirit of that wind whose soft step deepens slumber

Motionless as a plumb line

Mountains like frozen wrinkles on a sea

Moving in the same dull round, like blind horses in a mill

Mute as an iceberg

My age is as a lusty Winter

My body broken as a turning wheel

My breath to Heaven like vapor goes

My head was like a great bronze bell with one thought for the clapper

My heart is as some famine-murdered land

My heart is like a full sponge and must weep a little

My heart like a bird doth hover

My heart will be as wind fainting in hot grass

My life floweth away like a river

My life was white as driven snow

My love for thee is like the sovereign moon that rules the sea

My love's like the steadfast sun

My lungs began to crow like chanticleer [chanticleer = rooster]

My mind swayed idly like a water-lily in a lake

My muscles are as steel

My skin is as sallow as gold

My soul was as a lampless sea

My spirit seemed to beat the void, like the bird from out the ark

My thoughts came yapping and growling round me like a pack of curs

My thoughts ran leaping through the green ways of my mind like fawns at play

N

Night falls like fire

No longer shall slander's venomed spite crawl like a snake across his perfect name

Now every nerve in my body seemed like a strained harp-string ready to snap at a touch

Now like a wild nymph she veils her shadowy form

Now like a wild rose in the fields of heaven slipt forth the slender figure of the Dawn

Now memory and emotion surged in my soul like a tempest

Now thou seemest like a bankrupt beau, stripped of his gaudy hues

O

Obscured with wrath as is the sun with cloud

Odorous as all Arabia

Often enough life tosses like a fretful stream among rocky boulders

Oh, lift me as a wave, a leaf, a cloud

Old as the evening star

Old happy hours that have long folded their wings

Once again, like madness, the black shapes of doubt swing through his brain

One bleared star, faint glimmering like a bee

One bright drop is like the gem that decks a monarch's crown

One by one flitting like a mournful bird

One deep roar as of a cloven world

One winged cloud above like a spread dragon overhangs the west

Oppressed by the indefiniteness which hung in her mind, like a thick summer haze

Or shedding radiance like the smiles of God

Our enemies were broken like a dam of river reeds

Our hearts bowed down like violets after rain

Our sail like a dew-lit blossom shone

Overhead the intense blue of the noonday sky burst like a jewel in the sun

P

Pale and grave as a sculptured nun

Pale as a drifting blossom

Passed like a phantom into the shadows

Passive and tractable as a child

Peaceful as a village cricket-green on Sunday

Peevish and impatient, like some ill-trained man who is sick

Perished utterly, like a blown-out flame

Philosophy evolved itself, like a vast spider's loom

Pillowed upon its alabaster arms like to a child o'erwearied with sweet toil

Polished as the bosom of a star

Poured his heart out like the rending sea in passionate wave on wave

Pouting like the snowy buds o' roses in July

Presently she hovered like a fluttering leaf or flake of snow

Pride and self-disgust served her like first-aid surgeons on the battlefield

Proud as the proudest of church dignitaries

Pure as a wild-flower

Pure as the azure above them

Pure as the naked heavens

Pure as the snowy leaves that fold over the flower's heart

Purple, crimson, and scarlet, like the curtains of God's tabernacle

Put on gravity like a robe

Q

Quaking and quivering like a short-haired puppy after a ducking

Questions and answers sounding like a continuous popping of corks

Quiet as a nun's face

Quietly as a cloud he stole

Quietude which seemed to him beautiful as clear depths of water

Quivering like an eager race-horse to start

R

Rage, rage ye tears, that never more should creep like hounds about God's footstool

Ran like a young fawn

Rattle in the ear like a flourish of trumpets

Rays springing from the east like golden arrows

Red as the print of a kiss might be

Redolent with the homely scent of old-fashioned herbs and flowers

Reflected each in the other like stars in a lake

Refreshed like dusty grass after a shower

Refreshing as descending rains to sunburnt climes

Remote as the hidden star

Restless as a blue-bottle fly on a warm summer's day

Revealed his doings like those of bees in a glass hive

Rich as the dawn

Ride like the wind through the night

Rivers that like silver threads ran through the green and gold of pasture lands

Roared like mountain torrents

Rolling it under the tongue as a sweet morsel

Round my chair the children run like little things of dancing gold

Ruddy as sunrise

Ruddy his face as the morning light

Ruffling out his cravat with a crackle of starch, like a turkey when it spreads its feathers

Running to and fro like frightened sheep

Rushing and hurrying about like a June-bug

S

Sanctuaries where the passions may, like wild falcons, cover their faces with their wings

Sayings that stir the blood like the sound of a trumpet

Scattered love as stars do light

Sea-gulls flying like flakes of the sea

Sentences level and straight like a hurled lance

Shadowy faces, known in dreams, pass as petals upon a stream

Shake like an aspen leaf

Shaken off like a nightmare

Shapeless as a sack of wool

Shattered like so much glass

She brightened like a child whose broken toy is glued together

She could summon tears as one summons servants

She danced like a flower in the wind

She disclaimed the weariness that dragged upon her spirits like leaden weights

She exuded a faint and intoxicating perfume of womanliness, like a crushed herb

She felt like an unrepentant criminal

She fled like a spirit from the room

She flounders like a huge conger-eel in an ocean of dingy morality

She gave him a surprised look, like a child catching an older person in a foolish statement

She gave off antipathies as a liquid gives off vapor

She has great eyes like the doe

She heard him like one in a dream

She let the soft waves of her deep hair fall like flowers from Paradise

She looked like a tall golden candle

She looked like the picture of a young rapt saint, lost in heavenly musing

She moved like mirth incarnate

She nestles like a dove

She played with a hundred possibilities fitfully and discursively as a musician runs his fingers over a key-board

She played with grave cabinets as a cat plays with a mouse

She saw this planet like a star hung in the glistening depths of even

She seemed as happy as a wave that dances on the sea

She shall be sportive as the fawn

She stood silent a moment, dropping before him like a broken branch

She that passed had lips like pinks

She walked like a galley-slave

She walks in beauty like the night

She was as brilliant, and as hard too, as electric light

She was silent, standing before him like a little statuesque figure

Shining like the dewy star of dawn

Shivering pine-trees, like phantoms

Showy as damask-rose and shy as musk

Shrill as the loon's call

Shrivel like paper thrust into a flame

Shy as the squirrel

Sights seen as a traveling swallow might see them on the wing

Silence deep as death

Silence now is brooding like a gentle spirit o'er the still and pulseless world

Silence that seemed heavy and dark; like a passing cloud

Sinks clamorous like mill-waters at wild play

Sits like the maniac on his fancied throne

Skies as clear as babies' eyes

Sleek and thick and yellow as gold

Slender and thin as a slender wire

Slowly as a tortoise

Slowly as the finger of a clock, her shadow came

Slowly moved off and disappeared like shapes breathed on a mirror and melting away

Slowly, unnoted, like the creeping rust that spreads insidious, had estrangement come

Small as a grain of mustard seed

Smooth as a pond

Smooth as the pillar flashing in the sun

Snug as a bug in a rug

Soaring as swift as smoke from a volcano springs

So elusive that the memory of it afterwards was wont to come and go like a flash of light

So my spirit beat itself like a caged bird against its prison bars in vain

Soft as a zephyr

Soft as sleep the snow fell

Soft as Spring

Soft as the down of the turtle dove

Soft as the landscape of a dream

Soft as the south-wind

Soft in their color as gray pearls

Soft vibrations of verbal melody, like the sound of a golden bell rung far down under the humming waters

Some gleams of feeling pure and warm as sunshine on a sky of storm

Some like veiled ghosts hurrying past as though driven to their land of shadows by shuddering fear

Some minds are like an open fire—how direct and instant our communication with them

Something divine seemed to cling around her like some subtle vapor

Something resistant and inert, like the obstinate rolling over of a heavy sleeper after he has been called to get up

Something sharp and brilliant, like the glitter of a sword or a forked flash of lightning

Sorrowful eyes like those of wearied kine spent from the plowing [kine = cows]

Spread like wildfire

Squirrel-in-the-cage kind of movement

Stamping like a plowman to shuffle off the snow

Stared about like calves in a pen

Steadfast as the soul of truth

Steals lingering like a river smooth

Still as death

Stood like a wave-beaten rock

Straight as a ray of light

Straight as an arrow

Streamed like a meteor through the troubled air

Streamed o'er his memory like a forest flame

Streaming tears, like pearl drops from a flint

Striking with the force of an engine of destruction

Strong as a bison

Style comes, if at all, like the bloom upon fruit, or the glow of health upon the cheek

Subtle as jealousy

Sudden a thought came like a full-blown rose, flushing his brow

Sudden sprays of rain, like volleys of sharp arrows, rattled gustily against the windows

Suddenly, like death, the truth flashed on them

Sunbeams flashing on the face of things like sudden smilings of divine delight

Sunday mornings which seem to put on, like a Sabbath garment, an atmosphere of divine quietude

Supple and sweet as a rose in bloom

Sway like blown moths against the rosewhite flame

Sweet as a summer night without a breath

Sweet as music she spoke

Sweet as the rain at noon

Sweet as the smile of a fairy

Swift as a swallow heading south

Swift as lightning

Swift as the panther in triumph

Swifter than the twinkling of an eye

T

Talking and thinking became to him like the open page of a monthly magazine

Tall lance-like reeds wave sadly o'er his head

That like a wounded snake drags its slow length along

The anemone that weeps at day-break, like a silly girl before her lover

The army blazed and glowed in the golden sunlight like a mosaic of a hundred thousand jewels

The army like a witch's caldron seethed

The beating of her heart was like a drum

The beauty of her quiet life was like a rose in blowing

The billows burst like cannon down the coast

The birds swam the flood of air like tiny ships

The boat cuts its swift way through little waves like molten gold and opal

The boom of the surf grew ever less sonorous, like the thunder of a retreating storm

The breast-plate of righteousness

The breathless hours like phantoms stole away

The breeze is as a pleasant tune

The calm white brow as calm as earliest morn

The camp fire reddens like angry skies

The chambers of the house were haunted by an incessant echoing, like some dripping cavern

The church swarmed like a hive

The city is all in a turmoil; it boils like a pot of lentils

The clouds that move like spirits o'er the welkin clear [welkin = sky]

The clustered apples burnt like flame

The colored bulbs swung noon-like from tree and shrub

The crimson close of day

The curl'd moon was like a little feather

The curling wreaths like turbans seem

The dark hours are swept away like crumbling ashes

The dark mass of her hair shook round her like a sea

The dawn is rising from the sea, like a white lady from her bed

The dawn had whitened in the mist like a dead face

The dawn with silver-sandaled feet crept like a frightened girl.

The day stunned me like light upon some wizard way

The day was sweeter than honey and the honey-comb

The day have trampled me like armed men

The dead past flew away over the fens like a flight of wild swans

The deep like one black maelstrom round her whirls

The deepening east like a scarlet poppy burnt

The desolate rocky hills rolled like a solid wave along the horizon

The dome of heaven is like one drop of dew

The dreams of poets come like music heard at evening from the depth of some enchanted forest

The eagerness faded from his eyes, leaving them cold as a winter sky after sunset

The earth was like a frying-pan, or some such hissing matter

The eternal sea, which like a childless mother, still must croon her ancient sorrows to the cold white moon

The evening sky was as green as jade

The excitement had spread through the whole house, like a piquant and agreeable odor

The excitement of the thought buoyed his high-strung temperament like a tonic

The feathery meadows like a lilac sea

The firm body like a slope of snow

The first whiff of reality dissipated them like smoke

The floor, newly waxed, gleamed in the candle-light like beaten moonbeams

The fragrant clouds of hair, they flowed round him like a snare

The gathering glory of life shone like the dawn

The gesture was all strength and will, like the stretching of a sea-bird's wings

The girl's voice rang like a bird-call through his rustling fancies

The glimmer of tall flowers standing like pensive moon-worshipers in an ecstasy of prayerless bloom

The guides sniffed, like chamois, the air

[chamois = extremely agile goat antelope]

The heavens are like a scroll unfurled

The hills across the valley were purple as thunder-clouds

The hoofs of the horses rang like the dumb cadence of an old saga

The hours crawled by like years

The hum of the camp sounds like the sea

The hurrying crowds of men gather like clouds

The ideas succeeded each other like a dynasty of kings

The impalpable presence of the new century rose like a vast empty house through which

no human feet had walked

- The inexorable facts closed in on him like prison-warders handcuffing a convict
- The lake glimmered as still as a mirror
- The land of gold seemed to hold him like a spell
- The land was like a dream
- The level boughs, like bars of iron across the setting sun
- The light of London flaring like a dreary dawn
- The lights blazed up like day
- The lilies were drooping, white, and wan, like the head and skin of a dying man
- The mellowing hand of time
- The melody rose tenderly and lingeringly like a haunting perfume of pressed flowers
- The Milky Way lay like diamond-dust upon the robe of some great king
- The monk's face whitened like sea-foam
- The moon drowsed between the trees like a great yellow moth
- The moon on the tower slept soft as snow
- The moonbeams rest like a pale spotless shroud
- The moonlight lay like snow
- The moonlight, like a fairy mist, upon the mesa spreads
- The mortal coldness of the soul, like death itself comes down
- The mountain shadows mingling, lay like pools above the earth
- The mountains loomed up dimly, like phantoms through the mist
- The music almost died away, then it burst like a pent-up flood
- The name that cuts into my soul like a knife
- The nervous little train winding its way like a jointed reptile

- The new ferns were spread upon the earth like some lacy coverlet
- The night like a battle-broken host is driven before
- The night yawned like a foul wind
- The ocean swelled like an undulating mirror of the bowl of heaven
- The old books look somewhat pathetically from the shelves, like aged dogs wondering why no one takes them for a walk
- The old infamy will pop into daylight like a toad out of fissure in the rock
- The penalty falls like a thunderbolt from heaven
- The phrase was like a spear-thrust
- The pine trees waved as waves a woman's hair
- The place was like some enchanted town of palaces
- The plains to northward change their color like the shimmering necks of doves
- The poppy burned like a crimson ember
- The prime of man has waxed like cedars
- The public press would chatter and make odd ambiguous sounds like a shipload of monkeys in a storm
- The purple heather rolls like dumb thunder
- The rainbows flashed like fire
- The river shouted as ever its cry of joy over the vitality of life, like a spirited boy before the face of inscrutable nature
- The roofs with their gables like hoods
- The roses lie upon the grass like little shreds of crimson silk
- The satire of the word cut like a knife
- The scullion with face shining like his pans
- The sea reeled round like a wine-vat splashing

The sea-song of the trampling waves is as muffled bells

The sea spread out like a wrinkled marble floor

The sea, that gleamed still, like a myriad-petaled rose

The sea was as untroubled as the turquoise vault which it reflected

The setting of the sun is like a word of peace

The sharp hail rattles against the panes and melts on my cheeks like tears

The ships, like sheeted phantoms coming and going

The silence seemed to crush to earth like a great looking-glass and shiver into a million pieces

The silvery morning like a tranquil vision fills the world

The sky burned like a heated opal

The sky gleamed with the hardness and brilliancy of blue enamel

The sky was as a shield that caught the stain of blood and battle from the dying sun

The sky was clear and blue, and the air as soft as milk

The sky was like a peach

The sky where stars like lilies white and fair shine through the mists

The solid air around me there heaved like a roaring ocean

The solid mountains gleamed like the unsteady sea

The soul is like a well of water springing up into everlasting life

The sound is like a noon-day gale

The sound is like a silver-fountain that springeth in a golden basin

The sound of a thousand tears, like softly pattering wings

The sound of your running feet that like the sea-hoofs beat

The spear-tongued lightning slipped like a snake

The Spring breaks like a bird

The stacks of corn in brown array, like tattered wigwams on the plain

The stars come down and trembling glow like blossoms on the waves below

The stars lay on the lapis-lazuli sky like white flower-petals on still deep water
[lapis-lazuli = opaque to translucent blue, violet-blue, or greenish-blue gemstone]

The stars pale and silent as a seer

The strange cold sense of aloofness that had numbed her senses suddenly gave way like snow melting in the spring

The sudden thought of your face is like a wound when it comes unsought

The sun, like a great dragon, writhes in gold

The sun on the sea-wave lies white as the moon

The surf was like the advancing lines of an unknown enemy flinging itself upon the shore

The terrible past lay afar, like a dream left behind in the night

The tide was in the salt-weed, and like a knife it tore

The time, gliding like a dream

The torrent from the hills leaped down their rocky stairways like wild steeds

The tree whose plumed boughs are soft as wings of birds

The uproar and contention pierced him like arrows

The veiled future bowed before me like a vision of promise

The velvet grass that is like padding to earth's meager ribs

The villa dips its foot in the lake, smiling at its reflection like a bather lingering on the brink

The voice of Fate, crying like some old Bellman through the world

The voice that rang in the night like a bugle call

The warm kindling blood burned her cheeks like the breath of a hot wind

The waves were rolling in, long and lazy, like sea-worn travelers

The whole truth, naked, cold, and fatal as a patriot's blade

The wind all round their ears hissed like a flight of white-winged geese

The wind comes and it draws its length along like the genii from the earthen pot

The wine flows like blood

The woman seemed like a thing of stone

The words kept ringing in my ears like the tolling of a bell

The words of the wise fall like the tolling of sweet, grave bells upon the soul

The world had vanished like a phantasmagoria

The world is bitter as a tear

The world is in a simmer, like a sea

The world wavers within its circle like a dream

The years stretched before her like some vast blank page out to receive the record of her toil

The years vanished like a May snowdrift

The yellow apples glowed like fire

Their glances met like crossed swords

Their joy like sunshine deep and broad falls on my heart

Their minds rested upon the thought, as chasing butterflies might rest together on a flower

Their music frightful as the serpent's hiss

Their touch affrights me as a serpent's sting

Then fall unheeded like the faded flower

Then felt I like some watcher of the skies

Then it swelled out to rich and glorious harmonies like a full orchestra playing under the sea

Then the lover sighing like furnace

Theories sprouted in his mind like mushrooms

There is an air about you like the air that folds a star

There, like a bird, it sits and sings

There seemed to brood in the air a quiet benevolence of a Father watching His myriad children at play

There she soars like a seraph

There she stood straight as a lily on its stem

There slowly rose to sight, a country like a dragon fast asleep

There streamed into the air the sweet smell of crushed grass, as though many fields had been pressed between giant's fingers and so had been left

These eyes like stars have led me

These final words snapped like a whip-lash

These thoughts pierced me like thorns

They are as cruel as creeping tigers

They are as white foam on the swept sands

They are as white swans in the dusk, thy white hands

They are painted sharp as death

They broke into pieces and fell on the ground, like a silvery, shimmering shower of hail

They dropped like panthers

They fly like spray

They had hands like claws

They had slipped away like visions

They have as many principles as a fish has bones

They have faces like flowers

They hurried down like plovers that have heard the call [plovers = wading birds]

They look like rose-buds filled with snow

They seem like swarming flies, the crowd of little men

They seemed like floating flowers

They shine as sweet as simple doves

They stand like solitary mountain forms on some hard, perfectly transparent day

They vanished like the shapes that float upon a summer's dream

Thick as wind-blown leaves innumerable

Thickly the flakes drive past, each like a childish ghost

Thine eyes like two twin stars shining

This life is like a bubble blown up in the air

This love that dwells like moonlight in your face

This thought is as death

This tower rose in the sunset like a prayer

Those ancestral themes past which so many generations have slept like sea-going winds over pastures

Those death-like eyes, unconscious of the sun

Those eyelids folded like a white rose-leaf

Those eyes like bridal beacons shine

Thou art to me but as a wave of the wild sea

Thou as heaven art fair and young

Thou hadst a voice whose sound was like the sea

Thou must wither like a rose

Thou shalt be as free as mountain winds

Thou wouldst weep tears bitter as blood

Though bright as silver the meridian beams shine

Though thou be black as night

Thoughts vague as the fitful breeze

Three-cornered notes fly about like butterflies

Through the forest, like a fairy dream through some dark mind, the ferns in branching beauty stream

Through the moonlit trees, like ghosts of sounds haunting the moonlight, stole the faint tinkle of a guitar

Through the riot of his senses, like a silver blaze, ran the legend

Thy beauty like a beast it bites

Thy brown benignant eyes have sudden gleams of gladness and surprise, like woodland brooks that cross a sunlit spot

Thy carven columns must have grown by magic, like a dream in stone

Thy favors are but like the wind that kisses everything it meets

Thy heart is light as a leaf of a tree

Thy name burns like a gray and flickering candle flame

Thy name will be as honey on men's lips

Till death like sleep might steal on me

Till he melted like a cloud in the silent summer heaven

Time drops in decay, like a candle burnt out

Time like a pulse shakes fierce

To drag life on, which like a heavy chain lengthens behind with many a link of pain

To forsake as the trees drop their leaves in autumn

Toys with smooth trifles like a child at play

Transitory as clouds without substance

Transparent like a shining sun

Tree and shrub altered their values and became transmuted to silver sentinels

Trees that spread their forked boughs like a stag's antlers

Trembling like an aspen-leaf

Truths which forever shine as fixed stars

Turning easily and securely as on a perfect axle

U

Unbends like a loosened bow

Unbreakable as iron

Unconscious as an oak-tree of its growth

Under the willow-tree glimmered her face like a foam-flake drifting over the sea

Unheralded, like some tornado loosed out of the brooding hills, it came to pass

Unknown, like a seed in fallow ground, was the germ of a plan

Unmoving as a tombstone

Untameable as flies

Unutterable things pressing on my soul like a pent-up storm craving for outlet

Upcast like foam of the effacing tide

Uplifting the soul as on dovelike wings

Uplifting their stony peaks around us like the walls and turrets of a gigantic fortress

Urgent as the seas

Uttering wild cries like a creature in pain

V

Vague as a dream

Vague thoughts that stream shapelessly through her mind like long sad vapors through the twilight sky

Vanish into thin air, like ghosts at the cockcrow

Vanished like snow when comes a thaw

Vanished like vapor before the sun

Vibrations set quivering like harp strings struck by the hand of a master

Vociferous praise following like a noisy wave

W

Walking somewhat unsteadily like a blind man feeling his way

Waves glittered and danced on all sides like millions of diamonds

We left her and retraced our steps like faithless hounds

Weak and frail like the vapor of a vale

Wearing their wounds like stars

Weary wind, who wanderest like the world's rejected guest

When a draft might puff them out like a guttering candle [guttering = To melt through the side of the hollow in a candle formed by a burning wick; to burn low and unsteadily; flicker]

When arm in arm they both came swiftly running, like a pair of turtle-doves that could not live asunder day or night

When cards, invitations, and three-corn'd notes fly about like white butterflies

When she died, her breath whistled like the wind in a keyhole

When the fever pierced me like a knife

Where a lamp of deathless beauty shines like a beacon

Where heroes die as leaves fall

Where the intricate wheels of trade are grinding on, like a mill

Where the source of the waters is fine as a thread

Whilst the lagging hours of the day went by like windless clouds o'er a tender sky

Whistled sharply in the air like a handful of vipers

White as a ghost from darkness

White as chalk

White as dove or lily, or spirit of the light

White as the driven snow

White as the moon's white flame

White as the sea-bird's wing

White clouds like daisies

White hands she moves like swimming swans

White hands through her hair, like white doves going into the shadow of a wood

White like flame

White sails of sloops like specters

Whose bodies are as strong as alabaster

Whose hair was as gold raiment on a king

Whose laugh moves like a bat through silent haunted woods

Whose little eyes glow like the sparks of fire

Whose music like a robe of living light reclothed each new-born age

Windy speech which hits all around the mark like a drunken carpenter

Winged like an arrow to its mark

With a sting like a scorpion

With all the complacency of a homeless cat

With an angry broken roar, like billows on an unseen shore, their fury burst

With hate darkling as the swift winter hail

With music sweet as love

With sounds like breakers

With strength like steel

With the whisper of leaves in one's ear

With words like honey melting from the comb

Wits as sharp as gimlets
  [gimlet = small hand tool for boring holes]

Women with tongues like polar needles

Words as fresh as spring verdure
  [verdure = lush greenness of flourishing vegetation]

Words as soft as rain

Words like the gossamer film of the summer

Words sweet as honey from his lips distill'd

Words were flashing like brilliant birds through the boughs overhead

Wordsworth, thy music like a river rolls

Worthless like the conjurer's gold

Wrangle over details like a grasping pawnbroker

Wrinkled and scored like a dried apple

Writhing with an intensity that burnt like a steady flame

Y

Yielding like melted snow

Yonder flimsy crescent, bent like an archer's bow above the snowy summit

You are as gloomy to-night as an undertaker out of employment

You are as hard as stone

You gave me such chill embraces as the snow-covered heights receive from clouds

Your blood is red like wine

Your charms lay like metals in a mine

Your eyes are like fantastic moons that shiver in some stagnant lake

Your eyes as blue as violets

Your eyes they were green and gray like an April day

Your frail fancies are swallowed up, like chance flowers flung upon the river's current

Your hair was golden as tints of sunrise

Your heart is as dry as a reed

Your locks are like the raven

Your love shall fall about me like sweet rain

Your step's like the rain to summer vexed farmer

Your thoughts are buzzing like a swarm of bees

Your tongue is like a scarlet snake

Your voice had a quaver in it just like the linnet [linnet = small finch]

Youth like a summer morn

SECTION IX

CONVERSATIONAL PHRASES

A

A most extraordinary idea!

A thousand hopes for your success

Accept my best wishes

All that is conjecture

Allow me to congratulate you

An unfortunate comparison, don't you think?

And even if it were so?

And how am I to thank you?

And in the end, what are you going to make of it?

And yet the explanation does not wholly satisfy me

Apparently I was wrong

Are we wandering from the point?

Are you a trifle—bored?

Are you fully reconciled?

Are you not complicating the question?

Are you prepared to go to that length?

Are you still obdurate?
   [obdurate = Hardened in wrongdoing; stubbornly impenitent]

As it happens, your conjecture is right

Assuredly I do

At first blush it may seem fantastic

B

Banish such thoughts

But are you not taking a slightly one-sided point of view?

But consider for a moment

But I look at the practical side

But I wander from my point

But now I'll confide something to you

But perhaps I'm hardly fair when I say that

But seriously speaking, what is the use of it?

But surely that is inconsistent

But that's a tremendous hazard

But the thing is simply impossible

But there's one thing you haven't said

But, wait, you haven't heard the end

But what do you yourself think about it?

But who could foresee what was going to happen?

But you are open to persuasion?

But you do not know for certain

But you must tell me more

By a curious chance, I know it very well

By no means desirable, I think

C

Can I persuade you?
Can you imagine anything so horrible?
Certain circumstances make it undesirable
Certainly not, if it displeases you
Certainly, with the greatest pleasure
Come, where's your sense of humor?
Consult me when you want me—at any time

D

Decidedly so
Dine with me to-morrow night?—if you are free?
Do I presume too much?
Do I seem very ungenerous?
Do not misunderstand me
Do not the circumstances justify it?
Don't be so dismal, please
Don't delude yourself
Don't let me encroach on your good nature
Don't think I am unappreciative of your kindness
Do you attach any particular meaning to that?
Do you know, I envy you that
Do you know what his chief interests are now?
Do you mind my making a suggestion?
Do you press me to tell?

Do you really regard him as a serious antagonist?
Do you think there is anything ominous in it?
Does it please you so tremendously?
Does it seem incredible?

E

Either way is perplexing
Eminently proper, I think
Everyone looks at it differently
Excuse my bluntness

F

Fanciful, I should say
For the simplest of reasons
Forgive me if I seem disobliging
Fortunate, to say the least
Frankly, I don't see why it should
Frugal to a degree
Fulsome praise, I call it

G

Give me your sympathy and counsel
Glorious to contemplate
Good! that is at least something
Gratifying, I am sure

H

Happily there are exceptions to every rule

Has it really come to that?

Have I incurred your displeasure?

Have you any rooted objection to it?

Have you anything definite in your mind?

Have you reflected what the consequences might be to yourself?

He does me too much honor

He feels it acutely

He has a queer conception of the proprieties

He is a poor dissembler
  [dissemble = conceal behind a false appearance]

He is anything but obtuse

He is so ludicrously wrong

He is the most guileless of men

He was so extremely susceptible

He writes uncommonly clever letters

Heaven forbid that I should wound your sensibility

His sense of humor is unquenchable

How amiable you are to say so

How can I tell you how much I have enjoyed it all?

How can I thank you?

How can you be so unjust?

How delightful to meet you

How does the idea appeal to you?

How droll you are!

How extraordinary!

How intensely interesting!

How perfectly delightful!

How utterly abominable

How very agreeable this is!

How very interesting

How very surprising

How well you do it!

However, I should like to hear your views

Human nature interests me very much indeed

I

I admire your foresight

I admit it most gratefully

I agree—at least, I suppose I do

I agree that something ought to be done

I always welcome criticism so long as it is sincere

I am absolutely bewildered

I am afraid I am not familiar enough with the subject

I am afraid I cannot suggest an alternative

I am afraid I've allowed you to tire yourself

I am afraid I must confess my ignorance

I am afraid you will call me a sentimentalist

I am always glad to do anything to please you

I am anxious to discharge the very onerous debt I owe you

I am appealing to your sense of humor

I am at your service

I am bound to secrecy
I am compelled to, unluckily
I am curious to learn what his motive was
I am deeply flattered and grateful
I am delighted to hear you say so
I am dumb with admiration
I am entirely at your disposal
I am extremely glad you approve of it
I am far from believing the maxim
I am fortunate in being able to do you a service
I am glad to be able to think that
I am glad to have had this talk with you
I am glad to say that I have entirely lost that faculty
I am glad you can see it in that way
I am glad you feel so deeply about it
I am giving you well-deserved praise
I am going to make a confession
I am grateful for your good opinion
I am honestly indignant
I am, I confess, a little discouraged
I am in a chastened mood
I am inclined to agree with you
I am incredulous
I am indebted to you for the suggestion
I am listening—I was about to propose
I am lost in admiration
I am luckily disengaged to-day
I am more grieved than I can tell you

I am naturally overjoyed

I am not a person of prejudices

I am not an alarmist

I am not as unreasonable as you suppose

I am not at all in the secret of his ambitions

I am not capable of unraveling it

I am not going into sordid details

I am not going to let you evade the question

I am not going to pay you any idle compliments

I am not impervious to the obligations involved

I am not in sympathy with it

I am not in the least surprised

I am not inquisitive

I am not prepared to say

I am not sure that I can manage it

I am not vindictive

I am overjoyed to hear you say so

I am perfectly aware of what I am saying

I am persuaded by your candor

I am quite convinced of that

I am quite discomfited

I am quite interested to see what you will do

I am quite ready to be convinced

I am rather of the opinion that I was mistaken

I am ready to make great allowances

I am really afraid I don't know

I am really gregarious

I am sensible of the flattery

I am seriously annoyed with myself about it
I am so glad you think that
I am so sorry—so very sorry
I am sorry to disillusionize you
I am sorry to interrupt this interesting discussion
I am sorry to say it is impossible
I am speaking plainly
I am still a little of an idealist
I am suppressing many of the details
I am sure it sounds very strange to you
I am sure you could pay me no higher compliment
I am sure you will hear me out
I am surprised, I confess
I am sustained by the prospect of a good dinner
I am vastly obliged to you
I am vastly your debtor for the information
I am very far from being a fanatic
I am very glad of this opportunity
I am very grateful—very much flattered
I am wholly in agreement with you
I am willing to accept all the consequences
I am wonderfully well
I am wondering if I may dare ask you a very personal question?
I am your creditor unawares
I anticipate your argument
I appreciate your motives
I assure you it is most painful to me
I assure you my knowledge of it is limited

I bear no malice about that
I beg your indulgence
I beg your pardon, but you take it too seriously
I brazenly confess it
I can easily understand your astonishment
I can explain the apparent contradiction
I can find no satisfaction in it
I can hardly agree with you there
I can never be sufficiently grateful
I can only tell you the bare facts
I can scarcely accept the offer
I can scarcely boast that honor
I can scarcely imagine anything more disagreeable
I can sympathize with you
I cannot altogether acquit myself of interested motives
I cannot explain it even to myself
I cannot find much real satisfaction in it
I cannot forbear to press my advantage
I cannot imagine what you mean
I cannot precisely determine
I can't pretend to make a jest of what I'm going to say
I cannot say definitely at the moment
I cannot say that in fact it is always so
I cannot see how you draw that conclusion
I cannot thank you enough for all your consideration
I compliment you on your good sense
I confess, I find it difficult
I could ask for nothing better

I could never forgive myself for that
I dare say your intuition is quite right
I decline to commit myself beforehand
I detest exaggeration
I didn't mean that—exactly
I do not comprehend your meaning
I don't deny that it is interesting
I don't doubt it for a moment
I do not doubt the sincerity of your arguments
I do not exactly understand you
I do not feel sure that I entirely share your views
I don't feel that it is my business
I do not find it an unpleasant subject
I don't insist on your believing me
I don't justify my presumption
I don't know quite why you should say that
I don't know that I can do that
I don't know when I have heard anything so lamentable
I don't know why you should be displeased
I don't make myself clear, I see
I don't pretend to explain
I don't see anything particularly wonderful in it
I don't underrate his kindness
I don't want to disguise that from you
I don't want to exaggerate
I don't want to seem critical
I doubt the truth of that saying
I endorse it, every word

I entirely approve of your plan
I fancy it's just that
I fear I cannot help you
I fear that's too technical for me
I feel a certain apprehension
I feel an unwonted sense of gaiety
   [unwonted = unusual]
I feel it my duty to be frank with you
I feel myself scarcely competent to judge
I feel very grateful to you for your kind offer
I find it absorbing
I find it rather monotonous
I find this agreeable mental exhilaration
I frankly confess that
I generally trust my first impressions
I give my word gladly
I give you my most sacred word of honor
I had better begin at the beginning
I had no intention of being offensive
I hadn't thought of it in that light
I hardly think that could be so
I have a hundred reasons for thinking so
I have a peculiar affection for it
I have an immense faith in him
I have been constrained by circumstances
I have been decidedly impressed
I have been longing to see more of you
I have been puzzling over a dilemma

I have every reason to think so
I have given you the best proof of it
I have gone back to my first impressions
I have known striking instances of the kind
I have never heard it put so well
I have no delusions on that score
I have not succeeded in convincing myself of that
I have not the influence you think
I have not the least doubt of it
I haven't the remotest idea
I have often a difficulty in deciding
I have often marveled at your courage
I have quite changed my opinion about that
I have something of great importance to say to you
I have sometimes vaguely felt it
I have the strongest possible prejudice against it
I heartily congratulate you
I hope it will not seem unreasonable to you
I hope we may meet again
I hope you will forgive an intruder
I hope you will not think me irreverent
I hope you will pardon my seeming carelessness
I indulge the modest hope
I know it is very presumptuous
I know my request will appear singular
I like it immensely
I like your frankness
I make no reflection whatever

I mean it literally

I might question all that

I mistrust these wild impulses

I most certainly agree with you

I most humbly ask pardon

I must add my congratulations on your taste

I must apologize for intruding upon you

I must ask you one more question, if I may

I must confess I have never thought of that

I must refrain from any comment

I must respectfully decline to tell you

I must take this opportunity to tell you

I need not remind you that you have a grave responsibility

I never heard anything so absurd

I offer my humblest apologies

I owe the idea wholly to you

I partly agree with you

I personally owe you a great debt of thankfulness

I place myself entirely at your service

I place the most implicit reliance on your good sense

I prefer to reserve my judgment

I purposely evaded the question

I quite appreciate the very clever way you put it

I quite see what the advantages are

I really am curious to know how you guessed that

I realize how painful it must be to you

I recollect it clearly

I rely on your good sense

FIFTEEN THOUSAND USEFUL PHRASES

I remember the occasion perfectly
I resent that kind of thing
I respect you for that
I respect your critical faculty
I say it in all modesty
I see disapproval in your face
I see it from a different angle
I see you are an enthusiast
I see your point of view
I seem to have heard that sentiment before
I shall at once proceed to forget it
I shall await your pleasure
I shall be glad if you will join me
I shall be interested to watch it develop
I shall be most proud and pleased
I shall certainly take you at your word
I shall feel highly honored
I shall make a point of thinking so
I shall never forget your kindness
I shall respect your confidence
I should appreciate your confidence greatly
I should be very ungrateful were I not satisfied with it
I should feel unhappy if I did otherwise
I should like your opinion of it
I should not dream of asking you to do so
I should think it very unlikely
I simply cannot endure it
I spoke only in jest

I stand corrected

I suppose I ought to feel flattered

I surmised as much

I sympathize deeply with you

I take that for granted

I think extremely well of it

I think he has very noble ideals

I think I can answer that for you

I think I know what you are going to say

I think it has its charm

I think it is superb!

I think it quite admirable

I think its tone is remarkably temperate

I think that is rather a brilliant idea

I think what you say is reasonable

I think you are quibbling

I think you are rather severe in your opinions

I think you have great appreciation of values

I think you have summed it up perfectly

I think your candor is charming

I thoroughly agree with you

I thought it most amusing

I thought you were seriously indisposed

I trust you will not consider it an impertinence

I understand exactly how you feel about it

I understand your delicacy of feeling

I venture to propose another plan

I very rarely allow myself that pleasure

I want to have a frank understanding with you
I was at a loss to understand the reason for it
I was hoping that I could persuade you
I was on the point of asking you
I was speaking generally
I watched you with admiration
I will answer you frankly
I will listen to no protestations
I will take it only under compulsion
I will tell you what puzzles me
I will think of it, since you wish it
I will, with great pleasure
I wish I could explain my point more fully
I wish I knew what you meant by that
I wish to be perfectly fair
I wish to put things as plainly as possible
I wonder how much truth there is in it?
I wonder if you have the smallest recollection of me?
I would agree if I understood
I wouldn't put it just that way
If ever I can repay it, command me
If I mistake not you were there once?
If I speak strongly, it is because I feel strongly
If I were disposed to offer counsel
If I were sure you would not misunderstand my meaning
If you don't mind my saying so
If you insist upon it
If you will pardon me the frankness

In a manner that sometimes terrifies me

In one respect you are quite right

In that case let me rob you of a few minutes

In what case, for example?

Incredible as it sounds, I had for a moment forgotten

Indeed, but it is quite possible

Indeed! How?

Indeed, you are wholly wrong

Indifferently so, I am afraid

Irony was ten thousand leagues from my intention

Is it sane—is it reasonable?

Isn't it amazing?

Isn't it extraordinarily funny?

Isn't it preposterous?

Isn't that a trifle unreasonable?

Isn't that rather a hasty conclusion?

Is that a fair question?

It always seemed to me impossible

It amuses you, doesn't it?

It blunts the sensibilities

It could never conceivably be anything but popular

It depends on how you look at it

It depends upon circumstances

It doesn't sound plausible to me

It has a lovely situation as I remember it

It has amused me hugely

It has been a relief to talk to you

It has been an immense privilege to see you

It has never occurred to me
It is a curious fact
It is a great pleasure to meet you
It is a huge undertaking
It is a most unfortunate affair
It is a perfectly plain proposition
It is a rather melancholy thought
It is a truth universally acknowledged
It is all very inexcusable
It is all very well for you to be philosophical
It is altogether probable
It is an admirable way of putting it
It is an error of taste
It is an extreme case, but the principle is sound
It is an ingenious theory
It is an uncommonly fine description
It is extremely interesting, I can assure you
It is for you to decide
It is historically true
It is I who should ask forgiveness
It is incredible!
It is indeed generous of you to suggest it
It is inexplicable
It is interesting, as a theory
It is literally impossible
It is merely a mood
It is most unfortunate
It is my deliberately formed opinion

It is my opinion you are too conscientious
It is nevertheless true
It is not a matter of the slightest consequence
It is not always fair to judge by appearances
It is not so unreasonable as you think
It is often very misleading
It is one of the grave problems of the day
It is only a fancy of mine
It is perfectly defensible
It is perfectly trite
It is permissible to gratify such an impulse
It is possible, but I rather doubt it
It is quite an easy matter
It is quite conceivable
It is quite too absurd
It is rather startling
It is really impressive
It is really most callous of you to laugh
It is sheer madness
It is sickening and so insufferably arrogant
It is simply a coincidence
It is the most incomprehensible thing in the world
It is to you that I am indebted for all this
It is true, I am grieved to say
It is true none the less
It is very amusing
It is very far from being a fiction
It is very good of you to do this for my pleasure

It is very ingenious

It is very splendid of you

It is wanton capriciousness

It is your privilege to think so

It's a difficult and delicate matter to discuss

It's a matter of immediate urgency

It's absolute folly

It's absurd—it's impossible

It's all nonsense

It's as logical as it can be under the circumstances

It's been a strange experience for you

It's deliciously honest

It's going to be rather troublesome

It's inconceivable that it should ever be necessary

It's mere pride of opinion

It's my chief form of recreation

It's not a matter of vast importance

It's past my comprehension

It's quite wonderful how logical and simple you make it

It's really very perplexing

It's so charming of you to say that

It's so kind of you to come

It's such a bore having to talk about it

It's the natural sequence

It's too melancholy

It's very wonderful

It makes it all quite interesting

It may sound strange to you

It must be a trifle dull at times
It must be fascinating
It must be very gratifying to you
It must have been rather embarrassing
It seems an age since we've last seen you
It seems entirely wonderful to me
It seems incredible
It seems like a distracting dream
It seems preposterous
It seems the height of absurdity
It seems to me that you have a perfect right to do so
It seems unspeakably funny to me
It seems very ridiculous
It shall be as you wish
It should not be objectionable
It sounds plausible
It sounds profoundly interesting
It sounds rather appalling
It sounds very alluring
It strikes me as rather pathetic
It was an unpardonable liberty
It was inevitable that you should say that
It was most stupid of me to have forgotten it
It was not unkindly meant
It was peculiarly unfortunate
It was really an extraordinary experience
It was so incredible
It was the most amazing thing I ever heard

It was very good of you to come out and join us
It will create a considerable sensation
It will divert your thoughts from a mournful subject
It will give me pleasure to do it
It will not alter my determination
It would be ill-advised
It would interest me very much
It would seem to be a wise decision
It would take too long to formulate my thought

J

Join us, please, when you have time
Just trust to the inspiration of the moment
Justify it if you can

L

Let me persuade you
Let me say how deeply indebted I feel for your kindness
Let me speak frankly
Let us grant that for the sake of the argument
Let us take a concrete instance

M

Many thanks—how kind and good you are!
May I ask to whom you allude?

May I be privileged to hear it?
May I speak freely?
May I venture to ask what inference you would draw from that?
Might I suggest an alternative?
Most dangerous!
My attitude would be one of disapproval
My confidence in you is absolute
My idea of it is quite the reverse
My information is rather scanty
My meaning is quite the contrary
My point of view is different, but I shall not insist upon it
My views are altered in many respects

N

No, I am speaking seriously
No, I don't understand it
Not at all
Not to my knowledge
Nothing could be more delightful
Now is it very plain to you?
Now you are flippant

O

Obviously the matter is settled
Of course, but that again isn't the point
Of course I am delighted

Of course I don't want to press you against your will
Of course you will do what you think best
Oh, certainly, if you wish it
Oh, do not form an erroneous impression
Oh, I appreciate that in you!
Oh, that's mere quibbling
Oh, that's splendid of you!
Oh, that was a manner of speaking
Oh, yes, I quite admit that
Oh, yes, you may take that for granted
Oh, you are very bitter
Oh, you may be as scornful as you like
On the contrary, I agree with you thoroughly
On the face of it, it sounds reasonable
One assumption you make I should like to contest
One has no choice to endure it
One must be indulgent under the circumstances
One thing I beg of you

P

Pardon me, but I don't think so
Pardon me, I meant something different
Perhaps I am indiscreet
Perhaps not in the strictest sense
Perhaps you do not feel at liberty to do so
Perhaps you think me ungrateful
Personally I confess to an objection

Please continue to be frank
Please do not think I am asking out of mere curiosity
Please forgive my thoughtlessness
Please make yourself at home
Pray don't apologize
Pray forgive me for intruding on you so unceremoniously
Pray go on!
Precisely, that is just what I meant
Put in that way it certainly sounds very well

Q

Question me, if you wish
Quibbling, I call it
Quite so
Quite the wisest thing you can do

R

Rather loquacious, I think
   [loquacious = very talkative]
Reading between the lines
Really? I should have thought otherwise
Really—you must go?
Reassure me, if you can
Reflect upon the possible consequences
Relatively speaking
Reluctantly I admit it

Reverting to another matter

S

Shall we have a compact?
She has an extraordinary gift of conversation
She is easily prejudiced
She seems uncommonly appreciative
She will be immensely surprised
Show me that the two cases are analogous
So far so good
So I inferred
So much the better for me
So you observe the transformation?
Something amuses you
Sometimes the absurdity of it occurs to me
Speaking with all due respect
Still, you might make an exception
Strangely it's true
Such conduct seems to me unjustifiable
Surely there can be no question about that
Surely we can speak frankly
Surely you sound too harsh a note
Surely you would not countenance that

T

Tell me in what way you want me to help you

Thank you for telling me that
Thank you for your good intentions
That, at least, you will agree to
That depends on one's point of view
That doesn't sound very logical
That is a counsel of perfection
That is a fair question, perhaps
That is a question I have often proposed to myself
That is a stroke of good fortune
That is a superb piece of work
That is a very practical explanation
That is admirably clear
That is certainly ideal
That is eminently proper
That is hardly consistent
That is inconceivable
That is just like you, if you will forgive me for saying so
That is most fortunate
That is most kind of you
That is most unexpected and distressing
That is not fair—to me
That is not to be lightly spoken of
That is precisely what I mean
That is quite true, theoretically
That is rather a difficult question to answer
That is rather a strange request to make
That is rather awkward
That is really good of you

That is the prevailing idea
That is tragic
That is true and I think you are right
That is very amiable in you
That is very curious
That is very felicitous
That is very gracious
That is what I call intelligent criticism
That is what I meant to tell you
That is a humiliating thought
That is a most interesting idea
That is such a hideous idea
That is the most incredible part of it
That might involve you in life-long self-reproach
That must be exceedingly tiresome
That ought to make you a little lenient
That reassures me
That shows the infirmity of his judgment
That theory isn't tenable
That was exceedingly generous
That was intended ironically
That was very thoughtful of you
That was very well reasoned
That will blast your chances, I am afraid
That will suit me excellently
That would be somewhat serious
That would be very discreditable
The agreement seems to be ideal

The idea is monstrous

The inference is obvious

The notion is rather new to me

The pleasure is certainly not all on your side

The reason is not so far to seek

The same problem has perplexed me

The sentiment is worthy of you

The simplest thing in the world

The situation is uncommonly delicate

The story seems to me incredible

The subject is extremely interesting

The tone of it was certainly hostile

The very obvious moral is this

The whole thing is an idle fancy

Then I have your permission?

Then you're really not disinclined?

Then you merely want to ask my advice?

There are endless difficulties

There are reasons which make such a course impossible

There is a good deal of sense in that

There is a grain of truth in that, I admit

There is food for reflection in that

There is my hand on it

There is no resisting you

There is nothing I should like so much

There is one inevitable condition

There is something almost terrifying about it

There must be extenuating circumstances

They amuse me immensely
This is a most unexpected pleasure
This is charmingly new to me
This is indeed good fortune
This is really appalling
This is really not a laughing matter
Those are my own private feelings
Those things are not forgotten at once
To me it's simply outrageous
To speak frankly, I do not like it
True, I forgot!

U

Undeniably true
Unfortunately I must decline the proposal
Unlikely to be so
Unquestionably superior
Unwholesome influence, I would say

V

Very good, I'll do so
Very well, I will consent
Vivacity is her greatest charm
Virtually accomplished, I believe
Vouch for its truth

W

We are all more or less susceptible

We are drifting away from our point

We are impervious to certain rules

We are merely wasting energy in this duel

We can safely take it for granted

We couldn't have a better topic

We had better agree to differ

We have had some conclusions in common

We must judge it leniently

We must not expose ourselves to misinterpretation

We owe you a debt of gratitude

We shall be glad to see you, if you care to come

We will devoutly hope not

Well, as a matter of fact, I have forgotten

Well done! I congratulate you

Well, I'm not going to argue that

Well, I call it scandalous

Well, I confess they don't appeal to me

Well, more's the pity

Well, perhaps it is none of my affair

Well, that is certainly ideal!

Well, this is good fortune

Well, yes—in a way

Well, you are a dreamer!

What a beautiful idea

What a charming place you have here

What a curious coincidence!

What a pretty compliment!

What a tempting prospect!

What an extraordinary idea!

What are your misgivings?

What can you possibly mean?

What conceivable reason is there for it?

What do you imagine my course should be?

What do you propose?

What is the next step in your argument?

What is there so strange about that?

What, may I ask, is your immediate object?

What unseemly levity on his part

What very kind things you say to me

What would you expect me to do?

What you have just said is even truer than you realize

What you propose is utterly impossible

Who is your sagacious adviser?
   [sagacious = sound judgment, wise]

Why ask such embarrassing questions?

Why did you desert us so entirely?

Why do you take it so seriously?

Will you allow me to ask you a question?

Will you be more explicit?

Will you have the kindness to explain?

Will you pardon my curiosity?

Will you permit me a brief explanation?

Would you apply that to everyone?
Would you mind telling me your opinion?

Y

Yes and no
Yes, but that is just what I fail to comprehend
Yes, I dare say
Yes, if you will be so good
Yes, it was extraordinarily fine
Yes, that is my earnest wish
Yes, that's undeniable
Yes? You were saying?
You agree with me, I know
You are a profound philosopher
You are a severe critic
You are delightfully frank
You are greatly to be envied
You are heartily welcome
You are incomprehensible
You are incorrigible
You are kind and comforting
You are most kind
You are not consistent
You are not serious, I hope
You are not seriously displeased with me?
You are quite delightful
You are rather puzzling to-day

You are right to remind me of that

You are unduly distressing yourself

You are very complimentary

You are very gracious

You're so tremendously kind about it

You're succeeding admirably

You're taking it all much too seriously

You're talking nonsense!

You're very good, I'm sure

You ask me—but I shouldn't wonder if you knew better than I do

You astonish me greatly

You behaved with great forbearance

You can hardly be serious

You cannot regret it more than I do

You could not pay me a higher compliment

You did it excellently

You did not clearly understand what I meant

You don't seem very enthusiastic

You excite my curiosity

You flatter my judgment

You have a genius for saying the right thing

You have asked me a riddle

You have asked the impossible

You have been wrongly informed

You have done me a great service

You have had a pleasant time, I hope

You have my deepest sympathy

You have my unbounded confidence
You have received a false impression
You have such an interesting way of putting things
You interest me deeply
You judge yourself too severely
You know I'm in an agony of curiosity
You know I'm not given to sentimentality
You know the familiar axiom
You leave no alternative
You look incredulous
You may be sure of my confidence
You may rely on me absolutely
You might make an exception
You must have misunderstood me
You must not fail to command me
You overwhelm me with your kindness
You really insist upon it?
You rebuke me very fairly
You say that as though you were surprised
You see how widely we differ
You see, it's all very vague
You see things rose-colored
You seem to be in a happy mood
You seem to take a very mild interest in what I propose
You shock me more than I can say
You speak in enigmas
You speak with authority
You surely understand my position

You take a great deal for granted
You take a pessimistic view of things
You take me quite by surprise
You will admit I have some provocation
You will become morbid if you are not careful
You will have ample opportunity
You will, of course, remember the incident
You will please not be flippant
You will understand my anxiety
Your argument is facile and superficial
Your consideration is entirely misplaced
Your judgments are very sound
Your logic is as clever as possible
Your opinion will be invaluable to me
Your request is granted before it is made
Your statement is somewhat startling

SECTION X

PUBLIC SPEAKING PHRASES

A

A fact of vast moment

A few words will suffice to answer

A further objection is

A great many people have said

A little indulgence may be due to those

A majority of us believe

A man in my situation has

A more plausible objection is found

A proof of this is

A servile mind can never know

A short time since

A specific answer can be given

A thought occurred to me

Able men have reasoned out

Above all things, let us not forget

Absolutely true it is

Abundant reason is there

Accordingly by reason of this circumstance

Add this instance to
After a careful study of all the evidence
After full deliberation
After reminding the hearer
After this it remains only to say
Again, can we doubt
Again, I ask the gentleman
Again, in this view
Again, it is quite clear that
Again, it is urged
Again, let us compare
Again, very numerous are the cases
Again, we have abundant instances
Against all this concurring testimony
All confess this to be true
All I ask is
All of us know
All that I will say now
All the facts which support this
All the signs of the time indicate
All these things you know
All this being considered
All this is historical fact
All this is very well
All this suggests
All this we take for granted
Allow me for a moment to turn to
Allow me to tell a story

Altho I say it to myself
Amazing as it may seem
Am I mistaken in this
Among many examples
Among the distinguished guests who honor
Among the problems that confront us
An answer to this is now ready
An argument has often been put forward
An example or two will illustrate
An indescribably touching incident
An opinion has now become established
And again, it is said
And again, it is to be presumed
And coming nearer to our own day
And did a man try to persuade me
And do you really think
And everybody here knows
And for myself, as I said
And further, all that I have said
And hence the well-known doctrine
And here again, when I speak
And here allow me to call your attention
And here I am led to observe
And here I come to the closing evidence
And here I have an opportunity
And here I reproach
And here I wish you to observe
And here let me define my position

And here let me give my explanation
And here let us recall to mind
And how is it possible to imagine
And I am bound to say
And I beg of you
And I call on you
And I might say this
And I refuse assent
And I rejoice to know
And I say, it were better for you
And I should in like manner repudiate
And I speak with reverence
And I submit to you
And I trust that you will consider
And I will make a practical suggestion
And I will tell you why
And I would, moreover submit
And if a man could anywhere be found
And if any of you should question
And if I know anything of my countrymen
And if I may presume to speak
And if I take another instance
And if this be true
And if you come to a decision
And if you think it your duty
And in conclusion
And in like manner
And in order to see this

And in thus speaking, I am not denying
And is not this lamentable
And is there not a presumption
And it happens
And it is certainly true
And it is doubtful if
And it is not difficult to see
And it is not plain
And it is one of the evidences
And it is precisely in this
And it is strikingly suggested to us
And it is undeniable, I say
And it is well that this should be so
And last of all
And lest anyone should marvel
And let it be observed
And lo! and behold
And more than this
And next I would ask
And now allow me to call attention
And now behold a mystery
And now consider
And now having discussed
And now I beg that I may be permitted
And now I go back to the statement
And now I have completed my review
And now I have said enough to explain
And now I must touch upon one point

And now if I may take for granted
And now it would be very pleasant for me
And now observe how
And now, sir, what I had first to say
And now supposing this point to be settled
And now that I have mentioned
And now the chief points of it
And now the question is asked me
And now, to close, let me give you
And now, to what purpose do I mention
And, of course, you are aware
And of this I am perfectly certain
And quite as difficult is it to create
And right here lies the cause
And, sir, a word
And so, again, as regard
And so I am reminded of a story
And so I leave these words with you
And so I may point out
And so I might recount to you
And so, in the other cases, I have named
And so in the present case
And so on
And so through all phases
And so, upon every hand
And sometimes it will be difficult
And that gave another distorted view
And the reason is very obvious

And the same holds good
And then again
And then hastily to conclude
And then I may be reminded
And then there is another thought
And then when it is said
And there are reasons why
And there is also this view
And therefore am I truly glad
And therefore it is not unfrequently quoted
And therefore it is not without regret
And this brings me to the last thing
And this is really the sense
And this leads me to say a word
And thus consistently
And thus it is conceivable
And thus it seems to me
And thus we are led on then to further question
And to all this must be added
And to return to the topic
And to this conclusion you must come
And unquestionably
And we are brought to the same conclusion
And what do you suppose will be
And when I have shown to you
And when I recall that event
And when we pass beyond the bounds of
And where, let me ask

And why should I insist
And will you still insist
And with these thoughts come others
And yet I can not but reflect
And yet I feel justified in believing
And yet I think we all feel
And yet let me say to you
And yet one more quotation
And yet this notion is, I conceive
And yet though this be true
And yet we ought, if we are wise
And you may also remember this
Another circumstance that adds to the difficulty
Another consideration which I shall adduce
    [adduce = cite as an example]
Another instance of signal success
Another of these presumptions
Another point is made as clear as crystal
Another reason of a kindred nature
Another reflection which occurs to me
Another sign of our times
Another signal advantage
Another striking instance
Answers doubtless may be given
Are there not many of us
Are we content to believe
Are we forever to deprive ourselves
Are we not startled into astonishment

Are we satisfied to assume
As a general rule I hold
As a last illustration
As a matter of fact
As a proof of this
As an illustration of this truth
As briefly as I may
As far as my limits allow
As far as this is true
As far as this objection relates
As far as we know
As for the rest
As I have now replied to
As I look around on this assembly
As I rise to respond to the sentiment
As I understand this matter
As memory scans the past
As society is now constituted
As some one has well said
As the foregoing instances have shown
As to the particular instance before us
As well might we compare
As we shall see in a few moments
Assuredly it is this
At the outset of this inquiry
At the risk of digression
At the same time, I candidly state
At the utmost we can say

At this juncture
At this solemn moment
Away then with the notion

B

Be assured, then
Be confident, therefore
Be it so
Be not deceived
Be sure that in spite of
Be these things as they may
Be your interests what they may be
Bear with me for a few moments
Bearing on this point
Before attempting to answer this question
Before going further
Before I close I will particularly remark
Before I come to the special matter
Before I proceed to compare
Being fully of the opinion
Being persuaded then
Believing, as I do
Beyond all question we
Bidden by your invitation to a discussion
Broadly speaking
But, above all things, let us
But after all, I think no one can say

But again, when we carefully consider

But am I wrong in saying

But apart from the fact

But besides these special facts

But can this question

But depend upon it

But despite all this

But do not let us depend

But do you imagine

But doubts here arise

But even admitting these possibilities

But everyone who deserves

But first of all, remark, I beg you

But, further, I shall now demonstrate

But, gentlemen, I must be done

But grave problems confront us

But here I am discussing

But here let me say

But how can we pass over

But how shall I describe my emotions

But however that may be

But I am bound to say

But I am certain from my own experience

But I am very sorry to say

But I am willing enough to admit

But I can at least say

But I can not conceive

But I can promise

But I cherish the hope
But I confess that I should be glad
But I digress
But I do not propose all these things
But I do say this
But I have been insisting simply
But I have heard it argued
But I have no fear of the future
But I leave this train of thought
But I may be permitted to speak
But I may say in conclusion
But I need hardly assert
But I pass that over
But I propose to speak to you
But I repeat
But I resist the temptation
But I return to the question
But I shall go still further
But I simply ask
But I submit the whole subject
But I trust that you will all admit
But I venture to assure you
But I will allude
But I will not further impress any idea
But I would earnestly impress upon you
But if I may even flatter myself
But if I seek for illustrations
But if you want more evidence

But if you wish to know
But in making this assertion
But in my opinion there is no need
But in the course of time
But is it quite possible to hold
But is this any reason why
But it does not follow from this
But it happens very fortunately
But it has been suggested to me
But it is a fact
But it is impossible for one
But it is necessary to explain
But it is no use protesting
But it is not fair to assert
But it is not my intention
But it is not necessary to suppose
But it is not possible to believe
But it is not really so
But it is otherwise with
But it is sometimes said
But it may be doubted whether
But it may happen that I forgot
But it will be a misfortune
But it will naturally be asked
But it will perhaps be argued
But it would be vain to attempt
But let me ask you to glance
But let me before closing refer

But let none of you think
But let us also keep ever in mind
But let us look a little further
But lo! all of a sudden
But mark this
But more than all things else
But my allotted time is running away
But my answer to this objection
But, my friends, pause for a moment
But never was a grosser wrong
But not for one moment
But notwithstanding all this
But now look at the effect
But now take notice of
But on the other hand
But on what ground are we
But passing these by
But perhaps I ought to speak distinctly
But perhaps you are not yet weary
But putting these questions aside
But quite contrary to this, you will find
But recollect, I pray you, how
But, sir, it is manifest
But some other things are to be noted
But some will ask me
But sooner or later
But still, I repeat
But suppose the fact

But surely, you can not say
But that I may not divert you from
But that is not all
But that must be always the impression
But the fact is
But the final value
But the greatest proof of all
But the most formidable problem
But the necessity of the case
But the question may arise
But, then, let us ask ourselves
But there is another duty imposed
But there is much more than this
But this I do not hesitate to say
But this I fearlessly affirm
But this I know
But this is a circuitous argument
But this is no place for controversy
But this is not all
But this is what I mean
But this much I affirm as true
But this warns me
But this we may put aside
But to go still further
But to say the truth
But we are met with the assertion
But we are to recollect
But we ask, perhaps

But we may depend upon it
But we think it is not wise
But we want something more for explanation
But what a blunder would be yours
But what is the fact
But what we must needs guard against
But when it is declared
But when we look a little deeper
But while it may be admitted
But who has not seen
But why do I numerate these details
But with these exceptions
But yet nothing can be more splendid
But you should know
By no means
By the way, I have not mentioned
By this time it will be suspected

C

Can it be supposed
Can the long records of humanity teach us
Can there be a better illustration
Can we pretend
Can you lightly contemplate
Can you yield yourselves
Cautious and practical thinkers ask
Certain it is

Certainly I am not blind to the faults

Certainly, one can conceive

Clearly enough

Coming back to the main subject

Coming down to modern times

Coming to present circumstances

Common sense indicates

Consequently, I am not discussing this matter

Consider, I beg you, what

Contemplating these marvelous changes

D

Delude not yourselves with the belief

Depend upon it

Did it ever occur to you

Difficult then as the question may be

Do I need to describe

Do me the honor of believing

Do not imagine

Do not let us conceal from ourselves

Do not suppose for a moment

Do not talk to me of

Do not think me guilty of

Do we not know

Do what you will

Do you ask how that can be

Do you believe this can be truthfully said

Do you not know I am speaking of
Do you remember a concrete instance
Do you think, then
Does any man say
Does it ever occur to you
Does it not seem something like idiocy to
Does it not shock you to think
Does not the event show
Does not the nature of every man revolt
Doubtless the end is sought

E

Every now and then you will find
Every one has asked himself
Every one therefore ought to look to
Every reader of history can recall

F

Far from it
Few indeed there are
Few subjects are more fruitful
Few things impress the imagination more
Finally, it is my most fervent prayer
First in my thoughts are
First of all I ask
For, be assured of this

For behold

For I must tell you

For if any one thinks that there is

For, in truth, if you please to recollect

For instance, I can fancy

For is it not true

For it is not right to

For let it be observed first

For mark you

For my own part, I believe

For myself, certainly I think

For observe what the real fact is

For one I deny

For, perhaps, after all

For, perhaps, some one may say

For so it generally happens

For the sake of my argument

For this is what I say

For this reason, indeed, it is

For we all know

Fortunately for us

Fortunately I am not obliged

From one point of view we are

From the circumstances already explained

From the standpoint of

From this statement you will perceive

G

Generally speaking
God be praised
Grant this true
Granting all this

H

Had I time for all that might be said
Had my limits allowed it
Happily for us
Hardly less marvelous
Hardly will anyone venture to say
Have I exaggerated
Have you ever noticed
Having taken a view of
Having thus described what appears to me
He is the best prophet who
He seems at times to confuse
He was an eminent instance of
He who is insensible to
Hence arises a grave mischief
Hence, as I have said
Hence it follows
Here again the testimony corroborates
Here arises the eternal question

Here comes the practical matter
Here for a moment I seem
Here, however, it may be objected
Here I am considering
Here I end my illustrations
Here I must pause for a moment
Here I only insist upon
Here I ought to stop
Here is another strange thing
Here is good hope for us
Here is no question
Here let me meet one other question
Here, then, I am brought to the consideration
Here then I take up the subject
Here then is the key
Here, then, it is natural at last
Here then, we are brought to the question
Here, then, we are involved
Here undoubtedly it is
Here we can not but pause to contemplate
Here we come into direct antagonism with
Here we come to the very crux of
Here we have it on high authority
History is replete with predictions
Hitherto I have spoken only of
Holding this view, I am concerned
How can we help believing
How do you account for

How does it happen
How human language staggers when
How infinitely difficult it is
How infinitely superior must it appear
How is this to be explained
How many a time
How momentous, then
How much better, I say, if
How much more rational it would be
How shall I attempt to enumerate
How shall I describe to you
However, I am viewing the matter
However, I will not in any way admit
However, it is to me a very refreshing thing

I

I abide by my statement
I add a few suggestions
I adduce these facts
   [adduce = cite as an example]
I admire the main drift of
I admit, of course, at once
I admit the extreme complexity
I again ask
I allude to
I always delight to think
I always will assert the right to

I am a great admirer
I am a little at a loss to know
I am about to supplement
I am agitated by conflicting emotions
I am alarmed, indeed, when I see
I am also bound to say
I am also satisfied
I am apprehensive
I am asked to-night to propose
I am assured and fully believe
I am at a loss for adequate terms
I am bold to say
I am but saying
I am by no means certain
I am certain that you will give me credit
I am certainly in earnest sympathy
I am confronted by the hope
I am conscious of the fact
I am convinced by what I have seen
I am deeply imbued with the conviction
I am deeply insensible of the compliment
I am determined
I am even bold enough to hazard
I am exceeding my necessary limits
I am exceedingly glad of this opportunity
I am extremely obliged to you
I am familiar with
I am far from asserting

I am filled with admiration
I am firmly convinced
I am free to admit
I am fully convinced
I am giving voice to what you all feel
I am glad of this public opportunity
I am glad to answer to the toast
I am glad to express the belief
I am glad to notice
I am going to spare you and myself
I am grateful to you for this honor
I am greatly alarmed
I am greatly indebted to you
I am happy to be with you
I am here by the favor of your invitation
I am here the advocate of
I am here to introduce
I am in favor of
I am in sympathy with
I am inclined sometimes to believe
I am inclined to suspect
I am indebted for the honor
I am, indeed, most solicitous
I am informed
I am led on by these reflections
I am led to believe
I am mainly concerned
I am most deeply sensible of the welcome

I am most grateful for the opportunity
I am myself greatly indebted
I am nevertheless too sensible
I am not a stranger to
I am not at liberty to discuss
I am not at present concerned
I am not about to defend
I am not advocating
I am not altogether clear
I am not aware of a single instance
I am not blind to the faults of
I am not bold enough to
I am not catching at sharp arguments
I am not concerned to argue
I am not defending myself
I am not dreaming of denying
I am not going into vexed questions
I am not going to reproach
I am not here to defend
I am not insensible
I am not of those who pretend
I am not prepared to dispute the word
I am not presumptuous to assert
I am not proposing to set forth
I am not ripe to pass sentence
I am not so unreasonable as to tell you
I am not surprised
I am not taking into account

I am not unaware
I am not undertaking to deliver
I am now going to attempt
I am obliged to add
I am obliged to go still further
I am often reminded
I am old enough to remember
I am one of those who believe
I am only too sensible of the fact
I am perfectly willing to admit
I am persuaded
I am prepared to back that opinion by
I am privileged to speak to
I am quite conscious that
I am rather disposed to think
I am ready to do battle
I am reassured by the presence here
I am reluctantly but forcibly reminded
I am resolved not to permit
I am sensible, sir
I am simply endeavoring to show
I am so surrounded on every hand
I am sometimes inclined to think
I am somewhat relieved to know
I am sorry to say
I am suggesting the reason why
I am sure, at any rate
I am sure every impartial man will agree

I am sure I feel no hostility
I am sure that I echo the sentiment
I am sure this generous audience will pardon me
I am sure you all hope
I am sure you feel the truth
I am sure you will acquit me
I am sure you will be kind enough
I am sure you will do me the justice
I am sure you will not be surprised
I am surely not here to assert
I am tempted further to offer to you
I am thankful for the privilege
I am thoroughly convinced
I am to speak to you this evening
I am to urge the interest of
I am told occasionally
I am told on authority
I am too well aware of the difficulties
I am totally at a loss to conceive
I am trespassing too long on your time
I am unable to understand
I am unconscious of intentional error
I am under a very great obligation
I am under the deepest feeling of gratitude
I am under the impression
I am unwillingly bound to add
I am uttering no paradox when I say
I am very far from thinking.

FIFTEEN THOUSAND USEFUL PHRASES

I am very glad to have the honor
I am very happy to be here
I am very much in the condition of
I am very sure that if you ponder
I am very sure you will believe
I am well aware
I am willing to know
I anticipate with pleasing expectation
I appeal in the first place
I appeal to any man to say
I appeal to the better judgment
I appreciate the significance
I argue this cause
I ask again
I ask no greater blessing
I ask permission to speak to you
I ask the attention
I ask the audience
I ask the audience to return with me
I ask this of you
I ask you calmly and dispassionately
I ask you gentlemen, do you think
I ask you if it is possible
I ask you, if you please, to rise and give the toast
I ask you in all candor
I ask you now to follow me
I ask you to consider
I ask you to join me in drinking a toast

I ask you to pledge with me
I ask your attention
I ask your indulgence
I assert, sir, that it is
I assure myself
I assure you, of my own personal knowledge
I attribute it to
I avail myself of the opportunity
I beg again to thank you for the honor
I beg all to remember
I beg and implore of you
I beg emphatically to say
I beg leave to make some observations
I beg of you to remember
I beg to tender my most fervent wishes
I beg you not to mistake my meaning
I beg you to accept my grateful expression
I begin by observing
I begin with expressing a sentiment
I believe from my own personal experience
I believe I can speak for all
I believe I shall make it clear to you
I believe I voice the sentiment
I believe it to be the simple truth
I believe most profoundly
I believe that I am within the mark
I believe that in this instance
I bid you a most cordial and hearty welcome

I bow with you in reverent commemoration
I call on you to answer
I call to mind how
I can by no calculation justify
I call hardly conceive
I can make allowance for
I can most truthfully assure you
I call never sufficiently express my gratitude
I can not allow myself to believe
I can not avoid confessing
I can not be content with
I can not believe, I will not believe
I can not better illustrate this argument
I can not better sum up
I can not boast of
I can not bound my vision
I can not but reflect
I can not but see what mischief
I can not charge myself with
I can not close without giving expression
I can not conceive a greater honor
I can not feel any doubt myself
I can not forbear from offering
I can not give you a better illustration
I can not help expressing a wish
I can not help speaking urgently
I can not here go into details
I can not hesitate to say

I can not hope adequately to respond
I can not justly be responsible because
I can not let this opportunity pass
I can not persuade myself
I can not prevail on myself
I can not refrain from saying for myself
I can not resist the train of thought
I can not say how glad I am
I can not say with confidence
I can not stop to give in detail
I can not sufficiently thank you
I can not take back my word
I can not take it for granted
I can not thank you enough
I can not well avoid saying
I can only congratulate you
I can only hope for indulgence
I can readily understand
I can scarcely concede anything more important
I can scarcely find fitting words
I can strongly recommend
I can understand, moreover
I can with propriety speak here
I certainly have not so good an opinion
I challenge any man
I cheerfully own
I cheerfully submit myself
I claim a share also for

FIFTEEN THOUSAND USEFUL PHRASES

I class them altogether under the head
I close with the words
I close with this sentiment
I come at length to
I come next to the question of
I come to the other assumption
I conceive this to be
I confess I feel not the least alarmed
I confess I have had my doubts
I confess I have little sympathy
I confess it affects me very deeply to
I confess it is very difficult to
I confess that I do not entirely approve
I confess that it is a comfort to me
I confess that my notions are widely different
I confess to a little embarrassment
I confess to you that I have no fear
I confine myself to saying
I congratulate you upon the auspicious character
I consider I have said enough in proof
I consider it amply explains
I contend
I content myself with pursuing
I could do no less than
I could easily mention
I could enlarge upon it
I could never understand
I could wish that this belief

I dare say you know
I dare venture the remark
I declare to you
I deem it both necessary and just
I deem it proper here to remind
I deem myself honored
I deny, once and for all
I deny the inference
I desire to be brief
I desire to bear my testimony
I desire to call attention
I desire to know
I desire to lay emphatic stress
I dissent from the opinion
I distrust all general theories of
I do again and again urge upon you
I do, indeed, recollect
I do not absolutely assert
I do not advocate
I do not argue
I do not ask you to
I do not at this moment remember
I do not believe it possible
I do not belong to those who
I do not choose to consume
I do not complain of
I do not consider it necessary
I do not contend

FIFTEEN THOUSAND USEFUL PHRASES

I do not countenance for a moment
I do not deem it incumbent upon me
I do not depreciate for a moment
I do not desire to call in question
I do not desire to put too much emphasis
I do not despair of surmounting
I do not disguise the fact
I do not enter into the question
I do not fail to admire
I do not fear a contradiction
I do not feel at liberty
I do not forget the practical necessity
I do not hesitate to say
I do not imagine
I do not in the least degree
I do not indeed deny
I do not indulge in the delusion
I do not know how anyone can believe
I do not know whether you are aware of it
I do not know why
I do not know with what correctness
I do not mean anything so absurd
I do not mean now to go further than
I do not mean to impute
I do not merely urge
I do not mistrust
I do not myself pretend to be
I do not need to remind you

I do not, of course, deny
I do not pretend to argue
I do not propose to take up your time
I do not question for a moment
I do not recount all
I do not say anything about the future
I do not say this with any affectation
I do not see how it is possible
I do not see much difference between
I do not seek to palliate
I do not speak exclusively
I do not stop to discuss
I do not, therefore, wonder
I do not think it necessary to warn you
I do not think it possible
I do not think it unfair reasoning
I do not think myself obliged to dwell
I do not think that I need further discuss
I do not think this at all an exaggeration
I do not think we can go far wrong
I do not think you will often hear
I do not understand how it can apply
I do not vouch for
I do not want to discourage you
I do not wish to be considered egotistic
I do not wish to be misrepresented
I do not wonder
I doubt very much whether

I dwell with pleasure on the considerations

I earnestly maintain

I embrace with peculiar satisfaction

I end as I began

I entertain great apprehension for

I entertain no such chimerical hopes
    [chimerical = highly improbable]

I entertain the hope and opinion

I entirely dissent from the view

I especially hail with approval

I even add this

I even venture to deny

I fancy I hear you say

I fear I may seem trifling

I fear lest I may

I fearlessly appeal

I fearlessly challenge

I feel a great necessity to

I feel bound to add my expression

I feel constrained to declare

I feel entirely satisfied

I feel I have a right to say

I feel it a proud privilege

I feel keenly myself impelled by every duty

I feel only a great emotion of gratitude

I feel respect and admiration

I feel some explanation is due

I feel sure

I feel tempted to introduce here
I feel that I have a special right to
I feel that it is not true
I feel the greatest satisfaction
I feel the task is far beyond my power
I fervently trust
I find it difficult to utter in words
I find it more easy
I find my reference to this
I find myself called upon to say something
I find myself in the position of
I find no better example than
I find no fault with
I find numberless cases
I flatter myself
I, for my part, would rather
I, for one, greatly doubt
I forbear to inquire
I foresaw the consequence
I fully recognize
I gave notice just now
I give you, in conclusion, this sentence
I go further
I grant all this
I grant with my warmest admiration
I gratefully accept
I greatly deplore
I had a kind of hope

I had almost said

I had in common with others

I had occasion to criticize

I happen to differ

I hardly dare to dwell longer

I hardly know anything more strange

I hasten to concede

I have a dark suspicion

I have a great admiration for

I have a pleasing and personal duty

I have a profound pity for those

I have a right to consider

I have a strong belief

I have a very high respect for

I have abstained from

I have acquired some useful experience

I have all along implied

I have all but finished

I have already alluded to

I have already shown the ground of my hope

I have already stated, and now repeat

I have always been under the impression

I have always listened with the greatest satisfaction

I have always maintained

I have another objection

I have another observation to add

I have anticipated the objection

I have assumed throughout

I have attempted thus hastily
I have barely touched some of the points
I have been allowed the privilege
I have been asked several times
I have been extremely anxious
I have been given to understand
I have been glad to observe
I have been heretofore treating
I have been insisting then on this
I have been interested in hearing
I have been pointing out how
I have been profoundly moved
I have been requested to say a word
I have been told by an eminent authority
I have been too long accustomed to hear
I have been touched by the large generosity
I have been trying to show
I have before me the statistics
I have but one more word to add
I have demonstrated to you
I have depicted
I have endeavored to emphasize
I have enlarged on this subject
I have felt it almost a duty to
I have found great cause for wonder
I have frequently been surprised at
I have gazed with admiration
I have generally observed

I have gone so far as to suggest

I have good reason for

I have had steadily in mind

I have had the honor

I have had to take a long sweep

I have heard it objected

I have heard with relief and pleasure

I have hitherto been adducing instances
    [adduce = cite as an example]

I have hitherto been engaged in showing

I have in a measure anticipated

I have in my possession

I have incidentally dwelt on

I have introduced it to suggest

I have labored to maintain

I have laid much stress upon

I have lately observed many strong indications

I have listened with the utmost interest

I have little hope that I can add anything

I have lived to see

I have long ago insisted

I have long been of the conviction

I have never heard it suggested

I have never whispered a syllable

I have no acquaintance with

I have no doubt whatever

I have no excuse for intruding

I have no fear of myself

I have no fears for the success
I have no hesitation in asserting
I have no intention to moralize
I have no particular inclination
I have no prejudice on the subject
I have no pretention to be regarded
I have no reason to think
I have no scruple in saying
I have no such gloomy forebodings
I have no sympathy with the men
I have no thought of venturing to say
I have no wish at all to preach
I have not accustomed myself
I have not allowed myself
I have not been able to deny
I have not particularly referred to
I have not said anything yet
I have not the means of forming a judgment
I have not the right to reproach
I have not time to present
I have nothing more to say
I have noticed of late years
I have now explained to you
I have now made bold to touch upon
I have now rather more than kept my word
I have now said all that occurs to me
I have often been impressed with
I have often been struck with the resemblance

I have often lingered in fancy

I have one step farther to go

I have only partially examined

I have partly anticipated

I have pleasant memories of

I have pointed out

I have pride and pleasure in quoting

I have racked this brain of mine

I have read with great regret

I have said and I repeat

I have said over and over again

I have said what I solemnly believe

I have scant patience

I have seen for myself

I have seen it stated in a recent journal

I have seen some signs of encouragement

I have shown

I have some sort of fear

I have sometimes asked myself

I have sometimes fancied

I have sometimes wondered whether

I have still two comments to make

I have taken pains to know

I have the confident hope

I have the greatest possible confidence

I have the honor to propose

I have then to investigate

I have thought it incumbent on me

I have thought it right on this day
I have thought it well to suggest
I have throughout highly appreciated
I have thus been led by my feelings
I have thus stated the reason
I have to confess with a feeling of melancholy
I have to force my imagination
I have touched very cursorily
I have tried to convey to you
I have undertaken to speak
I have very much less feeling of
I have watched with some attention
I have witnessed the extraordinary
I have yet a more cogent reason
I have yet to learn
I hazard nothing in saying
I hear it sometimes said
I hear you say to yourselves
I heartily feel the singular claims
I hesitate to take an instance
I hold it to be clearly expedient
I hold myself obliged to
I hold the maxim no less applicable
I hold this to be a truth
I hold to the principle
I hope by this time we are all convinced
I hope for our own sakes
I hope I have expressed myself explicitly

I hope I may be allowed to intimate
I hope I shall not be told
I hope it is no disparagement
I hope most sincerely and truly
I hope none who hear me
I hope not to occupy more than a few minutes
I hope that I shall not be so unfortunate
I hope the day may be far distant
I hope the time may come again
I hope to be excused if
I hope to be forgiven if
I hope we may forget
I hope you will not accuse me
I imagine that no one will be disposed
I insist upon it
I intend to propose
I know from experience how
I know full well
I know I am treading on thin ice
I know it has been questioned
I know it is said
I know it will be said
I know many reasons why
I know not how else to express
I know not in what direction to look
I know not of my own knowledge
I know not where else to find
I know perfectly well

I know that it is impossible for me to
I know that this is the feeling
I know that what I may say is true
I know there are some who think
I know there is a theory among us
I know too well
I know very well the difference between
I know well it is not for me
I know well the sentiments
I know you are all impatient to hear
I know you will do all in your power
I know you will interpret what I say
I labor under a degree of prejudice
I lately heard it affirmed
I lay it down as a principle
I leave history to judge
I leave it to you
I leave the arduous task
I leave to others to speak
I long to speak a word or two
I look hopefully to
I look in vain
I look with encouragement
I look with inexpressible dread
I look with mingled hope and terror
I make my appeal to
I make no extravagant claim
I make this abrupt acknowledgment

I marvel that
I may add, speaking for my own part
I may be allowed to make one remark
I may be permitted to add
I may confess to you
I may safely appeal
I may say to you calmly
I may seem to have been diffuse
I may take as an instance
I may venture upon a review
I mean by this
I mean, moreover
I mean something more than that
I mention it to you to justify
I mention these facts because
I mention this, not by way of complaint
I might bring you another such case
I might deny that
I might enter into such detail
I might go further
I might go on indefinitely
I might go on to illustrate
I might of course point first
I might reasonably question the justice
I might try to explain
I might venture to claim
I might well have desired
I might well think

I must ask an abrupt question
I must be careful about what I say
I must be contented with
I must be excused if I say
I must bow in reverence
I must call your attention for a moment
I must conclude abruptly
I must confess that I became rather alarmed
I must consider this as
I must crave your indulgence
I must express to you again
I must fairly tell you
I must find some fault with
I must for want of time omit
I must here admit
I must lament
I must leave any detailed development
I must mention with praise
I must not allow myself to indulge
I must not for an instant be supposed
I must not overlook
I must now beg to ask
I must pause a moment to
I must proceed
I must qualify the statement
I must remind my hearers of
I must reply to some observations
I must return to the subject

FIFTEEN THOUSAND USEFUL PHRASES

I must say that I am one of those
I must speak plainly
I must suppose, however
I must take occasion to say
I must thank you once more
I must try to describe to you
I myself have boundless faith
I need not assure this brilliant company
I need not dwell
I need not enter into
I need not follow out the application
I need not, I am certain, assure you
I need not say how much I thank you
I need not show how inconsistent
I need not specially recommend to you
I need not wander far in search
I need only to observe
I need say nothing in praise
I need scarcely observe
I need to guard myself right here
I neither affirm nor deny
I next come to the implicit assumption
I note with particular pleasure
I notice it as affording an instance
I noticed incidentally the fact
I now address you on a question
I now come, sir, to the second head
I now have the pleasure of presenting to you

I now pass to the question of
I now proceed to inquire
I now reiterate
I object strongly to the use
I observe, then, in the first place
I only ask a favorable construction of
I only marvel
I only wish you to recognize
I open the all-important question
I ought to give an illustration
I own I can not help feeling
I particularly allude to
I pass on from that
I pass then to our second division
I pause for a moment to say
I pause to confess once more
I pay tribute to
I personally know that it is so
I pray God I may never
I predict that you will
I prefer a practical view
I presume I shall have to admit
I presume that I shall not be disbelieved
I proceed to another important phase
I profess
I propose briefly to glance at
I propose, therefore to consider
I protest I never had any doubt

I purposely have avoided

I question whether

I quite endorse what has been said

I rather look forward to a time

I readily grant

I really can not think it necessary to

I really do not know

I really thought that you would excuse me

I recall another historical fact

I recognize the high compliment conveyed

I recollect hearing a sagacious remark
  [sagacious = sound judgment]

I refer especially

I refuse to believe

I regard as an erroneous view

I regard it as a tribute

I regard it as a very great honor

I regret that I am not able to remember

I regret that it is not possible for me

I regret the time limits me

I regret this the less

I rejoice in an occasion like this

I rejoice that events have occurred

I rejoice to think I remark here

I remember a reference made

I remember an intimation

I remember full well

I remember the enjoyment with which

I remember to have heard

I repeat, I am not speaking

I repeat my statement in another form

I respectfully counsel

I respectfully submit

I rest my opinion on

I rise in behalf

I rise to express my disapprobation
   [approbation = warm approval; praise]

I rise to thank you

I rise with some trepidation

I return, in conclusion, to

I return you my most grateful thanks

I said a little way back

I said it would be well

I said that I thought

I salute with profound reverence

I sanction with all my heart

I saw an ingenious argument the other day

I say frankly

I say in moderation

I say it is extremely important

I say it most confidently

I say no more of these things

I say not one syllable against

I say, then, my first point is

I say this is no disparagement of

I say this the more gladly

I say without fear of contradiction

I see around me

I see as clearly as any man possibly can

I see little hope of

I see no exception

I see no possibility of

I see no reason for doubting

I seem to hear you say

I seize upon this opportunity

I seriously desire

I set out with saying

I shall add a few words

I shall address myself to a single point

I shall ask you to look very closely

I shall be told

I shall best attain my object

I shall bestow a little attention upon

I shall certainly admit

I shall consider myself privileged

I shall desist from

I shall endeavor to be guided

I shall give it in the words of

I shall here briefly recite the

I shall here use the word to denote

I shall hope to interest you

I shall invite you to follow me

I shall just give the summary of

I shall never believe

I shall never cease to be grateful
I shall not acknowledge
I shall not attempt a detailed narrative
I shall not end without appealing
I shall not enlarge upon
I shall not force into the discussion
I shall not go so far as to say
I shall not hesitate to say something
I shall not tax your patience
I shall not undertake to prophesy
I shall not weary your patience
I shall now give you some instances
I shall now proceed to show
I shall often have to advert to
I shall pass by all this
I shall presently show
I shall proceed without further preface
I shall recur to certain questions
I shall say all this without entering into
I shall show that I am not
I shall speak first about
I shall speak with becoming frankness
I shall take a broader view of the subject
I shall take it for granted here
I shall therefore endeavor
I shall touch upon one or two questions
I shall waste no time in refuting
I shall with your sanction

I should be false to my own manhood
I should be surprised if
I should be the last man to deny
I should fail in my duty if
I should find it hard to discover
I should have forfeited my own self-respect
I should like at least to mention
I should like to emphasize
I should like to go a step farther
I should like to refer to two events
I should like to see that view answered
I should like to-day to examine briefly
I should much prefer
I should not be satisfied with myself
I should think it too absurd
I shrink from the contemplation
I shudder at the doctrine
I simply lay my finger on a fact
I simply pause here to ask
I sincerely regret the absence
I sincerely wish it were in my power
I solemnly declare
I sometimes hear a wish expressed
I sorrowfully call to mind
I speak forth my sentiment
I speak from no little personal observation
I speak of this to show
I speak the fact when I tell you

I speak the secret feeling of this company
I speak what I know when I say
I speak wholly without authority
I speak with feeling upon this point
I speak with some degree of encouragement
I speak with the utmost sincerity
I speak within the hearing of
I stand in awed amazement before
I stand in the midst of men
I still view with respect
I submit it to every candid mind
I submit that in such a case
I submit that it is high time
I submit this proposition
I summon you to do your share
I suppose it is right to answer
I suppose it to be entirely true
I suppose most men will recollect
I suppose that everyone who listens to me
I suppose there is no one here
I suppose we are all of one opinion
I suspect that is why we so often
I sympathize most heartily
I take a broader and bolder position
I take it for granted
I take leave to say
I take one picture as an illustration
I take pleasure in saying

FIFTEEN THOUSAND USEFUL PHRASES

I take the liberty of observing
I take this instance at random
I take two views of
I tell him in reply
I tell you, gentlemen
I tender my thanks to you
I thank you for having allowed me
I thank you for the appreciative tone
I thank you for the honor
I thank you for your most generous greeting
I thank you for your thoughtful courtesy
I thank you from the bottom of my heart
I thank you very gratefully
I thank you very sincerely for the honor
I think I am correct in saying
I think I am not the first to utter
I think I can claim a purpose
I think I can sincerely declare
I think I have a right to look upon
I think I have rightly spoken
I think I might safely say
I think I need not say more
I think it is not too much to say
I think it is quite right
I think it may be necessary to consider
I think it might be said with safety
I think it my duty to
I think it observable

I think it probable
I think it will astonish you
I think it will be granted
I think no Wise man can be indifferent
I think, on the contrary
I think something may be said in favor of
I think that all will agree
I think that I can explain
I think that I can venture to say
I think that, in these last years
I think that none of us will deny
I think there is no better evidence
I think there is no call on me to listen
I think we are justified
I think we can hardly hope
I think we may all easily see
I think we may ask in reply
I think we may safely conclude
I think we may say, therefore
I think we may well be proud of
I think we may well congratulate each other
I think we must draw a distinction
I think we need neither doubt nor fear
I think we ought to recur a moment to
I think we shall all recognize
I think we should do well to call to mind
I think we take too narrow a view
I think when we look back upon

I think you may well rejoice in
I think you will all agree
I think you will pardon my saying
I think you will see
I thus explicitly reply
I tremble at the task
I tremble to think
I trust I may be indulged
I trust it is not presumptuous
I trust that as the years roll on
I trust that I shall have the indulgence
I trust that this will not be regarded as
I turn, gentlemen, to the case
I use the word advisedly
I use the word in the sense
I use very plain language
I utter this word with the deepest affection
I value very much the honor
I venture to ask permission
I venture to say
I verily believe
I very confidently submit
I view that prospect with the greatest misgiving
I want to bespeak your attention
I want to know the character
I want to make some simple applications
I want to say just a few words
I want to say one word more

I want to say to you seriously
I want to think with you
I warn and exhort you
I was astonished to learn
I was constantly watchful to
I was exceedingly interested
I was honored with the acquaintance
I was lost in admiration
I was not slow to accept and believe
I was not without some anxiety
I was overwhelmed
I was sincerely astonished
I was very much interested
I was very much thrilled
I well recollect the time
I well remember an occasion
I will accept the general proposition
I will add the memorable words
I will ask the indulgence
I will ask you to accompany me
I will ask you to bear witness
I will dwell a little longer
I will endeavor in a brief way
I will endeavor to illustrate
I will endeavor to show you
I will enlarge no further
I will even express a hope at the outset
I will even go further and say

FIFTEEN THOUSAND USEFUL PHRASES

I will first call your attention to
I will give one more illustration
I will illustrate this point by
I will merely mention
I will neither affirm nor deny
I will not allude
I will not argue this
I will not attempt to note
I will not be content until
I will not condescend to
I will not enumerate at present
I will not pause to maintain
I will not positively say
I will not pretend to inquire into
I will not quarrel with
I will not relinquish the confidence
I will not repeat the arguments here
I will not try to gauge
I will now consider with you
I will now leave this question
I will now take an instance
I will only speak to one point
I will only sum up my evidence
I will only take an occasion to express
I will only venture to remind you
I will point out to your attention
I will say at once
I will speak but a word or two more

I will speak plainly
I will state with perfect distinctness
I will suppose the objection to be
I will take one more instance
I will take the precaution to add
I will tell you what I think of
I will try to make the thing intelligible
I will venture a single remark
I will venture to add
I will venture to express the hope
I will yield the whole question
I willingly admit
I wish also to declare positively
I wish at the outset
I wish emphatically to reaffirm
I wish I had the time and the power
I wish it first observed
I wish rather to call your attention
I wish, sir, that justice might be done
I wish to ask if you honestly and candidly believe
I wish to be allowed to enforce in detail
I wish to begin my statement
I wish to confine what I have to say
I wish to do full justice to
I wish to draw your attention
I wish to express my profound gratification
I wish to give these arguments their full weight
I wish to know whether

I wish to offer a few words relative to
I wish to remind you in how large a degree
I wish to say a word or two
I wish to state all this as a matter of fact
I wish you success and happiness
I wish you to observe
I would also gratefully acknowledge
I would as soon believe
I would desire to speak simply and directly
I would enter a protest
I would further point out to you
I would have you understand
I would infinitely rather
I would like to say one word just here
I would not be understood as belittling
I would not dwell upon that matter if
I would not push the suggestion so far
I would now gladly lay before you
I would rather a thousand times
I would recommend to your consideration
I would suggest first of all
I would that my voice could reach the ear
I would urge and entreat you
I would urge upon you
I would venture to point out
I yielded to the earnest solicitations
If any man be so persuaded
If anyone could conceive

If anyone is so dim of vision
If any other answer be made
If at first view this should seem
If, however, you determine to
If I am asked for the proof
If I am wrong
If I can carry you with me
If I can succeed in describing
If I could find words
If I have done no more than view the facts
If I have in any way deserved
If I may be allowed a little criticism
If I may be allowed modestly to suggest
If I may be allowed to refer
If I may reverently say so
If I may say so without presumption
If I may so speak
If I may take for granted
If I may venture to say anything
If I mistake not the sentiment
If I recollect aright
If I understand the matter at all
If I venture a few remarks
If I were asked
If I were to act upon my conviction
If I were to recapitulate
If I wished to prove my contention
If, in consequence we find it necessary

If in the glow of conscious pride
If in the years of the future
If it be difficult to appreciate
If it be so
If it be true
If it is contended
If it means anything, it means this
If more were needed to illustrate.
If my opinions are true
If on the contrary, we all foresee
If, on the other hand, I say
If one seeks to measure
If only we go deep enough
If still you have further doubt
If the bare facts were studied
If the experience of the world is worth anything
If, then, I am asked
If, then, I should here rest my cause
If there be any among us
If there be one lesson more than another
If this be so
If this seems doubtful to anyone
If, unhappily, the day should ever come
If we accept at all the argument
If we are not blind to
If we are rightly informed
If we are to reason on the fact
If we cast our glance back

If we embark upon a career
If we had the whole case before us
If we isolate ourselves
If we may trust to experience
If we pursue a different course
If we pursue our inquiries through
If we sincerely desire
If we survey
If we would not be beguiled
If what has been said is true
If you remain silent
If you seek the real meaning of
If you think for a moment
If you want to look
If you were asked to point out
If you will allow me to prophesy
If you will forgive me the expression
If you wish for a more interesting example
If you wish to get at the bottom of facts
If you would see the most conclusive proof
If your view is right
In a significant paragraph
In a wider sense
In a word, gentlemen
In a word, I conceive
In actual life, I suspect
In addition to these arguments
In addressing myself to the question

In addressing you I feel
In agreement with this obvious conclusion
In all ages of the world
In all or any of these views
In all times and places
In an unguarded moment
In answering the inquiry
In any view of the case
In closing my speech, I ask each of you
In conclusion, let me say
In conclusion, may I repeat
In consequence it becomes a necessity
In contemplating the causes
In days to come
In examining this part of the subject
In fine, it is no extravagance to say
In former ages and generations
In further illustration
In further proof of my assertion
In illustration of what I have said
In like manner are to be explained
In like manner I would advise
In listening to the kind words
In looking about me
In many instances
In meeting this difficulty, I will not urge
In most cases I hold
In my estimation

In my humble opinion
In my view
In offering to you these counsels
In one other respect
In one point I wish no one to mistake me
In one sense this is undoubtedly true
In order to appreciate the force of
In order to complete the proof
In order to do justice to the question
In order to prove plainly and intelligibly
In order to realize adequately
In other words
In our estimate of the past
In point of fact
In precisely the same way
In pursuance of these views
In pursuing the great objects
In regard to
In rising to return my sincere thanks
In saying all of this, I do not forget
In saying this, I am not disposed to deny
In short, I say
In solving this difficulty
In something of a parallel way
In spite of the fact
In such cases, strictly speaking
In support of this assertion
In that matchless epitome

FIFTEEN THOUSAND USEFUL PHRASES

In that mood of high hope
In the anomalies of fortune
In the course of these remarks
In the existing circumstances
In the first place, therefore, I consider
In the first place we see
In the first place, we should be all agreed
In the fullest sense
In the fullness of time
In the last suggestion
In the meantime I will commend to you
In the next place, be assured
In the presence of this vast assembly
In the present situation
In the progress of events
In the remarks I have made
In the same manner I rely
In the second place it is quite clear
In the suggestion I have made
In the very brief space at our disposal
In these extraordinary circumstances
In these sentiments I agree
In this brief survey
In this connection, I may be permitted to refer
In this connection I remind myself
In this necessarily brief and imperfect review
In this rapid and slight enumeration
In this respect

In this sense only
In this there is no contradiction
In very many instances
In very truth
In view of these reflections
In what has now been said
In what I have now further to say
In widening our view
Indeed, can anyone tell me
Indeed, I am not convinced
Indeed, I can not do better
Indeed, I have heard it whispered
Indeed, I may fairly say
Indeed, it will generally be found
Indeed we know
Instances abound
Is it logically consistent
Is it not legitimate to recognize
Is it not marvelous
Is it not obvious
Is it not quite possible
Is it not, then, preposterous
Is it not universally recognized
Is it not wise to argue
Is it possible, can it be believed
Is it, then, any wonder
Is not that the common sentiment
Is there any evidence here

FIFTEEN THOUSAND USEFUL PHRASES

Is there any language of reproach

Is there any possibility of mistaking

Is there any reason in the world

It affords me gratification

It also pleases me very much

It amounts to this

It appears from what has been said

It appears to me, on the contrary

It can rightly be said

It certainly follows, then

It comes to this

It could not be otherwise

It does not necessarily follow

It exhibits a state of mind

It follows as a matter of course

It follows inevitably

It gives us an exalted conception

It grieves me to relate

It hardly fits the character

It has at all times been a just reproach

It has been a very great pleasure for me

It has been generally assumed

It has been justly objected

It has been my privilege

It has been suggested fancifully

It has been well said

It has ever been my ambition

It has struck me very forcibly

It is a circumstance of happy augury
  [augury = sign of something coming; omen]

It is a common error

It is a curious trait

It is a fact well known

It is a falsehood to say

It is a familiar charge against

It is a good augury of success
  [augury = sign of something coming; omen]

It is a great pleasure to me

It is a living truth

It is a matter of absorbing interest

It is a matter of amusement

It is a matter of fact

It is a matter of just pride

It is a melancholy story

It is a memory I cherish

It is a mischievous notion

It is a mistake to suppose

It is a most extraordinary thing

It is a most pertinent question

It is a noble thing

It is a peculiar pleasure to me

It is a perversion of terms

It is a pleasing peculiarity

It is a popular idea

It is a rare privilege

It is a recognized principle

It is a remarkable and striking fact

It is a strange fact

It is a sure sign

It is a theme too familiar

It is a thing commonly said

It is a touching reflection

It is a true saying

It is a very significant fact

It is a vision which still inspires us

It is a wholesome symptom

It is, all things considered, a fact

It is all very fine to think

It is all very well to say

It is almost proverbial

It is also possible

It is also probably true

It is always pleasant to respond

It is amazing how little

It is an easy matter

It is an egregious mistake
  [egregious = conspicuously and outrageously reprehensible]

It is an established rule

It is an incredible thing

It is an interesting fact

It is an unforgivable offense

It is an unquestionable truth

It is appropriate that we should celebrate

It is asserted

It is assumed as an axiom
It is at once inconsistent
It is but fair to say
It is but too true
It is by no means my design
It is certainly especially pleasant
It is certainly remarkable
It is common in these days to lament
It is commonly assumed
It is comparatively easy
It is curious sophistry
It is curious to observe
It is desirable for us
It is difficult for me to respond fitly
It is difficult to avoid saying
It is difficult to describe
It is difficult to overstate
It is difficult to put a limit
It is difficult to surmise
It is doubtful whether
It is easy enough to add
It is easy to instance cases
It is easy to understand
It is eminently proper
It is every man's duty to think
It is evident that the answer to this
It is evidently supposed by many people
It is exceedingly gratifying to hear

It is exceedingly unfortunate
It is fair that you should hear
It is fair to suppose
It is far from me to desire
It is fatal to suppose
It is fitting
It is for me to relate
It is for others to illustrate
It is for this reason
It is for us to ask
It is greatly assumed
It is gratifying to have the honor
It is hardly for me
It is hardly necessary to pass judgment
It is idle to think of
It is immaterial whether
It is impossible to avoid saying
It is in every way appropriate
It is in the highest degree worthy
It is in this characteristic
It is in vain
It is in your power to give
It is indeed a strange doctrine
It is indeed not a little remarkable
It is indeed true
It is indeed very clear
It is indispensable to have
It is interesting and suggestive

It is interesting to know

It is just so far true

It is likewise necessary

It is made evident

It is manifest

It is manifestly absurd to say

It is merely common sense to say

It is more than probable

It is my agreeable duty

It is my belief

It is my earnest wish

It is my grateful duty to address you

It is my hope

It is my present purpose

It is natural to ask the question

It is necessary to refer

It is necessary to take some notice

It is needful to a complete understanding

It is needless before this audience to repeat

It is no doubt true

It is no exaggeration to say

It is no part of my business

It is no significant thing

It is no small indication

It is no wonder

It is not a practical question

It is not altogether satisfactory

It is not an unknown occurrence

It is not by any means
It is not difficult to comprehend
It is not difficult to discern
It is not easy for me to find words
It is not enough to say
It is not entirely clear to me
It is not evident
It is not for me on this occasion
It is not given to many men
It is not likely that any of you
It is not logical to say
It is not my intention to enter into
It is not my purpose to discuss
It is not necessarily true
It is not necessary for me even to sketch
It is not necessary for our purpose
It is not often in these modern days
It is not ours to pronounce
It is not out of place to remind you
It is not possible to recount
It is not quite clear
It is not to me so very surprising
It is not too much to say
It is not unknown to you
It is not within the scope of this address
It is now high time for me
It is now perfectly plain
It is observable enough

It is obvious

It is of course difficult

It is of great importance to show

It is of no moment

It is of very little importance

It is often remarked

It is on these grounds

It is one of the burning questions of the day

It is one of the most natural visions

It is one of the most significant things

It is one of the queerest freaks of fate

It is only a few short years since

It is only just to say

It is our duty to examine

It is ours to bear witness

It is owing to this truth

It is peculiarly befitting at this time

It is perfectly apparent

It is pitiable to reflect

It is pleasant to meet this brilliant company

It is rather a pleasant coincidence

It is rather an arduous task

It is rather startling

It is related

It is ridiculous to say

It is said, and I think said truly

It is said to be impossible

It is satisfactory to notice

FIFTEEN THOUSAND USEFUL PHRASES

It is scarcely necessary to insist

It is scarcely questioned

It is self-evident

It is sometimes hard to determine

It is still an open question

It is still more surprising

It is substantially true

It is surely necessary for me

It is the clear duty of

It is the doctrine of

It is the fashion to extol

It is the universal testimony

It is therefore evident

It is therefore necessary

It is this which lies at the foundation

It is to be expected

It is to be remembered

It is to me a very sincere satisfaction

It is told traditionally

It is too plain to be argued

It is true

It is unnecessary for me to remind you

It is upon this line of reasoning

It is very common to confuse

It is very doubtful whether

It is very interesting and pleasant

It is well known

It is with great pleasure

It is with pity unspeakable
It is within the memory of men now living
It is worth while to notice
It may appear absurd
It may at first sight seem strange
It may be added
It may be conjectured
It may be imagined
It may be plausibly objected
It may be rightly said
It may be useful to trace
It may be worth your while to keep in view
It may indeed be unavoidable
It may not be altogether certain
It may not be uninteresting to any of you
It may or may not be true
It may, perhaps, seem wonderful
It may seem a little strange
It may still more probably be said
It must be a cause of delight
It must be borne in mind
It must be the verdict of history
It must create astonishment
It must doubtless be admitted
It must ever be recollected
It must never be forgotten
It must not be supposed
It must seem to every thoughtful man

FIFTEEN THOUSAND USEFUL PHRASES

It needs scarcely be said
It now becomes my pride and privilege
It only remains now to speak
It ought to animate us
It proves a great deal
It remains only to speak briefly
It remains that I inform you of
It remains that I should say a few words
It reminds me of an anecdote
It reminds one of the compliment
It requires no effort of imagination
It scarcely seems to be in keeping
It seems almost desperate to think of
It seems almost incredible
It seems now to be generally admitted
It seems strange to be told
It seems then that on the whole
It seems to me a striking circumstance
It seems to me idle to ask
It seems to me singularly appropriate
It seems to me the primary foundation
It seems to me unphilosophical
It should always be borne in mind
It should be remembered
It so happens
It sometimes seems to me
It still remains to be observed
It strikes me with wonder

It suggests at the outset

It summons our imagination

It surely is not too much to expect

It therefore astonishes me

It used to be a reproach

It was a brilliant answer

It was a fine and delicate rebuke

It was a fit and beautiful circumstance

It was a propitious circumstance
    [propitious = auspicious, favorable]

It was certainly a gracious act

It was in the full understanding

It was my good fortune

It was not to be expected

It was said by one who ought to know

It was, therefore, inevitable

It was under these circumstances

It will appeal to

It will appear from what has been said

It will be asked me how

It will be easy to say too much

It will be easy to trace the influence

It will be evident to you

It will be idle to imply

It will be interesting to trace

It will be just as reasonable to say

It will be rather to our advantage

It will be recollected

It will be seen at a glance
It will be well and wise
It will carry out my meaning more fully
It will, I suppose, be denied
It will not be expected from me
It will not be safe
It will not do for a man to say
It will not, I trust, be concluded
It will not surely be objected
It will not take many words to sum up
It will thus be seen
It would be a misfortune
It would be a proud distinction
It would be a very remarkable fact
It would be absurd to pretend
It would be an inexcusable omission
It would be idle for me
It would be imprudent in me
It would be invidious for me
   [invidious = rousing ill will, animosity]
It would be natural on such an occasion
It would be no less impracticable
It would be out of place here
It would be preposterous to say
It would be presumptuous in me
It would be the height of absurdity
It would be unfair to praise
It would be unjust to deny

It would be well for us to reflect

It would indeed be unworthy

It would seem perhaps most fitting

J

Just the reverse is true

L

Language is inadequate to voice my appreciation

Lastly, I do not understand

Lastly, it can not be denied

Less than this could not be said

Lest I should be accused of quibbling

Let all of us labor in this work

Let anyone imagine to himself

Let anyone who doubts

Let everyone consider

Let it be clearly understood, I repeat it

Let it be remembered

Let it not be objected

Let it not be supposed that I impute
   [impute = relate to a particular cause or source]

Let me add another thing

Let me add my final word

Let me add one other hint

Let me also say a word in regard

Let me answer these questions

Let me ask you to imagine

Let me ask your leave to propose

Let me be allowed to devote a few words

Let me call attention to another fact

Let me commend to you

Let me direct your attention now to

Let me entreat you to examine

Let me give one more instance

Let me give one parting word

Let me give you an illustration

Let me here make one remark

Let me here say

Let me hope that I have said enough

Let me illustrate again

Let me make myself distinctly understood

Let me make use of an illustration

Let me not be thought offensive

Let me now conclude with

Let me once more urge upon you

Let me protest against the manner

Let me quite temperately defend

Let me rather make the supposition

Let me say a practical word

Let me simply declare

Let me tell you an interesting reminiscence

Let me thank you once more

Let me urge you earnestly

Let no man congratulate himself
Let our conception be enlarged
Let our object be
Let that question be answered by
Let the facts be granted
Let these instances suffice
Let this be the record made
Let this inspire us with abhorrence of
Let us approach the subject from another side
Let us attempt a survey
Let us be perfectly just
Let us be quite practical
Let us bear perpetually in mind
Let us begin at the beginning
Let us begin by examining
Let us briefly review
Let us brush aside once for all
Let us cherish
Let us confirm our opinion
Let us consider for a moment
Let us devote ourselves
Let us discard all prejudice
Let us do all we can
Let us draw an illustration
Let us endeavor to understand
Let us enumerate
Let us figure to ourselves
Let us for the moment put aside

Let us get a clear understanding

Let us heed the voice

Let us hope and believe

Let us hope that future generations

Let us imitate

Let us inquire also

Let us labor and pray

Let us likewise remember

Let us look briefly at a few particulars

Let us look nearer home

Let us not be fearful

Let us not be misled

Let us not be misunderstood

Let us not flatter ourselves

Let us not for a moment forget

Let us not limit our view

Let us now apply the views presented

Let us now consider the characteristics

Let us now see the results

Let us now turn our consideration

Let us observe this analogy

Let us pass on to another fact

Let us pause a moment

Let us push the inquiry yet further

Let us rather listen to

Let us reflect how vain

Let us remember this

Let us remind ourselves

Let us resolve

Let us scrutinize the facts

Let us suppose, for argument's sake

Let us suppose the case to be

Let us take, for instance

Let us, then, be assured

Let us, then, be worthy of

Let us, therefore, say once for all

Let us try to form a mental picture

Let us turn to the contemplation of

Let your imagination realize

Like all citizens of high ideals

Likely enough

Little wonder therefore

Long have I been convinced

Look at it in another way

Look at some of these questions

Look at the situation

M

Mainly, I believe

Making allowances for differences of opinion

Many of us have had the good fortune

Many of you, perhaps, recollect

May I ask you to believe

May I not speak here

May I try to show that every effort

May I venture to suggest
May it not also be advanced
May the day come quickly
Meantime it is encouraging to think
Meanwhile let us freely recognize
Men are in the habit of saying
Men are telling us nowadays
Men everywhere testify
More and more it is felt
More than once have I had to express
More than this need not be said
Moreover, I have insisted
Moreover, I would counsel you
Moreover, when we pass judgment
Much has been said and written about
My appreciation has been quickened
My belief, therefore, is
My duty is to endeavor to show
My experience tells me
My first duty is to express to you
My friends, do you really believe
My friends, I propose
My heart tells me
My idea, therefore, is
My last criticism upon
My mind is not moved by
My mind most perfectly acquiesces
My next objection is

My own private opinion is
My present business is
My regret is intensified by the thought

N

Nay, I boldly say
Nay, it will be a relief to my mind
Nay, there is a general feeling
Need I say that I mean
Neither should you deceive
Never before have I so strongly felt
Never can I cease to feel
Never did there devolve
Never for a moment believe
Never have I felt so forcibly
Never was a weaker defense attempted
Never was there a greater mistake
Never was there an instance
Nevertheless we can admit
Next, from what has been said it is plain
Next, I consider
Next, it will be denied
No argument can overwhelm a fact
No defense is to be found
No distinct test can be named
No doubt, in the first instance
No doubt there are many questions

No doubt to most of us
No finer sentence has come down to us
No greater service could be rendered
No longer do we believe
No man regrets more than I do
No one can feel this more strongly
No one can, I think, pretend
No one can see the end
No one here, I am sure
No one, I suppose, would say
No one, I think, can fail to observe
No one, I think, will dispute the statement
No one need to exaggerate
No one will accuse me
No true man ever believes
None can have failed to observe
Nor am I disparaging or discouraging
Nor can I forget either
Nor can it justly be said
Nor can we afford to waste time
Nor can we forget how long
Nor can we now ask
Nor do I believe
Nor do I doubt
Nor do I pretend
Nor do I think there can be found
Nor does it matter much
Nor has there been wanting

Nor indeed am I supposing
Nor is it a fair objection
Nor is it probable
Nor is this all
Nor let me forget to add here
Nor must I be understood as saying
Nor must it be forgotten
Nor need we fear to speak
Nor should any attempt be made
Nor will history fail to record
Nor will I enlarge on the matter
Not at all
Not only so
Not that I quarrel with
Nothing but the deepest sense
Nothing can be further from the truth
Nothing could be clearer
Nothing could be more striking
Nothing is more common in the world
Nothing that you can do
Notwithstanding all that has been said
Notwithstanding all this, I hold
Now, bear with me when I say
Now comes the question
Now, comparing these instances together
Now, from these instances it is plain
Now, having spoken of
Now, I admit

Now, I am far from denying
Now, I am far from undervaluing
Now, I am justified in calling this
Now, I am obliged to say
Now, I do not wish you to believe
Now, I have a closing sentence or two
Now, I pass on to consider
Now, I shall not occupy your time
Now, I understand the argument
Now, I will undertake to say
Now, I wish to call your attention
Now, if you will clearly understand
Now, is there any ground or basis for
Now, it is an undoubted fact
Now, it is evident
Now, it is not at all strange
Now, it is unquestioned
Now, let me speak with the greatest care
Now, let me stop a moment
Now, let us consider
Now, observe, my drift
Now, sir, I am truly horrified
Now, the answer we should give
Now, the question here at issue
Now, the world will say
Now, there is a close alliance between
Now, this is precisely the danger
Now, this is to some extent

Now, understand me definitely
Now, we do not maintain
Now, we will inquire
Now, what I want you to realize
Now, with regard to
Now, you will allow me to state
Now, you will understand from this

O

Observe again
Occasionally you ought to read
Of course I am aware
Of course I am putting an impossible case
Of course I can not be taken to mean
Of course I do not maintain
Of course I do not stop here
Of course I would not allow
Of course much may be said
Of course these remarks hold good
Of course we may, if we please
Of course you will sympathize
Of one thing, however, I am certain
Of this briefly
Of this statement I will only say
Of this truth I shall convince you by
On a review of the whole subject
On occasions of this kind

On such a day as this
On the contrary, I am assuming
On the occasion to which I refer
On the other hand, it is clear
On the whole, then, I observe
On this auspicious occasion
On this point I do not mean to dwell
On this subject you need not suspect
Once again, there are those
Once more I emphasize
Once more let me try to put into words
One additional remark
One almost wishes
One can not decline to note
One concluding remark has to be made
One fact is clear and indisputable
One further word
One important topic remains
One is fairly tempted to wish
One lesson history may be said to repeat
One might be challenged to produce
One of the ancients said
One of the most commonly known
One of the most extraordinary incidents
One of the things I recollect with most pride
One of these signs is the fact
One or two points are made clear
One other circumstance

One other remark suggests itself
One remark I will make
One thing more will complete this question
One thing which always impressed me
One very striking tendency
One word in courtesy I must say
One word more in a serious vein
One would naturally suppose
Only so much do I know
Opinions are divided as to whether
Or to come nearer home
Or to take but one other example
Ordinarily speaking, such deductions
Others may hold other opinions
Ought we not to think
Our thoughts wander back
Over and above all this

P

Pardon me if
Perhaps another reason why
Perhaps, however, in speaking to you
Perhaps, however, some among you will be
Perhaps I may be best able to illustrate
Perhaps I ought to say
Perhaps it may be doubted
Perhaps, sir, I am mistaken in

Permit me frankly to say
Permit me to add another circumstance
Permit me to bring home to you
Personally, I am far too firm a believer
Pray, sir, let me say

R

Read but your history aright
Recollect, sir
Reflections such as these
Rely upon it
Remember, I do not seek to
Remembering some past occurrences
Returning, then, to the consideration

S

Seriously, then, do I beg you
Shall I tell you
Shall we complain
Should there be objection, I answer
Since, then, it is provided
Since, then, this is the case
Sir, with all my heart, I respond
So accustomed are we
So at least it seems to me
So far as I know

So far as my observation and experience goes
So far in general
So I say to you
So it comes to pass
So long as we continue to love truth and duty
So men are asking
So much at first sight
So much on this subject
So that I may venture to say
So that if you were persuaded
So then ought we also
So, to add one other example
So, too, I may go on to speak
So when I hear people say
Some have insisted
Some of you can recall the time
Some of you may think this visionary
Some of you will remember
Some one will perhaps object
Some prejudice is attached
Some writer has said
Sometimes I venture to think
Sometimes it may happen
Speaking in this place
Startling as this may appear to you
Stating only the truth, I affirm
Still another encouraging fact
Still further

Still I can not part from my subject
Still I have generally found
Still I imagine you would consider it
Still I know what answer I can make to
Still it may with justice be said
Still one thing more
Still we ought to be grateful
Strange as it may seem
Strictly in confidence, I do not think
Strictly speaking, there is no such thing
Such a doctrine is essentially superficial
Such are the rather tolerant ideas
Such considerations as these
Such, I believe, would be the consequences
Such illustrations are not frequent
Such, in brief, is the story
Such is steadfastly my opinion
Such is the deep prejudice now existing
Such is the intellectual view we take
Such is the lesson which I am taught
Such is the progress
Such is the truth
Such, sir, I conceive to be
Such, then, is the true idea
Such, too, is the characteristic of
Suffer me to point out
Suffice it to say here
Summing up what I have said

Suppose we turn our eyes to
Surely I do not misinterpret
Surely it is a paradox
Surely it is not too much for me to say

T

Take another instance
Take one of the most recent cases
Take the simple fact
Take this example
Taking a broader view
Taking the facts by themselves
That is a further point
That is a natural boast
That is a pure assumption
That is all that it seems necessary to me
That is all very good
That is far from my thoughts
That is final and conclusive
That is the lesson of history
That is the question of questions
That you may conceive the force of
The answer is easy to find
The answer is ready
The belief is born of the wish
The broad principle which I would lay down
The circumstances under which we meet

The climax of my purpose in this address
The common consent of civilized mankind
The conclusion is irresistible
The confusing assertion is sometimes made
The day is at hand
The decided objection is raised
The doctrine I am combating
The doctrine is admirable
The effect too often is
The evolution of events has brought
The fact has made a deep impression on me
The fact has often been insisted
The fact to be particularly noted
The facts are clear and unequivocal
The facts may be strung together
The first business of every man
The first counsel I would offer
The first great fact to remember is
The first point to be ascertained
The first practical thought is
The first remarkable instance was
The first thing I wish to note
The first thing that we have to consider
The future historian will, no doubt
The generous feeling that has promoted you
The great mass of the people
The hour is at hand
The illustration is analogous

The important thing is
The instance I shall choose
The irresistible tendency of
The kindness with which I have been received
The last and distinguishing feature is
The latest inclination I have seen
The lesson which we should take most to heart
The main cause of all this
The more you examine this matter
The most concise tribute paid
The most reasonable anticipation
The most remarkable step forward
The most striking characteristic
The most sublime instance that I know
The next point is
The next question to be considered is
The next thing I consider indispensable
The occasion that calls us together
The one central difference between
The only course that remains open
The only plea to be offered
The other day I observed
The paramount consideration is
The perils that beset us here
The pleasing duty is assigned me
The point I have urged upon you is
The point I wish a little further to speak of
The point to which I shall call your attention

The popular notion is
The practical inference from all this
The presence of this brilliant assemblage
The pressing question is
The prevalent opinion, no doubt
The proof of this statement is to be found
The question is deeply involved
The question, then, recurs
The remedy I believe to be
The result, I fancy, has been
The result of the whole
The rule will always hold good
The sacred voice of inspiration
The same is true in respect of
The scene all comes back
The sentiment to which I am to respond
The sentiment which you have expressed
The simple rule and test
The simple truth is
The soundness of this doctrine depends
The strongest proof I have
The subject of the evening's address
The subject which has been assigned to me
The task has been placed in my hands
The testimony of history is
The theory seems at first sight
The thought with which I shall close
The time has manifestly now arrived

The time is not far distant
The time is now come for me
The times are full of signs and warnings
The toast I am about to propose to you
The vain wish has sometimes been indulged
The view I have been enforcing
The view is more misleading
The warmth and kindness of your reception
The welcome that has been extended to me
The whole story of civilization
Then again, in corroboration
Then again, when men say
Then take the other side of the argument
Then the question arises
Then there is another story
Then, too, it must be remembered
There are certain old truths
There are few spectacles
There are hopeful signs of
There are, I believe, many who think
There are, indeed, exceptions
There are, indeed, persons who profess
There are many educated and intelligent people
There are people in every community
There are several reasons why
There are some slight modifications
There are some who are fond of looking at
There are some who have an idea

There are those of us who can remember
There are those who wish
There are two conflicting theories
There can be but one answer
There can be no doubt
There has been a great deal of discussion lately
There has been no period of time
There have been differences of opinion
There is a characteristic saying
There is a class of person
There is a common saying
There is a conviction
There is a degree of evidence
There is a genuine grief
There is a great deal of rash talking
There is a growing disposition
There is a large class of thinkers
There is a lesson of profound interest
There is a more important question
There is a most serious lesson
There is a multitude of facts
There is a question of vital importance
There is a very common tendency
There is a vital difference of opinion
There is an analogy in this respect
There is an ancient story to the effect
There is an eternal controversy
There is another class of men

There is another factor
There is another object equally important
There is another point of view
There is another remarkable analogy
There is another sense in which
There is, at any rate, to be said
There is but one consideration
There is certainly no reason
There is hardly any limit
There is, however, another opinion
There is, however, one caution
There is little truth in
There is no field of human activity
There is no good reason
There is no justification for
There is no mistaking the purpose
There is no more insidious peril
There is no more striking exemplification
There is no occasion to exaggerate
There is no page of history
There is no sense in saying
There is no worse perversion
There is not a shadow of evidence
There is nothing more repulsive
There is nothing overstated in this description
There is nothing to show
There is one story which it is said
There is only one sense in which

There is some difference of opinion
There is something strangely interesting
There is yet another distinction
There is yet one other remark
There ought certainly to be
There was but one alternative
There was one remarkable incident
There will always be a number of men
There will be no difficulty
There yet remains
Therefore, there is no possibility of a doubt
Therein lies your responsibility
These alone would not be sufficient
These are enough to refute the opinion
These are general counsels
These are generalizations
These are my reasons for
These are points for consideration
These considerations have great weight with me
These exceptions do not hold in the case of
These ideas naturally present themselves
These instances are far from common
These instances are indications
These last words lead me to say
These objections only go to show
These questions I shall examine
These various partial views
They mistake the intelligence

They would persuade you to
Think for a moment
Think of the cool disregard
This absurdity arises
This appeal to the common sense
This argument is especially cogent
    [cogent = powerfully persuasive]
This, at least, is sure
This being the case
This being true
This being undeniable, it is plain
This being understood, I ask
This brings me to a single remark
This brings us to a subject
This episode goes to prove
This fact was soon made manifest
This from the nature of the case
This I conceive to be the business
This I consider to be my own case
This I have told you
This is a general statement
This is a very one-sided conception
This is a very serious situation
This is an astonishing announcement
This is conceded by
This is contrary to all argument
This is doubtless the truth
This is especially the case

This is essentially an age of

This is in the main just

This is like saying

This is not all

This is not the main point of objection

This is not the occasion or the place

This is obvious

This is on the whole reasonable

This is only another illustration of

This is owing in great measure to

This is precisely what we ought to do

This is said in no spirit of

This is suggested to us

This is the design and intention

This is the great fact

This is the main point on which the inquiry turns

This is the meaning of

This is the obvious answer

This is the point I want to impress upon you

This is the point of view

This is the position of our minds

This is the radical question

This is the sentiment of mankind

This is the starting-point

This is the sum

This is to be found in the fact

This is what I am led to say

This is what may be objected

This is why I take the liberty
This language is plain
This leads me to the question
This leads us to inquire
This may be said without prejudice
This might be illustrated at length
This much is certain
This sentiment was well-nigh universal
This, surely, is the conclusion
This, then, is the answer
This, then, is the drift of my illustration
This, then, is what I mean by saying
This will be evident at once
This you can not deny
Those who have watched the tendencies
Thus a great deal may be done
Thus analogy suggests
Thus far, I willingly admit
Thus I am led on to another remark
Thus if you look into
Thus instances occur now and then
Thus it comes to pass
Thus my imagination tells me
Thus much, however, I may say
Thus much I may be allowed to say
Thus much may be sufficient to recall
Thus we see
Time would not permit me

To a man of the highest public spirit
To avoid all possibility of being misunderstood
To be more explicit
To be sure, we sometimes hear
To bring the matter nearer home
To convince them of this
To feel the true force of this argument
To illustrate
To make my story quite complete
To me, however, it would appear
To my way of conceiving such matters
To prevent misapprehension
To some it may sound like a paradox
To sum up all that has been said
To sum up in one word
To take a very different instance
To the conclusion thus drawn
To the enormous majority of persons
To these general considerations
To this I answer
To this it will be replied
To what other cause can you ascribe
To-day, as never before
Treading close upon the heels
Tried by this standard
True it is
True, there are difficulties
Truly it is a subject for astonishment

Two things are made very clear

U

Under all the circumstances
Under these favoring conditions
Under this head
Undoubtedly we may find
Unfortunately it is a truth
Unless I could be sure
Up to this moment I have stated

V

Very strange is this indeed

W

We all agree as to
We all feel the force of the maxim
We all in equal sincerity profess
We almost shudder when we see
We are accustomed to lay stress upon
We are all familiar with
We are approaching an era
We are apt to forget
We are assembled here to-day
We are beginning to realize

We are bound to give heed
We are constantly being told
We are fulfilling what I believe to be
We are in the habit of saying
We are met to-night
We are not able to prove
We are not disinterested
We are quite unable to speculate
We are told emphatically
We are tolerably certain
We believe with a sincere belief
We can but pause to contemplate
We can imagine the amazement of
We can not but be struck with
We can not escape the truth
We can not have this too deeply fixed
We can not too highly honor the temper of
We can not wonder
We can only applaud the sentiment
We can only bow with awe
We can presume
We can remember with pride
We can see to some extent
We continually hear nowadays
We deeply appreciate the circumstances of
We do not quarrel with those
We do not question the reality
We do well to recall

We easily persuade ourselves

We feel keenly about such things

We grope blindly along

We have a firm assurance

We have a right to claim

We have an overpowering sense

We have been accustomed to

We have been told by more than one

We have come together to-night

We have great reason to be thankful

We have heard lately

We have here plain proof

We have need to examine

We have no means of knowing

We have no other alternative

We have not yet solved the problem

We have sought on this occasion

We have the evidence of this

We have the good fortune to-night

We have to admit

We have witnessed on many occasions

We hear it is said sometimes

We hear no complaint

We heartily wish and mean

We hold fast to the principle

We laugh to scorn the idea

We may all of us agree

We may be permitted to remember

We may contemplate with satisfaction
We may have a deep consciousness
We may indeed consider
We may not know precisely how
We must also look
We must constantly direct our purpose
We must not be deceived
We must not mistake
We must realize conscientiously
We must remember
We need no proof to assure us
We need not look far for reasons
We need not trouble ourselves
We of this generation
We often hear persons say
We ought in strict propriety
We pride ourselves upon the fact
We rightly pay all honor
We see in a variety of ways
We shall all doubtless concede
We shall be blind not to perceive
We shall do well to remember
We shall have no difficulty in determining
We should be convinced
We should contemplate and compare
We should dread nothing so much
We should lend our influence
We should not question for a moment

We should not, therefore, question
We stand astonished at
We stumble and falter and fall
We take it for granted
We will not stop to inquire
Weighty as these conditions are
Well, gentlemen, it must be confessed
Well may we explain
Well, now, let us propose
Well, that being the case, I say
Were I to enter into a detailed description
Were I to speculate
What are the precise characteristics
What are we to think of
What are you going to do
What can avail
What can be more intelligible
What can be more monstrous than
What can I say better
What commonly happens is this
What could be more captivating
What could be more true
What do we gain by
What do we understand to have been
What I mean is this
What I now say is
What I object to is
What I propose to do is

What I shall actually attempt to show here
What I suggest is
What is more important
What is more remarkable
What is the pretext
What is this but to say
What more shall I say
What remains but to wish you
What strikes the mind so forcibly
What, then, are we to believe
What, then, can be the reason
What, then, I may be asked
What, then, is the use
What, then, was the nature of
What was the consequence of
What we are concerned to know is
What we have most to complain of
What would you say
Whatever a man thinks
Whatever difference of opinion may exist
Whatever opinion I may express
Whatever the truth may be
When I am told
When I hear it said
When I remember the history
When I review these circumstances
When I speak of this question
When I thus profess myself

When one remembers
When we consider the vastness
When we contemplate
When we get so far as this
When we look closely at
When will men understand
When you are assured
When you did me the honor to invite me
Whence it is, I say
Whence was the proof to come
While acknowledging the great value
While I feel most keenly the honor
While I have hinted to you
Whilst I am on this matter
Who can deny the effect
Who can say in a word
Who does not like to see
Who has not felt the contrast
Who that reads does not see
Who will accuse me
Why, again, should I take notice
Why need you seek to disprove
Will any gentleman say
Will anyone answer
Will it be whispered
Will it not be well for us
Will you allow me to present to you
Will you bear with me

Will you mistake this
Will you permit me to thank you
With all my heart I share
With possibly a single exception
With respect to what has been said
With this ideal clearly before us
With whatever opinions we come here
Without going into any details
Without my saying a word more

Y

Yet I am convinced
Yet I am willing to admit
Yet I am willing to conclude
Yet I feel quite free to say
Yet I, for one, do not hesitate to admit
Yet I have never been thoroughly satisfied
Yet I suppose it is worth while
Yet I would have to think
Yet if you were to ask the question
Yet it is instructive and interesting
Yet it is no less true
Yet it is perfectly plain
Yet let me consider what consequences must
Yet may I not remind you
You all know the history of
You and I are always contrasting

You are at a parting of the ways

You are now invited to do honor

You can never forget

You can not assert

You do not need to be told

You have all read the story

You have been gracious enough to assign to me

You have been mindful

You have been pleased to confer upon me

You have but to observe

You have done me great honor

You have no right

You have not forgotten

You have often pondered over

You have sometimes been astonished

You know that it is impossible to

You know the legend which has grown up

You know very well

You may also be assured

You may be acquainted with

You may be sure

You may depend upon it

You may remember

You may well be proud

You may well study the example

You might apply to yourselves

You must not forget

You must understand I do not mean to claim

FIFTEEN THOUSAND USEFUL PHRASES

You ought not to disregard what I say
You remember how
You will allow me to say with becoming brevity
You will be pleased to hear
You will bear me out when I say
You will clearly understand
You will expect me to say something about
You will forgive me
You will join with me, I trust
You will observe
You will pardon me, I am sure
You will scarcely be surprised
You would never dream of urging
You yourselves are the evidence
Your friendly and generous words
Your good sense must tell you
Your presence seems to say

SECTION XI

MISCELLANEOUS PHRASES

A

A bewildering labyrinth of facts

A blank absence of interest or sympathy

A bloodless diplomatist

A breach of confidence

A brilliant and paradoxical talker

A burning sense of shame and horror

A century of disillusionment

A certain catholicity of taste
 [catholicity = universality]

A cheap and coarse cynicism

A civilizing agency of conspicuous value

A cleanness and probity of life
 [probity = integrity; uprightness]

A commendable restraint

A condescending and patronizing spirit

A confused and troublesome time

A conscientious anxiety to do the right thing

A conspicuous and crowning service

A constant source of surprise and delight

A contemptible species of mockery
A convenient makeshift
A copious torrent of pleasantry
A course of arrogant obstinacy
A crumb of consolation
A crystallized embodiment of the age
A cynical and selfish hedonist
A dangerous varnish of refinement
A dead theological dogma
A decorous and well-intentioned person
A deep and most impressive solemnity
A deep and strange suggestiveness
A deep authentic impression of disinterestedness
A dereliction of duty
A disaster of the first magnitude
A distorted and pessimistic view of life
A dogmatic and self-righteous spirit
A duel of brains
A dull collocation of words
A fastidious sense of fitness
A fatal moral hollowness
A feeling of lofty remoteness
A feminine excess of inconsequence
A final and irrevocable settlement
A firmness tempered by the most scrupulous courtesy
A fitting interval for penitence
A flippant rejoinder
A flood of external impressions

A flourish of rhetoric

A fund of curious information

A furtive groping after knowledge

A gambler's desperate chance

A ghastly mixture of defiance and conceit

A glaring example of rapacity
  [rapacity = plundering]

A graceful nonentity

A great and many-sided personality

A great capacity for generous indignation

A great source of confusion

A gross piece of stupidity

A habit of riding a theory too hard

A habit of rigorous definition

A happy and compensating experience

A haughty self-assertion of equality

A hideous absurdity

A hideous orgy of massacre and outrage

A high pitch of eloquence

A homelike and festive aspect

A hopeless enigma

A hotbed of disturbance

A hushed rustle of applause testified to a widespread approbation
  [approbation = warm approval; praise]

A keenly receptive and intensely sensitive temperament

A kind of fantastic patchwork

A kind of surly reluctance

A laudable stimulus

A law of retributive justice

A less revolutionary innovation

A life of studious contemplation

A limpidity and lucidity of style
   [limpidity = transparent clearity; easily intelligible]

A lingering tinge of admiration

A lively sense of what is dishonorable

A long accumulating store of discontent and unrest

A long tangle of unavoidable detail

A look threatening and peremptory
   [peremptory = ending all debate or action]

A many-sided and far-reaching enthusiasm

A marvelous sharpener of the faculties

A melancholy preponderance of mischief

A memory-haunting phrase

A mercenary marriage

A mere conjectural estimate

A microscopic care in the search of words

A misconception which is singularly prevalent

A mixture of malignancy and madness

A modicum of truth

A monstrous travesty

A mood of hard skepticism

A more than ordinary share of baseness and depravity

A most laudable zeal

A most repulsive and incomprehensible idiom

A most unseasonable piece of impertinence

A multitude of groundless alarms
A murderous tenacity about trifles
A mysterious and an intractable pestilence
A mysterious and inscrutable power
A narrow and superficial survey
A nature somewhat frivolous and irresolute
A needlessly offensive manner
A nimble interchange of uninteresting gossip
A noble and puissant nation
 [puissant = with power, might]
A novel and perplexing course
A numerous company
A painful and disconcerting deformity
A partial disenchantment
A passage of extraordinary daring
A patchwork of compromises
A permanent and habitual state of mind
A pernicious and growing tendency
A perversion of judgment
A phantom of the brain
A piece of grotesque stupidity
A pleasant flow of appropriate language
A pompous failure
A potential menace to life
A powerful and persuasive orator
A prevalent characteristic of her nature
A prey to the tongue of the public
A pristine vigor of style

A profusion of compliments

A proposition inherently vicious

A puerile illusion
[puerile = immature; childish]

A quenchless thirst for expression

A rage akin to frenzy

A rare precision of insight

A rather desperate procedure

A reckless fashion

A recrudescence of superstition
[recrudescence = recurrence of a pathological symptoms after a period of improvement]

A relish for the sublime

A reversion to the boldest paganism

A rigid avoidance of extravagance and excess

A ripple of applause

A restraining and conservative force

A robust and consistent application

A sacred and indissoluble union

A sane philosophy of life

A secluded dreamer of dreams

A secret and wistful charm

A sense of deepening discouragement

A sense of indescribable reverence

A series of brief and irritating hopes

A settled conviction of success

A sharp difference of opinion

A sharp pang of regretful surprise

A shrewd eye to the main chance

A signal deed of justice

A skeptical suspension of judgment

A slight and superficial tribute

A slowly subsiding frenzy

A snare and a delusion

A somewhat complicated and abstruse calculation [abstruse = difficult to understand]

A sordid and detestable motive

A sort of incredulous stupefaction

A source of unfailing delight and wonder

A species of moral usurpation

A spirit inimical to learning

A spirit of complacent pessimism

A startling and unfortunate digression

A state of scarcely veiled insurrection

A state of urgent necessity

A stern decree of fate

A stern foe of snobbishness

A storm of public indignation

A strange mixture of carelessness, generosity, and caprice

A strangely perverse and poverty stricken imagination

A strong assumption of superiority

A subjugated and sullen population

A sudden revulsion

A supposed ground of affinity

A synonym for retrogression

A taunting accusation of falsehood

A tedious and needless drudgery
A temper which brooked no resistance
A temporary expedient
A tender tone of remonstrance
A theme of endless meditation
A thing of moods and moments
A thoroughly sincere and unaffected effort
A thousand mangled delusions
A tissue of dull excuses
A tone of exaggerated solicitude
A touch of exquisite pathos
A trace of obvious sarcasm
A transcript of the common conscience
A trifle prim and puritanic
A truth begirt with fire
A unique and overwhelming charm
A vague aversion
A variety of conflicting and profound emotions
A variety of enfeebling amendments
A vast multitude of facts
A vastly extended vision of opportunity
A vehement and direct attack
A very elusive and delicate thought
A very formidable problem
A vigilant reserve
A violent and base calumniator
   [calumniator = makes malicious or knowingly false statements]

A voice of matchless compass and eloquence
A warmth of seemingly generous indignations
A wealth of resource that seemed inexhaustible
A welcome release from besetting difficulties
A whole catalog of disastrous blunders
A whole whirlpool of various emotions
Abounding bodily vigor
Above and beyond and before all else
Absurd and inconsequential career
Abundant and congenial employment
Accidental rather than intentional
Accustomed to ascribe to chance
Acquired sentiments of propriety
Activities of the discursive intellect
Actuated by an unduly anxious desire
Acute sensibility coupled with quickness of intellect
Adhere too tenaciously to forms and modes
Admirable mastery of technique
Admit the soft impeachment
Admitted with a childlike cheerfulness
Advance by leaps and bounds
Advancing to dignity and honor
Adventitious aids to memory
   [adventitious = Not inherent; added extrinsically]
Affectation and superfluous ornament
Aggravated to an unspeakable degree
Agitated and perplexed by a dozen cross-currents of conflicting tendency

Agreeable and humanizing intercourse
Aided by strong mental endowments
Airy swiftness of treatment
Alien to the purpose
All sorts of petty tyrannies
All the resources of a burnished rhetoric
Allied by taste and circumstances
Allied with a marked imperiousness
    [imperious = arrogantly overbearing]
Almost incredible obtuseness
Altogether monstrous and unnatural
Always observant and discriminating
Amaze and confound the imagination
Amiable and indulgent hostess
Amid many and pressing avocations
Amid the homeliest details of daily life
Amid the rush and roar of life
Ample scope for the exercise of his astonishing gifts
An abandoned and exaggerated grief
An accidental encounter
An act of folly amounting to wickedness
An afternoon of painfully constrained behavior
An agreeable image of serene dignity
An air of artificial constraint
An air of round-eyed profundity
An alarmed sense of strange responsibilities
An almost excessive exactness
An almost sepulchral regularity and seclusion

An ample and imposing structure
An apostle of unworldly ardor
An appreciable menace
An ardent and gifted youth
An arid dictum
An artful and malignant enemy
An assumption entirely gratuitous
An assumption which proved erroneous
An atmosphere of sunny gaiety
An attitude of passive impartiality
An authoritative and conclusive inquiry
An egregious assumption
  [egregious = outrageously reprehensible]
An elaborate assumption of indifference
An endless field for discussion
An enervating and emasculating form of indulgence
An ennobling and invigorating influence
An entirely negligible quantity
An essentially grotesque and commonplace thing
An eternal and imperishable example
An exalted and chimerical sense of honor
  [chimerical = highly improbable]
An excess of unadulterated praise
An excessive refinement of feeling
An expression at once confident and appealing
An extensive and populous country
An habitual steadiness and coolness of reflection
An honest and unquestioning pride

An icy indifference

An idle and unworthy action

An ill-assorted vocabulary

An immeasurable advantage

An imminent and overmastering peril

An imperturbable demeanor and steadiness of mind

An implacable foe

An inborn and irresistible impulse

An incongruous spectacle

An incredible mental agility

An indefinable taint of priggishness
   [priggishness = exaggerated propriety]

An indescribable frankness and simplicity of character

An indolent surrender to mere sensuous experience

An indomitable and unselfish soul

An ineradicable love of fun and mystification

An inevitable factor of human conduct

An inexhaustible copiousness and readiness of speech

An insatiable appetite for trifles

An insatiable voracity

An inscrutable mystery

An intentional breach of politeness

An interchange of civilities

An intolerable deal of guesswork

An involuntary gesture of remonstrance

An irrelevant bit of magniloquence
   [magniloquence = extravagant in speech]

An irrepressible and impassioned hopefulness

An irritating and dangerous treatment
An itching propensity for argument
An object of indestructible interest
An obnoxious member of society
An ominous lull and silence
An open and violent rupture
An outburst of impassioned eloquence
An unaccountable feeling of antipathy
An unbecoming vehemence
An undisciplined state of feeling
An unerring sense of humor
An unparalleled and almost miraculous growth
An unparalleled atrocity
An unpatriotic and ignoble act
An unreasoning form of coercion
An utterly vile and detestable spirit
And now I address myself to my task
And the like
Announced in a tone of pious satisfaction
Another thought importuned him
    [importuned = insistent or repeated requests]
Anticipated with lively expectation
Apparent rather than real
Appeal to a tardy justice
Appreciably above the level of mediocrity
Arbitrary assumption of power
Ardently and enthusiastically convinced
Argued with immense force and feeling

Arrayed with scrupulous neatness
Arrogance and untutored haughtiness
As an impartial bystander
As belated as they are fallacious
As by a secret of freemasonry
As odious as it is absurd
As ridiculous as it was unnecessary
As we scan the vague unknown
Assailed by poignant doubts
Assume a menacing attitude
Assumed almost heroic proportions
At once epigrammatic and arresting
  [epigrammatic = terse and witty]
At once misleading and infelicitous
At the mercy of small prejudices
Attained by rigorous self-restraint
Attended by insuperable difficulties
Averted by some happy stroke of fortune
Await the sentence of impartial posterity
Awaited with feverish anxiety

B

Bandied to and fro
Based on a fundamental error
Beguile the tedium of the journey
Bemoaning and bewailing his sad fortune
Beset with external dangers

Betrayed into deplorable error
Bewildering multiplication of details
Beyond the dreams of avarice
Blended with courage and devotion
Blind leaders of the blind
Blunt the finer sensibilities
Blustering desire for publicity
Bound up with impossibilities and absurdities
Breathed an almost exaggerated humility
Bred in the tepid reticence of propriety
Brief ventures of kindliness
Brilliant display of ingenious argument
Bring odium upon the individual
Brisk directness of speech
Brutal recognition of failure
Bursts of unpremeditated frankness
But delusions and phantasmagoria
But that is beside the mark
But this is a digression
By a curious perversity of fate
By a happy turn of thinking
By a whimsical diversion
By common consent
By means of crafty insinuations
By no means inconsolable
By temperament incompatible
By the common judgment of the thinking world
By the sheer centripetal force of sympathy

By virtue of a common understanding
By way of rejoinder

C

Calculated to create disgust
Calm strength and constancy
Capable of a severe scientific treatment
Capacity for urbanity and moderation
Carried into port by fair winds
Caught unawares by a base impulse
Ceaseless tramp of humanity
Censured for his negligence
Championing the cause of religious education
Chastened and refined by experience
Checked by the voice of authority
Cherished the amiable illusion
Cherishing a huge fallacy
Childishly inaccurate and absurd
Chivalrous loyalty and high forbearance
Clever and captivating eloquence
Coarse and glittering ostentation
Coherent and continuous trend of thought
Commended by perfect suavity
Common ground of agreement
Complicated and infinitely embittered
Conceded from a sense of justice
Conceived with imperfect knowledge

Concentrated and implacable resolve
Conditions of unspeakable humiliation
Conducive to well-being and efficiency
Confused rumblings presaging a different epoch
Constrained by the sober exercise of judgment
Consumed by a demon of activity
Continuous and stubborn disregard
Contrary to the clearest conviction of his judgment
Couched in terms of feigned devotion
Credulous and emotionally extravagant
Creed of incredulity and derision
Criticized with unsparing vigor
Crude undigested masses of suggestion
Cruel and baseless calumnies
   [calumnies = maliciously false statements; slander]
Cynically repudiate all obligations

D

Daily usages and modes of thinking
Dangerously near snobbery
Darkly insinuating what may possibly happen
Dazzled by their novelty and brilliance
Debased by common use
Deep essentials of moral grandeur
Deeply engrossed in congenial work
Deeply moved as well as keenly stung
Deeply rooted in the heart of humanity

Defiant of analysis and rule

Degenerate into comparative feebleness

Degenerated into deadness and formality

Degrading and debasing curiosity

Deliberate and cautious reflection

Delicacy of perception and quick tact

Delude many minds into acquiescence

Dense to the point of stupidity

Descanting on them cursorily
 [descanting = discussion or discourse]

Devices generally held to be discreditable

Devious and perilous ways

Devoid of hysteria and extravagance

Dexterous modes of concealment

Dictated by an overweening partiality

Differ in degree only and not in kind

Difficult and abstruse questions
 [abstruse = incomprehensible]

Diffidence overwhelmed him

Diffusing beneficent results

Dignified by deliberation and privacy

Dimly implying some sort of jest

Discreditable and insincere support

Disdaining the guidance of reason

Disenchanting effect of time and experience

Disfigured by glaring faults

Disguised in sentimental frippery

Dispel all anxious concern

Displayed enormous power and splendor
Distinguish themselves by their eccentricities
Distracted by contending desires
Diversity of mind and temperament
Divested of all personal feelings
Dogged and shameless beyond all precedent
Dominated by no prevailing taste or fashion
Doomed by inexorable fate
Doomed to impermanence and transiency
Draw back in distrust and misgiving
Dreaded and detested rival
Driven towards disaffection and violence
Due to historical perspective
Dull and trite commonplaces
Dwindled to alarmingly small dimensions

E

Easy-going to the point of lethargy
Elementary principles of right and wrong
Embittered and fanatical agitation
Encrusted with pedantry and prejudice
   [pedantry = attention to detail]
Endless and intricate technicalities
Endowed with undreamed-of powers
Enforced by coercive measures
Enormities of crime and anomalies of law
Entangled in theological controversy

Entirely futile and negligible
Erroneous assumptions and sophistries
Espoused with extraordinary ardor
Essentially one-sided and incomplete
Eternally fruitful and stimulating
Evidently malicious and adroit
Evinces a hardened conscience and an insensibility to shame
Exact and resolute allegiance
Examples of terrific and explosive energy
Exasperating to the last degree
Excruciating cruelty and injustice
Exposed to damaging criticism
Exposing his arrogance and folly to merited contempt
Expressions of unrestrained grief
Exquisite lucidity of statement
Extraordinarily subtle and penetrating analysis
Exuberant rush of words

F

Facile and fertile literary brains
Faithfully and religiously eschewed
  [eschew = avoid; shun]
Fallen into the convenient oblivion of the waste-basket
Fanatical and dangerous excesses
Far off and incredibly remote
Fastidious correctness of form
Fate had turned and twisted a thousand ways

Fed by many currents from the long stream of human experience

Feigning a virtuous indignation

Fertility of argumentative resource

Fictitious and adventitious aid

Finely touched to the fine issues

Fit to stand the gaze of millions

Fits and starts of generosity

Fixed convictions of mankind

Flouted as unpractical

Foolish and inflexible superstition

Fostering and preserving order

Free from all controversial pettifogging
  [pettifogging = quibbling over insignificant details]

Freighted with the most precious cargoes

Frequently recurring forms of awkwardness

Fresh and unsuspected loveliness

From the standpoint of expediency and effectiveness

Full and tuneful diction

Full of ardent affection and gratitude

Full of presentiments of some evil

Full of singular freshness, insight and power

Full of speculation and a deep restrained excitement

Fumble and stumble in helpless incapacity

G

Gain the applause of future ages

Generous to a pathetic and touching degree
Give vent to his indignation
Giving an ear to a little neighborly gossip
Glances and smiles of tacit contempt
Gnawing at the vitals of society
Grace and gentleness of manner
Graceful succession of sentences
Gratuitous and arbitrary meddling
Greeted with unalloyed satisfaction
Grooves of intellectual habit
Growing sense of bewilderment and dismay
Guilty and baffled antagonists

H

Habits of unintelligent routine
Habitual self-possession and self-respect
Happy and gracious willingness
Hard-souled and joyously joyous
Haunted by blank misgivings
He affected neither pomp nor grandeur
He became more blandly garrulous
   [garrulous = excessive and trivial talk]
He declined the proffered hospitality
He dropped into an eloquent silence
He eludes analysis and baffles description
He glanced at her indulgently
He had the habit of self-engrossed silences

He harbored his misgivings in silence

He poured bitter and biting ridicule on his discomfited opponents

He spoke with sledgehammer directness

He suffers nothing to draw him aside

He took his courage in both hands

He turned on me a glance of stored intelligence

He was disheveled and untidy

He was inexhaustibly voluble

Heavily freighted with erudition
  [erudition = extensive learning]

Heights of serene contemplation

Her voice had a wooden resonance and a ghost of a lisp

Hidebound in official pedantry
  [pedantry = attention to detail]

High and undiscouraged hope

High-handed indifference to all restraint

His chin had too vanishing an aspect

His first zeal was flagging

His general attitude suggested an idea that he had an oration for you

His gestures and his gait were untidy

His mood was one of pure exaltation

His plea was irresistible

His tone verged on the ironical

His work was ludicrously perfunctory

Hopelessly belated in its appearance

I

I adjured him
   [adjured = command or enjoin solemnly, as under oath]

I am not without a lurking suspicion

I bemoaned my unlucky fate

I could almost allege it as a supreme example

I have somewhat overshot the mark

I lost myself in a reverie of gratitude

I made bold to retort

I must hazard the story

I was extremely perplexed

I will permit myself the liberty of saying

I would fain believe
   [fain = happily; gladly]

Illuminate with sinister effect

Immediate and effectual steps

Immense capacity for ceaseless progress

Immunity from criticism and control

Impartial and exacting judgment

Impatience of despotic influence

Impelled by strong conviction

Imperiled in a restless age

Imperious in its demands
   [imperious = arrogantly domineering]

Impotent outbreaks of unreasoning rage

Impromptu parades of noisy patriotism

In a diversity of application

In a fever of apprehension

In a frenzy of fussy excitement

In a frowning abstraction

In a great and fruitful way

In a high degree culpable

In a kind of confused astonishment

In a most commendable fashion

In a most impressive vein

In a position of undisputed supremacy

In a rapture of imagined ecstasy

In a secret and surreptitious way
   [surreptitious = done by clandestine or stealthy means]

In a spirit of friendliness and conciliation

In a state of mulish reluctance
   [mulish = stubborn and intractable]

In a state of nervous exacerbation

In a state of virtuous complacency

In a tone of uneasy interrogation

In a transport of ambitious vanity

In a whirlwind of feeling and memory

In accents embarrassed and hesitating

In alliance with steady clearness of intellect

In amazed ejaculation

In an eminent and unique sense

In an eminent degree

In deference to a unanimous sentiment

In extenuation of the past

In high good humor
In his customary sententious fashion
  [sententious = terse and energetic; pithy]
In its most odious and intolerable shape
In language terse yet familiar
In moments of the most imminent peril
In quite incredible confusion
In seasons of difficulty and trial
In spite of plausible arguments
In terms of imperishable beauty
In the dim procession of years
In the highest conceivable degree
In the local phrase
In the nature of things
In the ordinarily accepted sense
In the realm of conjecture
In the scheme of things
In the tone of one who moralizes
In the twinkling of an eye
In the world of letters
In tones of genuine admiration
Incapable of flashy make-believe
Incited by a lust for gain
Incomparable lucidity and penetrativeness
Inconceivable clumsiness of organization
Indulge a train of gentle recollection
Indulging a sickly and nauseating petulance
Ineffably dreary and unpicturesque

Infected with a feverish dissatisfaction

Infuse a wholesome terror

Inimical to true and determined principle
  [Inimical = harmful; adverse]

Inimitable grace and felicity
  [inimitable = defying imitation; matchless]

Injudicious and inelegant ostentation

Innumerable and incessant creations

Inordinate greed and love of wealth

Insatiably greedy of recognition

Insensibility to moral perspective and proportion

Insolent and riotous excess

Inspired by a vague malevolence

Inspirited by approval and applause

Instances might be multiplied indefinitely

Instantly alive to the slightest breach of decorum

Insufferable violence to the feelings

Intense and stubborn dogmatism

Intense sensitiveness to injustice

Intercourse with polished society

Intervals of respite and repose

Inveigh against established customs
  [inveigh = angry disapproval; protest vehemently]

Invested with a partial authority

Inveterate forces of opposition

Invincible jealousy and hate

Involuntary thrill of gratified vanity

Involved in profound uncertainty

Involving ourselves in embarrassments

Inward appraisal and self-renouncement

Irregulated and desultory education
  [desultory = haphazard; random]

Irrelevant to the main issue

Irresistibly impelled by conscience

Irritable bitterness and angry suspicion

It assumes the shape of malignity

It betrays a great want of prudence and discernment

It defies description

It dissipates every doubt and scruple

It enslaves the imagination

It extorted from him expressions of irritability

It gives one a little grip at the throat

It has been stigmatized as irrelevant

It has more than passing interest

It has seldom been surpassed

It imposes no constraint

It is a capital blunder

It is a common error among ignorant people

It is a consoling reflection

It is a mark of great instability

It is a staggering thought

It is always something vicious

It is an odd jealousy

It is an intolerable idea

It is impossible to resist acknowledging this

It is little more than a platitude

It is not consistent with elevated and dignified character
It is not wholly insignificant
It is notoriously easy to exaggerate
It is the common consent of men
It is unnecessary to multiply instances
It makes life insupportable
It must be a matter of conjecture
It occasions suspicion and discontent
It runs counter to all established customs
It was a matter of notoriety
It wears a ragged and dangerous front
It would be a fruitless and unthankful task
It would be superfluous to say
It would not seem an improbable conclusion
Its dominating and inspiring influence

J

Jealous and formidable foes
Justifiable in certain exigencies
   [exigencies = urgent situations]

K

Keen power of calculation and unhesitating audacity
Kindle the flames of genuine oratory
Knotty and subtle disquisitions
   [disquisitions = formal discourse]

L

Labored and far-fetched elocution

Laid down in a most unflinching and vigorous fashion

Lamentable instances of extravagance

Lash themselves into fury

Lax theories and corresponding practises

Lay hold of the affections

Leaden mood of dulness

Lend a critical ear

Lest the requirements of courtesy be disregarded

Links in the chain of reasoning

Little less than scandalous

Lofty and distinguished simplicity

Long-sighted continuity of thought and plan

Looking at the matter by and large

Looming large and ugly in the public view

Loose and otiose statement
   [otiose = lazy; indolent; of no use]

Lost in indolent content

Lovely beyond all words

Lucidity and argumentative vigor

Lulled into a sense of false satisfaction

M

Maddened by a jealous hate

Maintained with ingenuity and vigor
Manifestly harsh and barbarous
Marvelous copiousness of illustration
Marvelously suggestive and inspiring
Men of profound erudition
   [erudition = extensive learning]
Mere effects of negligence
Microscopic analysis of character
Mingled distrust and fear
Ministering to mere pleasure and indulgence
Minutely and rationally exposing their imperfections
Morbid and subjective brooding
More or less severe and prolonged
Moved to unaccustomed tears
My worst suspicions were confirmed
Mysterious and invincible darkness

N

Naked vigor of resolution
Naturally prone to believe
Necessity thus imposed by prudence
Nerveless and faithless folly
No more than brief palliatives or mitigations
Noble and sublime patience
Noisy torrent of talk
Not averse to a little gossip
Not so much polished as varnished

Noted for their quixotic love of adventure

Nothing could be more captious or unfair
    [captious = disposition to find and point out trivial faults]

Nothing remained but a graceful acquiescence

Notoriously distracted by internecine jealousies

O

Objects of general censure

Obscured beneath the rubbish of the age

Obsessed with an overweening pride

Obstacles that are difficult but not insuperable

Obviously at variance with facts

Occasioned by direct moral turpitude
    [turpitude = depravity; baseness]

Oddly amenable to the proposed innovations

Often employed promiscuously

Ominous and swift days

Omitting all compliments and commonplaces

On a noble and commanding scale

On sure ground of fact

On the edge of great irritability

On the horns of a dilemma

One of life's ironical adjustments

One of the foreseen and inevitable results

One tissue of rashness, folly, ingratitude, and injustice

Openly flouted and disavowed

Oppressed by some vague dread

Organs of party rage and popular frenzy
Our opinions were diametrically opposed
Our vaunted civilization
Outward mark of obeisance and humiliation
  [obeisance = attitude of deference]
Overcome by an access of misery
Overshadowed by a fretful anxiety
Overwhelmed with reproach and popular indignation

P

Painful and lamentable indifference
Palpably and unmistakably commonplace
Parading an exception to prove a rule
Paralyzed by infirmity of purpose
Paralyzing doubts and scruples
Paramount obligation and righteousness
Partial and fragmentary evidence
Passionately addicted to pleasure
Patently inimical to liberty
Patience under continual provocation
Peculiarly liable to misinterpretation
Peddling and pitiful compromises
Pelting one another with catchwords
Perfectly illustrated and exemplified
Perpetually excite our curiosity
Pierced to the quick
Pitiful shifts of policy

Plainly dictated by a lofty purpose

Pleading the exigencies of strategical interest
  [exigencies = urgent situations]

Plunged into tumultuous preoccupation

Pointed out with triumphant malice

Polished beauty of diction

Political storm and stress.

Position of titular command

Preached with a fierce unction
  [unction = exaggerated earnestness]

Precipitate and arbitrary changes

Predict the gloomiest consequences

Pregnant with a lesson of the deepest import

Presented with matchless vigor and courage

Princely generosity of praise

Prodigious and portentous events

Protracted to a vexatious length

Proud schemes for aggrandizement

Provocative of bitter hostility

Pruned of their excrescences and grotesque extremes
  [excrescences = abnormal growth, such as a wart]

Purged of glaringly offensive features

Pursued to a vicious extent

Q

Questioned and tested in the crucible of experience

Quickened into a stabbing suspicion

Quickness to conceive and courage to execute
Quite destitute of resources
Quixotically generous about money

R

Radiantly and transparently happy
Railed at the world
Rare candor and flexibility of mind
Rare fidelity of purpose and achievement
Rarely brought to pass
Reeling headlong in luxury and sensuality
Regarded with sincere abhorrence
Regulated by the fixed rules of good-breeding
Religious rights and ceremonies
Reluctant to appear in so equivocal a character
Render null and void
Rent by internal contentions
Repugnant alike to reason and conscience
Resigned to growing infirmities
Resist a common adversary
Resting on some collateral circumstance
Rhetorical and ambitious diction
Rich and exuberant complexities
Rigid and exact boundaries
Rooted in immeasurable error and falsity
Roused to tumultuous activity
Rude and blind criticism

S

Sadly counterbalanced by numerous faults

Said with epigrammatic point
　[epigrammatic = terse and witty]

Salutary in the extreme

Salutary tonic of a free current of public criticism

Sanity and quietness of soul

Scorned as an impracticable theory

Scornful of petty calculations

Screen themselves from punishment

Scrupulous and chivalrous loyalty

See with eagle glance through conventionalisms

Seem to savor of paradox

Seize the auspicious moment

Self-centered anxiety and preoccupation

Self-command born of varied intercourse

Self-interest of the most compelling character

Selfish and uselessly recondite
　[recondite = not easily understood]

Selfishness pampered by abundance

Senses of marvelous acuteness

Sensible diminution of our comfort

Sensitive and apprehensive temperament

Sentimental wailings for the past

Serve the innocent purposes of life

Set down with meticulous care

Shames us out of our nonsense
Sharp outbursts of hatred and bitterness
Sharp restrictions of duty and opportunity
Sharply and definitely conceived
She had lost her way in a labyrinth of conjecture
She took refuge in a passionate exaggeration of her own insufficiency
Sheer midsummer madness
Silly displays of cheap animosity
Simple and obvious to a plain understanding
Sinister and fatal augury
   [augury = sign of something coming; omen]
Skulking beneath a high-sounding benevolence
Slack-minded skimming of newspapers
Slavish doctrines of sectarianism
Slow and resistless forces of conviction
Smug respectability and self-content
Snatch some advantage
Socialized and exacting studies
Some very undignified disclosures
Something essentially inexpressible
Something stifling and over-perfumed
Spinning a network of falsehoods
Spiritual and moral significance
Staring in helpless bewilderment
Stealthily escaping observation
Stern determination to inflict summary justice
Stigmatized as moral cowards

Stimulated to profitable industry

Stopped as if on the verge of profundities

Strange frankness of cynical brutality

Strange streak of melancholy

Strangled by a snare of words

Strenuous and conscientious endeavor

Stretched out in dreary monotony

Strict and unalloyed veracity

Struck incessantly and remorselessly

Stupendous and awe-inspiring spectacle

Subject to the vicissitudes of fortune
   [vicissitudes = sudden or unexpected changes]

Subjected to the grossest cruelties

Subordination to the common weal

Subservient to the ends of religion

Sudden and inexplicable changes of mood

Suddenly and imperatively summoned

Suddenly swelled to unprecedented magnitude

Sufficient to repel vulgar curiosity

Suggestive sagacity and penetration
   [sagacity = farsighted; wise]

Suit the means to the end

Sullen and widespread discontent

Superior in strength and prowess

Supported by a splendid fearlessness

Supremely and undeniably great

Susceptible to every impulse and stimulus

Sustained dignity and mellifluous precision
  [mellifluous = flowing with honey; smooth and sweet]

Swamping every aspiration and ambition

Swift and vehement outbursts of feeling

T

Take root in the heart

Take vengeance upon arrogant self-assertion

Taken in their totality

Tamed and wonted to a settled existence

Tempered by the emotional warmth of high moral ideals

That way madness lies

The abysmal depths of despair

The accumulated bitterness of failure

The agonies of conscious failure

The air was full of the cry and clamor

The animadversions of critics
  [animadversions = Strong criticism]

The applause was unbounded

The best proof of its timeliness and salutariness
  [salutariness = favorable]

The bewildered and tumultuous world

The blackest abyss of despair

The blemishes of an extraordinary reputation

The bluntness of a provincial

The bogey of bad luck
  [bogey = evil or mischievous spirit; hobgoblin]

The bounding pulse of youth

The brunt of life

The capacity for refined pursuits

The charming omniscience of youth

The cloak of cowardice

The collective life of humanity

The combined dictates of reason and experience

The companion of a noble and elevated spirit

The complaining gate swung open

The complex phenomena of life

The consequence of an agitated mind

The consequence of ignorance and childish assumption

The constant pressure of anxieties

The creature and tool of a party

The critical eyes of posterity

The dead and dusty past

The delimitation is sufficiently definite

The dictates of plain reason

The disjointed babble of the chronicler

The dull derision of the world

The dullest and most vacant minds

The dumb forces of brute nature

The dupe of some imposture

The eager pretentiousness of youth

The ebb and flow of events

The everlasting deluge of books

The evil was irremediable

The exchange of harmless amenities

The exertion of an inherent power

The expression was keenly intellectual
The facile conjectures of ignorant onlookers
The facts took him by the throat
The fitful swerving of passion
The flabbiness of our culture
The flaccid moods of prose
The flame of discord raged with redoubled fury
The flattest and most obvious truisms
The flippant insolence of a decadent skepticism
The foe of excess and immoderation
The fog of prejudice and ill-feeling
The frustration of their dearest hopes
The garb of civilization
The general infusion of wit
The gift of prophecy
The golden years of youth and maturity
The gratification of ambition
The grim reality of defeat
The hall-mark of a healthy humanity
The handmaid of tyranny
The hint of tranquillity and self-poise
The hints of an imaginable alliance
The hobgoblin of little minds
The holiest and most ennobling sensations of the soul
The hollowest of hollow shams
The homely virtue of practical utility
The hubbub and turmoil of the great world
The huge and thoughtful night

The hurly-burly of events

The idea was utterly hateful and repugnant

The idle of all hobbledehoys
    [hobbledehoys = gawky adolescent boy]

The ignoble exploitation of public interests

The imminent fatality awaiting him

The impulse of prejudice or caprice

The incorrigibility of perverse human nature

The incursions of a venomous rabble

The indulgence of an overweening self-conceit

The inevitable climax and culmination

The inference is inescapable

The infirmity and fallibility of human nature

The inflexible serenity of the wheeling sun

The ingenuities of legal verbiage

The inmost recesses of the human heart

The insipidity of indifference

The insolence of power

The irony of circumstances

The jaded weariness of overstrained living

The jargon of well-handled and voice-worn phrases

The jostling and ugliness of life

The lawyer's habit of circumspection and delay

The long-delayed hour of retribution

The lowest grade of precarious mendacity
    [mendacity = untruthfulness]

The makeshifts of mediocrity

The malarious air of after-dinner gossip

The mazes of conflicting testimony
The mean and frivolous affections of the idle
The menacing shadow of want
The mere fruit of his distempered imagination
The mere reversal of the wheel of fortune
The merest smattering of knowledge
The meticulous preciosity of the lawyer and the logician [preciosity = extreme overrefinement]
The most absurd elementary questions
The most amazing impudence
The most exacting and exciting business
The most fallacious of all fallacies
The most implacable logic
The most preposterous pride
The multitudinous tongue of the people
The outcome of unerring observation
The outraged conscience of mankind
The overpowering force of circumstances and necessity
The overweening exercise of power
The panacea for the evils of society
The panorama of history
The pernicious doctrines of skeptics
The perpetrator of clumsy witticisms
The precarious tenure of fame
The precursor of violence
The pretty and delicate game of talk
The primitive instinct of self-preservation
The property of little minds

The prophecies of visionaries and enthusiasts

The proprieties of etiquette

The purse-proud inflation of the moneyed man

The question was disconcertingly frank

The ravening wolves of brute instinct

The remark was sternly uncompromising

The result of caprice

The rigor of the law

The sanction and authority of a great name

The severest shocks of adverse fate

The sharp and vehement assertion of authority

The sinister influence of unprincipled men

The speaker drew an indignant breath

The springs of human action

The staple of conversation

The stillness of finality

The stings of self-reproach

The straightforward path of inexorable logic

The strong hand of executive authority

The sum and fruit of experience

The sum total of her impressions was negative

The summit of excellence

The supernatural prescience of prophecy

The sweet indulgence of good-nature

The sycophants of the rich
  [sycophant = servile self-seeker attempting to win favor by flattery]

The taint of fretful ingratitude

The talk flowed

The target for ill-informed criticism

The tears welled up and flowed abundantly

The tediousness of inactivity

The tendency to evade implicit obligations

The ties of a common cause

The tranquil aspects of society

The tribute of affectionate applause

The ultimate verdict of mankind

The unbroken habit of a lifetime

The unimpeachable correctness of his demeanor

The unlicensed indulgence of curiosity

The unsophisticated period of youth

The utmost excitement and agitation

The vanishing thoughtlessness of youth

The vanity and conceit of insular self-satisfaction

The very texture of man's soul and life

The victim of an increasing irritability

The victorious assertion of personality

The virtue of taciturnity
  [taciturnity = habitually untalkative]

The voice was sharp and peremptory
  [peremptory = ending all debate or action]

The want of serious and sustained thinking

The widest compass of human life

The wonderful pageant of consciousness

The words stabbed him

Their authenticity may be greatly questioned

Their indignation waxed fast and furious
Themes of perennial interest
There was a blank silence
There was no sense of diminution
They affected the tone of an impartial observer
They rent the air with shouts and acclamations
Thoughts which mock at human life
Through ever-widening circles of devastation
Through the distortions of prejudice
Thwarted by seeming insuperable obstacles
Time was dissolving the circle of his friends
Times of unexampled difficulty
Tinseled over with a gaudy embellishment of words
To a practised eye
To be sedulously avoided
   [sedulously = persevering]
To prosecute a scheme of personal ambition
To state the case is to prove it
Too preposterous for belief
Too puerile to notice
Too sanguine a forecast
   [sanguine = cheerfully confident; optimistic]
Torn asunder by eternal strife
Totally detached from all factions
Touched with a sort of reverential gratitude
Transcend the bounds of human credulity
Transitory in its nature
Transparent and ridiculous self-importance

Treasured up with a timid and niggardly thrift
Treated the idea with lofty scorn
Tremendous exploits and thrilling escapades
True incentives to knowledge

U

Unamiable and envious attributes
Unbounded devotion and indulgence
Uncharted oceans of thought
Unconquerable fidelity to duty
Under all conceivable circumstances
Under the sway of arbitrary opinions
Undertaken under propitious circumstances
   [propitious = auspicious, favorable; kindly]
Uneasy sense of impending change
Unequaled simplicity and directness of purpose
Unexceptional in point of breeding
Unexpected obstacles and inextricable difficulties
Unfailing and miraculous foresight
Unfeigned astonishment and indignation
Unfounded and incredible calumnies
   [calumnies = maliciously false statements]
Unhampered by binding alliances
Universal in their signification
Unjust and unrighteous persecution
Unreasoning and unquestioning attachment
Unrivaled beauty and excellence

Unrivaled gift of succinct and trenchant speech
   [trenchant = forceful, effective, vigorous; incisive; distinct]

Unsparing industry and attention

Unspeakably alluring and satisfying

Unsurpassed in force and fitness

Unswerving and unselfish fidelity

Untiring enunciation of platitudes and fallacies

Unutterably trivial and paltry

Unwavering and unquestioning approbation
   [approbation = warm approval; praise]

Unworthy and ungenerous treatment

Upbraid ourselves with folly

Urgent warning and admonition

Utterly and essentially irreverent

V

Vast and vague aspirations

Vastly complex and far-reaching problems

Vehemently and indignantly repudiated

Venerable and dignified conservatism

Versatile and essentially original

Versed in the arts of exciting tumult and sedition
   [sedition = insurrection; rebellion]

Viewed in its general tenor and substance

Vigorous and well compacted

Violating all decency

Violent and unforeseen vicissitudes

   [vicissitudes = sudden or unexpected changes]
Vitiated by intolerance and shortsightedness

   [vitiated = reduce the value; corrupt morally; debase]
Vivid even to oppressiveness
Voracious and insatiable appetite
Vulgar eagerness for place

W

Warnings too pregnant to be disregarded
Warped by personal pretensions and self-consequence
We may parenthetically note
We must profoundly revere it
Weigh the merits and demerits
Welcomed at first with skeptical contempt
Well-concerted and well-timed stratagems
Whirled into rapid and ceaseless motion
Wholesale friction and discontent
Wholly devoid of public interest
Widely divergent social traits
Wield an unequaled and paramount authority
Wiser counsels prevailed
Withal decidedly handsome
Written in indelible characters upon his heart

Y

Yield to urgent representations

Z

Zealous in the cause he affected to serve

www.ingramcontent.com/pod-product-compliance
Lightning Source LLC
Chambersburg PA
CBHW031717230426
43669CB00007B/172